Inside Alabama

Fire Ant Books

Inside Alabama

A Personal History of My State

HARVEY H. JACKSON III

THE UNIVERSITY OF ALABAMA PRESS • *Tuscaloosa*

Copyright © 2004
The University of Alabama Press
Tuscaloosa, Alabama 35487–0380
All rights reserved
Manufactured in the United States of America

Typeface: Bembo
∞
The paper on which this book is printed meets the minimum requirements of American National Standard for Information Science–Permanence of Paper for Printed Library Materials, ANSI Z39.48–1984.

Library of Congress Cataloging-in-Publication Data

Jackson, Harvey H.
    Inside Alabama : a personal history of my state / Harvey H. Jackson III.
        p. cm.
    "Fire ant books."
Includes bibliographical references and index.
    ISBN 0-8173-5068-3 (alk. paper)
    1. Alabama—History. 2. Alabama—Politics and government. I. Title.
    F326 .J225 2003
    976.1—dc22

                                                    2003015331

For Anna: our newest Alabamian

Contents

Preface   ix

Acknowledgments   xv

1. Back When It Belonged to the Indians   1

2. Frontier Alabama   20

3. Becoming a State   41

4. Antebellum Alabama   54

5. Stumbling toward Secession   72

6. Secession and Civil War   86

7. After the War That Never Ended   103

8. A World Made by Bourbons, for Bourbons   124

9. White Man's Alabama   147

10. Depression and War   174

11. Alabama after the War: "Big Jim" and Beyond   200

12. Old Times There Should Not Be Forgotten   224

13. The Age of Wallace   249

14. The Age of Wallace and After   276

    Epilogue: To Sum It Up   303

    Bibliographical Essay   309

    Index   321

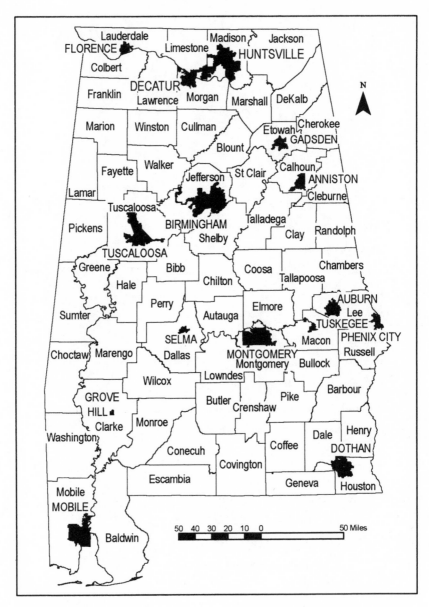

Counties and Major Cities (Courtesy Dr. M. H. Hill, PES, Jacksonville State University)

Preface

This is not the book I was supposed to write. Nor is it the book I set out to write. As it turned out, it is the book I wanted to write.

The plan was for me to produce a short, popular, illustrated history of Alabama. That was what I was asked to do. Thinking it an interesting idea, I agreed. But in the months that followed the project began to take on a life of its own. Soon I realized that I was using this opportunity to sort out some things, and say some things, that I have wanted to sort out and say for years. The result, therefore, is not so much a history as a commentary, an extended essay on events and attitudes that I think made and make Alabama what it is today.

Somewhere in the midst of the research and writing, I realized that I was approaching my subject much like John Gunther approached his. Gunther, for those who do not remember, was the author of a number of "Inside" books that were popular in the 1930s and 1940s. Noted for his willingness to meet his subject on its own ground, Gunther traveled the land, studied history and institutions, watched how things worked—and how they didn't. Gunther got personal with his topic, then got personal with his readers. His casual, conversational style made folks comfortable, which allowed him to lure them into darker corners where otherwise they might not have gone, places where they confronted situations some of them would rather have avoided.

Often Gunther made his points with humor, humor drawn from

those same situations, and from the ironies, absurdities they frequently contained. But he did not neglect the good things, the accomplishments, the triumphs, and the joys. Gunther wrote hopeful books. This was especially true of *Inside U.S.A.,* which I read first, and at an impressionable age. In it I saw how it was possible to be lovingly critical, bluntly honest, and warmly fair. Yet I really did not know what an impact he made and how much he influenced me until I pulled together this book. When that realization hit me, I had my title.

John Gunther wrote about more than countries and continents. He wrote about people. His books were held together lightly by peculiarities and prejudices shared by folks who lived and loved and had their being in a particular place. From these observations came what might be called themes. *Inside Europe,* for example, became a book about nationalism. *Inside Asia* spoke of imperialism. *Inside Latin America* found its focus in colonialism. *Inside U.S.A.* was about democracy.

Inside Alabama is about politics. Mostly.

I make no apology for this, mainly because I consider politics, especially as practiced in this state, to be the clearest expression of social, cultural, and economic forces you can find. The political stage is where it all, or at least most of it, comes together. That is how I understand Alabama. That is how I explain it here.

I realize now that I started researching this book before I was in my teens. Like so many of my generation, I was raised among storytellers and came to admire the art of the tale. My father, a raconteur without peer, filled me with stories of his family, pioneers who arrived in central Alabama in the 1830s to farm and fight and finally settle, calm and almost civilized. My mother was the quiet repository for her side, an archives of a woman, who not only remembered ours, but everyone else's, and who, when asked, could and would tell things we were warned not to repeat, and we didn't. And there were the others, especially the women, who would sit quietly and rock, shelling peas maybe, until someone called up a memory, and then it would come rolling out, and I would listen.

In the small southwest Alabama town where I grew up, these stories were spread on me, layer after layer, until past and present were difficult to separate. My father went into politics—that's how they said it, "went into politics," like he went into town, or into business, but not into church—and I began hanging around the courthouse, where officeholders accepted me and my questions with tolerant understanding. Watching and hearing, I learned that not only were past and present hard to divide, but often there wasn't much reason to do it, since fathoming one depended on grasping the other.

"Why," I asked Daddy during an election, "aren't we campaigning up in Mitcham Beat?"

"Because I'm married to your mama," he replied.

Then he told me how Mama's granddaddy, "Grandpa Bill," had been the sheriff that led the posse that cleaned out a nest of outlaws up there, only descendants of those attacked said it was no posse but a "mob" that terrorized good country folks because they didn't vote right, and over half a century later those descendants were still mad.

Tales like that I collected and blended with book-bound accounts read in and out of school, so that when I finally came to teaching I brought with me memories to add spice and zest and life and, in some cases, even insight to what I had to say to students who often cared less about the facts than they did about the tales. And when an occasional one asked if what I told was true I'd tell them "mostly."

By then I was "outside" Alabama. In 1966 Lurleen Wallace was elected governor, and I left the state. The two events were more than casually related. I had become tired of the Wallaces and all they represented, so when I was offered a job teaching in Florida, I took it. Four years there, then I moved to Georgia, finally settling in the Atlanta area, where looking down on Alabama was a popular pastime. But instead of joining in, I took to defending the state I had so happily left. Or when defense wasn't possible, at least explaining—which was often more difficult.

In order to explain to them, I had to explain to myself, and so I became a more careful student of Alabama than I had ever been before.

Then I came home. After a quarter of a century the expatriate returned to teach, among other things, Alabama history to Alabamians, and finally to use those things I had learned when I was teaching myself. So I put it all together, laid it out for my students, and after over a decade of teaching the tale, I got the opportunity to write it down.

Here it is.

I do not plead the cause of objectivity in this effort. I am not objective. There is much that I do not like about our history, as well as much that I do, and if I do not come right out and say so, I hope I imply my opinions so that you won't miss them. Yet my criticism should not cloud the fact that I love Alabama, draw strength from its strengths, delight in its foibles, am entertained by its eccentricities, treasure its contradictions, enjoy its ironies and ambiguities, and take pride in the fact that I am one of its citizens. Through some strange chemistry that I can neither explain nor fully understand, I have always felt that Alabama's history is my history. Maybe it is because my people came so early and stayed so long, because they did what other folk did, because they farmed, fought, preached, politicked, and philandered like their neighbors; maybe that's what gives me a sense of being part of the whole rather than apart from it. From this association has come the love, the devotion, that I believe gives me the right (as well as the privilege and the responsibility) to say some of the things I say.

But keep this in mind. What you have here is a narrowly focused, personal history, written for the general reader, not the specialist. And as the title says, it is written about things that happened "inside Alabama." This means, of course, that what Alabamians do outside the state, in Washington, D.C., for example, will not get the attention given to goings on back home. As a result, a great many things are left out. Just because I do not include a particular person, place, or thing, however, does not mean that I consider them, that, or it unimportant. A book of this nature cannot be inclusive. If you want the full account, go to *Alabama: The History of a Deep South State,* by William Warren Rogers, Robert David Ward, Leah Rawls Atkins, and Wayne Flynt. In my opinion it is the best single-volume history of a state (any state) yet written, and what I have done here is in no way an effort to supersede it.

In the final analysis, what I have tried to do is tell Alabama's story in a narrative of people and events that will interest readers, hold their attention, and maybe give them a sense of why the past is so important today. I leave it to you, the reader, to judge whether or not I have succeeded.

Acknowledgments

This book has been pre-read by more people than any I have written, so my debt to others is great.

When I was writing it as the text for a popular, illustrated history, Nicole Mitchell, then the director of the University of Alabama Press, sent chapters out to various people (one known to me and the other not), and their comments were particularly helpful. The reader whose name was revealed, Leah Atkins, read the whole manuscript and in her cheerful, scholarly way offered suggestions and warnings that brought the project into shape. During this initial phase I also sent copies of the work to Ed Williams of Auburn University and my father, Harvey H. Jackson Jr. of Grove Hill, Alabama. Both were careful critics whose observations and support meant a lot to me.

Once the manuscript was done, I sent it to the press, which sent it out to three anonymous readers. Two of these liked what I had done and recommended publication. One hated it and told the press to shelve the project. To Director Mitchell's credit, she decided to send it to a fourth reader who agreed with the more positive assessments but noted that embedded in the harsh criticism of that third reader were comments that might improve the manuscript. Deciding to follow that advice, I settled back to rework what I had written and, in the process, to write the book it seems that I wanted to write all along.

When that was done, I turned again to friends for insight and advice. Both Jerry Brown, a Clarke County, Alabama, boy who is dean of the School of Journalism at the University of Montana, and Sam Hodges, author and working journalist with the *Mobile Register,* read the manuscript and helped me through rough spots. You will note that while the press rightfully has sent my work out to historians, I have sent it to three journalists—Williams, Brown, and Hodges. Though they are writers with scholarly credentials, I hoped that their professional training and writing experience would make them more comfortable with the "voice" (my voice) employed here and less likely to reject what I say because of the way I say it.

That review done, I sent the manuscript back to the press. Again it went out to readers, and to my joy and satisfaction all three recommended publication. I sincerely thank them for their comments and suggestions. Then the manuscript went before the press's board of editors, which (I was later told), with "sympathy and understanding for what [I was] undertaking," unanimously approved the project. I was particularly heartened to learn that one member of the board requested that "the press take particular care in the copyediting process not to hinder the personal tone of the work." Thanks to the careful and sensitive attention given the manuscript by my editor, Jane Powers Weldon, that board member should be happy. I know I am.

So you can see, my debt is great. But the accounting does not end there. My students let me approach Alabama history in different ways, and their responses have a lot to do with what is included and what is left out of this work. Earl Wade, dean of Arts and Sciences at Jacksonville State University, provided the encouragement and flexibility necessary for me to keep the project going. Travel support came from the university's faculty research committee, and the Department of History and Foreign Languages helped with copying and such. My colleagues at JSU were a source of inspiration, while Lisa Green, departmental secretary, kept things on an even keel and made sure I met deadlines as they came due. She is a treasure.

My father not only read the manuscript but talked with me about it. He and I, and my Clarke County buddy Jim Cox, spent hours at Daddy's Poutin' House, cussing and discussing parts and participles of the past. My wife, Suzanne, listened to me moan and groan when things weren't going right. Snapped me back to reality time and time again. Offered suggestions and encouragement. Kept me from chunking the whole thing. And provided the support and comfort I needed when I needed it. She is my partner, and this is as much her book as mine.

My older daughter, Kelly, raised in Georgia, married and settled there, was not around much when this book was taking shape. But she contributed to it by joining me on my Black Belt wanderings. She may not be an Alabamian, but she is close. My son, Will, entered fourth grade and the study of Alabama history just as the final touches were being put on the manuscript. Watching him learn, talking with him about people long gone from the earth—what they did and why they did it—have given me a new appreciation of what makes the past interesting and important to the present. He taught me as much as I taught him.

Anna, to whom this book is dedicated, grew up as it did. She and Will represent Alabama's future. Maybe what I have written here will help them face it with hope, courage, tolerance, a sense of irony, and a sense of humor.

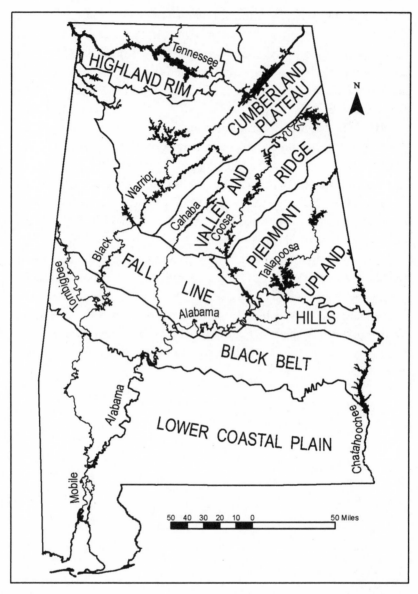

Regions and Rivers (Courtesy Dr. M. H. Hill, PES, Jacksonville State University)

1
Back When It Belonged
to the Indians

IN THE BEGINNING

It is hard to say, exactly, when or where Alabama's prehistoric founders wandered in, but they did. Maybe first into the Tennessee Valley, that rich divot of red land north of the river where part of Alabama's plantation system will later take root. Or maybe they followed hills and mountains of the Appalachian Plateau, tumbled south until they stood on the heights above the junction of the Coosa and Tallapoosa Rivers, and looked out across what later men in later times would call the Black Belt. Some surely came in from the west, into the canebrakes and prairies of that same half-moon stretch of dark, chalky-rich soil where one day a few who were white would live rich and many who were black would live as slaves. And others surely moved in along the coast, where they stayed to fish a little, eat a lot of oysters, fight among themselves, and generally do things that gulf people would do for centuries after them.

Wherever they settled these stone-age immigrants hunted and gathered. They followed the animals, lived in simple shelters or clustered under rock overhangs where today archeologists find their camps. In time they settled in small family units along streams and back in sheltered coves. They refined tools, made better use of food resources, established trade routes, and so stabilized their lives that populations grew, villages developed, and a social order emerged and flourished.

Sometime around 1000 B.C. they began to make pottery, an accomplishment for them and a big deal for anthropologists who use that development to mark the beginning of what they call the Woodland Period. Clay vessels enabled these natives to store and cook the food that made their lives better than that of their ancestors. In these pots they put plants—first nuts, seeds, and berries, which they picked (or picked up), and later corn or maize, which they grew to supplement the traditional hunters' diet, a diet that improved with the development of the bow and arrow. A more healthful (and more plentiful) supply of food resulted in a population explosion that turned family settlements into villages and, in some cases, villages into towns.

Influenced by contact with similar cultures to the north and west, Alabama's Woodland tribes laid the foundation for a complex religious system, marked by ceremonies far more elaborate than those conducted by Indians before them. Because the evidence of this is best preserved in the mass graves found beneath and within their large, dome-shaped burial mounds, our knowledge of these people is both extensive and at the same time less complete than we would hope. However, careful excavation and analysis have taught us that these were a rapidly developing people with their own social, political, artistic, and religious culture, a people who might appear primitive when compared to those who came later but, seen in context, were innovative, energetic, and advanced.

Toward the end of the two-thousand-year Woodland Period (around A.D. 1000), Alabama Indians came in contact with the vibrant cultures that were developing in the Mississippi Valley and in northern Florida, and this combination of influences from the south, west, and north helped create the region's last prehistoric period— the Mississippian (A.D. 1000 to 1550). Marking this transition was a significant change in the way people lived and were governed. Woodland culture, so we believe, was distinguished by a sociopolitical system based on shared resources, with power and authority distributed on the basis of individual accomplishments. The Mississippian period was characterized by chiefdoms, where political, religious, and even economic authority was in the hands of an elite group, bound together by bloodlines and served by the general population. It was a system that nineteenth- and twentieth-century Alabamians, white and black, would have recognized as similar to their own. This hierarchical culture matured over the centuries, and though the political system that grew from it appears to have declined toward the end of the Mississippian era, it was one of the few elements of Indian culture that Europeans found familiar when they arrived.

During the Mississippian epoch Indians developed shell-tempered ceramics, improved their stone tools, and created ceremonial objects that showed an artistic sophistication previously unknown in the region. We know this and more because evidence of their way of life, and way of death, has been preserved in large, flat-topped earthen mounds found in or near their towns and cities. Topped by temples or by the houses of their chiefs, the mounds were located around a plaza, which was the ceremonial center of the community. Excavations of these mounds have revealed a highly structured religion that functioned as an element of the social system, where priests and chief served complementary functions and in some instances may well have been the same people.

Two of the most important Mississippian sites located in what would become Alabama are found at Moundville, on the banks of the Black Warrior River, and at Bottle Creek, in the Mobile-Tensaw delta. Today Moundville is the more accessible. Around that site, on the rich flood plain along the Warrior, early Indians found plants, fish, and game enough to feed a growing community. Slowly, steadily, the population expanded, agriculture improved, corn was introduced, and the hierarchy associated with Mississippian culture took shape. Then, around A.D. 1000, they began to build their mounds. We don't know why. Maybe one of them saw some on a trading trip into the Ohio River Valley, came back and told his friends "what this place needs is mounds." Or maybe a chief got up one morning, decided he was tired of living on the same level with the common herd, and told them to pile up some dirt and put his house on top.

Maybe the motive was religious, maybe political, or maybe it was just one of those examples of vanity that was and is part of the human condition, but whatever motivated the builders, the structures became an important expression of who they were, so they kept building them.

Construction went on for some two hundred years, and when the builders finished, there were about twenty mounds in the complex. Although not primarily for burials, some did contain human remains along with ritual artifacts, many of them intricately engraved or carved with human and animal figures. Also found in these burials were objects made of copper and other materials that could have come to the region only through an extensive trading network of which the Alabama Indians were part. Indeed, Moundville's very location suggests that trade was an important part of the community's way of life. The river was a ready means of transportation, and dugout canoes found at other Mississippian sites reveal that these Indians knew well the value of streams. But Moundville is also located at or near some of the major trails that would later open the land to Spanish, French, English, and finally American traders. Moundville was at a crossroads, and its location reflected its importance.

The Bottle Creek site is less well known and less studied, largely because it is difficult to reach. Its location has also protected it from looters, who have defaced and destroyed many of the state's archaeological treasures. Bottle Creek Indians began building their mound complex on an island in the Mobile–Tensaw delta swamp, some time after work began in Moundville, and apparently the community was able to retain its supremacy as a political and cultural center longer than its counterpart to the north. At its zenith it contained at least eighteen mounds, and from that location much of the region to the south and east was governed.

We don't know why the Mississippian culture went into decline, or why the mound complexes at Moundville and Bottle Creek were abandoned. Some have suggested increased economic competition between chiefs and chiefdoms led to wars between the cities, and they point to evidence of defensive stockades that were built at many of the sites. What we do know is that about the same time mound building ceased, long-distance trade seemed to wane, and in burials there were fewer of the finely wrought ceremonial items that characterized Mississippian culture at its height. Not surprisingly, as the centers declined, the power and influence of the elites who governed declined as well, though it is impossible to say if one led to the other, or if all of this change was part of the general disintegration throughout the region. We can say, however, that when Europeans began to arrive, the Indians who met them were not the powerful force they once had been.

EUROPEANS IN ALABAMA

Europeans called America a "New World," and to them it was. But we should take care not to speak of the New World as if it were new only to the invaders. In the years that followed the white man's arrival, Indians witnessed their old way of life fade away and a new one take shape. Thus it became a New World for the Indians as well, and, in a very short time, it would become newer still.

We should admit up front that we are anything but sure about when and where the first Europeans arrived in Alabama or had their initial impact on native cultures. The Spanish captain Alonzo de Pineda was probably the first, with "probably" the operative word. In 1519 Pineda led an expedition west along the Gulf Coast, from Florida to Texas, stopping from time to time along the way. At his party's last landfall it was attacked by natives, who killed the commander and many of his men. Then the victors skinned and ate a few of the fallen and hung the human hides as trophies. Those who escaped brought back the grisly tale, along with maps that included a deep inlet that looks very much like Mobile Bay. Maybe it was.

Then came Panfilo Narvaez, who was either Spain's most unlucky or most incompetent explorer. Opinion seems to lean to the latter. Narvaez left Spain with five ships and a force of over six hundred, including African slaves. By the time he arrived at the Gulf of Mexico off the west coast of Florida in 1528, desertions and storms had reduced the fleet by two and his army by a third. Landing with some three hundred men, he sent his ships and the remaining crew off to find a safe harbor. Thus separated from supplies and a means of escape, the expedition set out across what would later be known as the Big Bend.

Believing a show of brutality would convince the natives to leave the expedition alone, the commander ordered the nose of a captured chief cut off, then had the mutilated Indian's mother killed by the expedition's dogs. But rather than cow the natives, these acts enraged them. Spanish scouts were ambushed, stragglers were attacked, arrows flew in without warning, and no one was safe. Finally Narvaez realized the march was futile. He returned to the gulf, constructed crude boats, then set sail, if sail it could be called, west along the coast. One by one the vessels sank. Sailors and soldiers drowned, and natives killed those who got to shore. The quickly dead were the lucky ones, for many on the remaining boats slowly starved. Drifting toward Mexico, the little flotilla might have entered Mobile Bay, though it is impossible to tell just where they went. Of the hundreds who set out on the expedition, only four survived. Panfilo Narvaez was not among them.

One who made it was Cabeza de Vaca, who returned to Spain with fantastic stories of his adventures and of rumors of cities of great wealth that lay in the interior. With the riches of Mexico and Peru in its treasury, Spain was ready to believe the tale.

This is where Hernando de Soto comes into the picture. De Soto has always fascinated Alabamians. One historian even went so far as to claim that Alabama history "begins" with him, which could be the case, if it is written history you mean. Journals and accounts scribbled out by members of the expedition do provide our first literary description of Alabama, although we are not exactly sure just where in Alabama the writers were writing about when they wrote, a mystery that is part of the fascination. While those interested pretty well agree that in 1540 the Spanish conquistador did travel through the heart of the state, no one has been able to prove conclusively where the expedition went. Back in the 1930s a federal commission marked what was then thought to be the "De Soto Trail," and many on that route accepted it as the final word on the subject, mainly because they wanted it to be. So it followed that when later research revealed that some of the commission's de Soto sites were mislabeled, many along the commission's route were angry. Some claimed politics was behind it all, others hinted at dark plots by communities along the new route, and others simply refused to accept the evidence.

So why all the fuss? Well, part of it was local pride. After years of believing your town or county was visited by a famous explorer, having a bunch of college professors tell you it wasn't could be quite a letdown.

And then there was money. In 1992, with all the hoopla surrounding the five hundredth anniversary of Columbus's "discovery," federal grants came available to those researching the Spanish exploration. All you had to do was prove you had something worth researching. So de Soto scholars began competing for the cash. Things got pretty nasty.

Some realized how ridiculous it all was and said so. One archeologist threatened to apply for a grant to dig a site near Childersburg where he claimed to have discovered a hubcap from a 1952 De Soto automobile—clear evidence of a Spanish presence. Another scholar, when asked by a South Alabama hunting club to confirm that de Soto had crossed the land they leased, wrote back with his own solution for determining the actual route. First, he suggested, find a bone from one of the pigs that the Spaniards took along. Then extract the DNA, clone a modern pig with the route imprinted in its genetic structure (the biology of it all gets a bit fuzzy here), and put the pig on the ground near Tampa Bay, where we think the expedition landed. Then follow the animal as it rambles through the Southeast. This could confirm once and for all the route taken by de Soto and his men. And when the pig arrives at its destination, its followers could barbecue it—not an inappropriate end to the noble animal, at least from an Alabama perspective.

Yet all this modern-day whoop-de-do notwithstanding, the fact remains that de Soto was and is an important part of Alabama history. If his route can be identified, then sites his chroniclers reported might be found and studied. This study would increase our knowledge of Native American culture long ago and would help us better understand changes in settlement patterns that followed in de Soto's wake.

THE INDIANS AND HERNANDO DE SOTO

Along his route de Soto found towns and villages large and prosperous and a native society that was vibrant and complex. This we know from the chroniclers who wrote of the expedition, and though they were generally condescending in their attitude toward the inhabitants, there remains a sort of grudging admiration in their accounts. From them we also get a hint of what the Indians thought of the clanging, banging, shouting, grumbling mass of foot soldiers, horsemen, craftsmen, priests, and drovers (remember the pigs) who, by the time they entered Alabama late in the summer of 1540, were surely wondering if their commander had a clue where he was going. De Soto, for his part, was willing to go wherever he might find riches like those his countrymen found in Mexico, so he asked in every village where the wealth lay. And every time he asked, the natives, who realized the sooner the Spaniards left the better off they would be, swore the expedition had not gone quite far enough and wished them good luck on their journey—or was it good riddance?

It is unlikely de Soto believed them, but since there was nothing where he was, the only alternative was to push ahead. So he took hostages—men to carry the baggage and women, as one historian diplomatically explained, "to entertain the Spaniards." They followed a river, the Coosa we think, south to where it joined another river, probably the Tallapoosa. There the expedition entered a region governed by Chief Tuscaluza (Tuscaloosa), who, "full of dignity" and seated on a large mound with retainers all about, received the invaders in a tableau created to impress the Spaniards, which it did, and discourage them from further aggression, which it did not. De Soto told the chief what he wanted—precious metal, more bearers to carry the riches, and women. Tuscaluza told him these things and more could be found at Mabila, a town a week or so farther downstream. To make sure the inducements actually existed, de Soto ordered Tuscaluza taken hostage, and with the chief (accompanied by an attendant carrying a sunshade) the army moved west. Making their way along the "craggy" gorge of a wide and winding river that must have been the Alabama, they reached their destination, which according to some modern scholars was near where Alabama's first state capital, Cahawba, would be built. Others claim the site was farther south. Some say it was off to the west. But nobody has ever found it, so nobody knows for sure.

Apparently Mabila was one of those fortified towns whose construction signaled the decline of Mississippian culture, and it was there that Tuscaluza and his allies planned to end the Spanish expedition once and for all. Within its walls natives from throughout the region assembled, planned, and waited. On 18 October 1540 de Soto with an advance party entered the main plaza, and the Indians sprang their trap. The fighting was brief and bloody, but the commander and most of his men were able to escape. The main army soon arrived, and the battle commenced in earnest. It was modern warfare—iron, steel, armor and gunpowder—against stone arrows, clubs, and spears, and as would happen often in years to come, modern technology carried the day. There were repeated assaults and heavy casualties before the walls were breached, but once inside the Spaniards put the town to the torch. One cannot know for sure how many Indians died—maybe three thousand, maybe more—but even by conservative estimates it was the bloodiest single day of battle on American soil until Union and Confederate soldiers slaughtered each other at Shiloh more than three hundred years later.

After binding their wounds and burying their dead, more than eighty by some accounts, the Spaniards headed west—out of the land of Tuscaluza. Had they marched south, they would have met a relief fleet waiting for them a week away at Achuse (Pensacola) Bay.

But de Soto, still determined to find wealth and fame, pushed his men on. Since many on the expedition had gambled everything they had on success, they had little choice but to obey. So they crossed out of Alabama, and finally, after months of wandering and fighting, reached the Mississippi River. There de Soto, stricken with fever, died, and to keep the Indians from desecrating his grave, his men sank his body in the stream. Survivors finally descended the river and eventually made it to Mexico and safety. By almost any measure, the great de Soto expedition was a failure.

ALABAMA AFTER DE SOTO

There is some justice in the fact that de Soto died of fever and not in battle, for in that sense his death was symbolic of the disaster his expedition, and others like it, brought to the Indians of the Alabama region. About twenty years after de Soto's passing, a new expedition, led by Tristan de Luna, made its way up from the gulf coast and into the interior, hoping to find the rich land described by de Soto's survivors. What they found instead was such a disappointment that they concluded the survivors' descriptions were simply "false and not true." But they had been true when the expedition came through; they just weren't true anymore. What had happened, we now know (or at least strongly believe) is that villages along the route had been devastated by a series of epidemics, fevers, for which the natives had no resistance. Measles, influenza, diphtheria, and smallpox, which had already appeared along the coast, were carried deeper into the interior by de Soto's troops, and these opened the door for a biological disaster of monumental proportions. A southeastern Indian population which may have been as great as 2 million in 1540 was, by the beginning of the eighteenth century, reduced to a fraction of that number—and a small fraction at that.

It did not happen overnight, or at least we suppose it did not, but once again, we don't know. For the centuries between de Luna's leaving and the arrival of the next Europeans who wrote down what they found, we have only scant and scattered archeological evidence to tell us what took place. Still, drawing parallels with other cultures that underwent such a transformation, we can make certain assumptions. The diseases decimated the chiefdoms, killing indiscriminately and leaving many towns without leaders and with few followers. Believing, sometimes rightly, that they could move away from the sickness, survivors began to migrate. Soon they joined with others also searching for safety. From their despair new alliances were made, and in time new tribes were formed.

By this process the Mississippian mound-building culture faded, and in its place emerged the modern Alabama tribes—Creeks, Cherokees, Choctaws, and Chickasaws. And while these new Indians continued to farm, hunt, and fish, continued to lay out towns, conduct rituals, and in some cases even govern in ways similar to their Mississippian predecessors, the differences were many and striking. Gone was the hierarchy with its priests and powerful chiefs, replaced by a sort of tribal democracy in which the arts of persuasion and diplomacy were as important as was the art of war. Gone too, or at least changed, were the political and religious ceremonies and customs that characterized the culture and gave reason to such matters as building mounds. The epidemics were critical to these alterations. When disease strikes, it strikes hardest at the weakest—the old and young—and so it was with the Indians. Losing the young was losing the future, and the deaths of so many children must have demoralized survivors. Losing the old was no less devastating. In an oral culture such as this, the old were the repositories of knowledge; they were the documents, the history, the law, the religion, and they explained why things were as they were or why they should be otherwise. To lose one of them before that knowledge was passed along was like losing a library, and there was no way to replace it.

Nor was there much incentive to do so. The past was not important. The future was what counted. So the Indians regrouped, retrenched, hung on to what they could of their old ways, and weathered the transition. At the end of the eighteenth century when the federal Indian agent Benjamin Hawkins arrived at the junction of the Coosa and Tallapoosa Rivers, upstream from present-day Montgomery, he saw mounds that may have been part of Tuscaluza's principal town. But when he asked nearby natives who built them, and why, he got no answer. So Hawkins concluded that they were constructed as a place of refuge from floods. Other whites looking at other mounds and getting no information from local Indians assumed they had been built by an earlier, superior race—perhaps (they believed in their conceit) built by, or at least at the direction of, Europeans. And the natives did not tell them otherwise, maybe because they did not know, or maybe because they did not want the Europeans to know.

It took nearly a hundred years, but by the middle of the seventeenth century the Indians had begun to recover from the epidemics. Increasingly resistant to diseases, their population growing and their society more stable, the tribes created a new and vibrant culture to replace the old. Villages, some of them quite large, rose along rivers and streams, and though the inhabitants no longer built mounds, they continued to lay out their towns around plazas where new political and religious ceremonies were conducted. Although governed by tribal consensus, chiefs and headmen were important spokesmen when there were negotiations between tribes and important leaders when there was war. Both of these conditions underscore the increased contact between tribal units and the alliances that were formed, alliances that in time bound villages into confederations. Significant in this transformation was the revival of the regional exchange system that was so important in the development and expansion of the Mississippian culture. Over trails and along rivers that had fallen into disuse, natives once again swapped goods and ideas. Prosperity came slowly, but it came, and with it came a cultural rejuvenation that must have given the Indians reason to believe that the future would indeed be better than the past.

What they could not have known is that this revival would invite a second European invasion, one that heralded the arrival of an economic system that would be as destructive to their way of life as the epidemics had been. The new chiefdoms were large enough to make commerce with them worthwhile, yet too small to effectively resist foreign intrusion. In short, they were ripe for exploitation, and in the late seventeenth century the exploiters arrived.

THE EUROPEANS RETURN

First came the Spanish, out from their Atlantic coast missions and up from the Apalachee province. A few French traders soon wandered down from Canada. Then the English arrived. Charleston was founded in 1670, and from that squalid settlement traders moved out into Carolina, Georgia, Alabama, and beyond. Englishmen with "packhorses loaded with all the apparatus of guns, muskets, powder, lead and . . . other merchandise" appeared in the villages and a brisk trade began. According to French reports the English wanted deerskins, furs, and, for a brief period early in the contact, Indian slaves. The natives obliged and soon were waging war on their neighbors, "killing the men," and "carrying away the women and children whom they sell to the English, each one for a gun."

Soon African slaves drove Indian slaves from the market, and the trade became one of "hides and peltries." As heavily laden pack trains followed timeworn trails across the region, Alabama became the crossroad of this commerce. Fords on the Tombigbee, Warrior, Coosa, and Tallapoosa Rivers were convenient spots for market centers, and there British traders, Scots mostly, built stores, stocked them, and settled in to barter. Such Europeans were soon fixtures on the frontier, and Charleston, as well as London, understood the importance of these posts. As Thomas Nairne, Carolina's first Indian agent, observed, the trade "attracts and maintains the obedience and friendship of the Indians," and that, to England's imperial planners, was as important as skins and pelts.

In the fall of 1698 the Spanish founded Pensacola, which a French expedition under the Le Moyne brothers, Iberville and Bienville, discovered to their surprise when they arrived at that spot three months later. So the French sailed further west and the next year planted their flag and a small colony near present-day Biloxi, Mississippi. Unhappy with that site, the French sent a party back east.

The men entered Mobile Bay, sailed to the northern end, and went up the river that fed it to a site that seemed better suited for the capital of what was being called French Louisiana. It followed that in 1702, with his brother Iberville sick, it fell to Bienville to take an expedition back up the bay, then up the river some twenty-seven miles to the bluff where they built Fort Louis de la Mobile. The town laid out beside the stockade was called, simply, Mobile.

Now there were the French, the Spanish, and the English to compete for the Indian trade. And compete they did. But the Indians were no innocents in the exchange. They let the Europeans know that "they Effect them most who sell best cheap," and whenever there was a choice to be made among merchants, the decision usually turned on that principle.

For its first two years Mobile was a garrison town of traders, soldiers, artisans, priests, and only a few families. It was a place of business for the most part, but it was a beginning, and like first settlements throughout America, a certain status is granted the founders and passed on to their descendants, whether they deserve it or not. Descendants would have been few had it not been for the arrival of the *Pelican,* for among its passengers were "twenty-three virtuous maidens" (some accounts say twenty-six), "young and well-bred" women who had been gathered from French orphanages and convents and sent abroad to marry settlers. Survival on the southern frontier was hard enough for a man, but women, whose lives were additionally threatened by the almost yearly cycle of pregnancy and birth, were understandably in short supply. So brides-to-be arrived, those who survived the voyage, sick and emaciated, to be greeted by a tumble of weather-beaten houses and their inhabitants, who were no more impressive than their dwellings. Once the girls recovered, many of them left for New Orleans, where pickings were better, but others married in Mobile and produced descendants who consider this lineage not unlike, or any less than, that linking first families to Virginia or to the *Mayflower.*

But Mobile did not stay long on the bluff. In 1710 the annual flood was greater that they had believed possible. The town and fort were inundated, and when the waters receded Bienville ordered the settlers downstream, to the mouth of the river, where the city sits today.

Not long after resettlement, French fortunes changed. In 1715 news arrived that the Yamasee Indians, a South Carolina tribe previously believed to be loyal to Charlestonians, had led an uprising that wiped out most of the English trading houses between the Atlantic and Alabama. So the window of opportunity was open. In 1717 the French sent an expedition up the Alabama River to the confluence of the Coosa and Tallapoosa—the "key to the country" according to imperial planners—and there they built a fort. Sometimes they called it Post aux Alibamons after the Indian village it sat hard against, sometimes Fort des Alibamons, and on formal occasions Fort Toulouse. The English referred to the outpost simply as the "mischievous French garrison *Alebamah.*"

So it was that three European nations—Spain, France, and England—set about to control Alabama. The advantage, so it seemed, lay with the French, who held the strategic spot near the fall line, the head of river navigation, where trading trails crossed the stream and where flatboats could be loaded with skins for an easy float down to Mobile. But soon the Yamasee were defeated, and the English were back, living in the villages and bettering French goods in quality, quantity, and cost. In a culture where power and status were measured by what a man had to trade, these gave Carolinians a distinct advantage. The Indians, for their part, made the most of the situation, and the Europeans could do little about it. As a disgusted South Carolina governor William Lyttleton noted, it was "a fix'd principle with [the natives] to observe neutrality between us and the French that they may get supplies and presents from both."

But the Indians could not remain neutral long. By 1756 England and France were at war, and the Carolina traders saw their opportunity and took it. French trade goods that made it past the British navy seldom got as far as the Alabama frontier, so the garrison at Toulouse had even less to offer the Indians for their loyalty. By 1759 the Alabama tribe was flying "the Suite of English Colours" in its village, a gesture confirming that Post aux Alibamons was little more than a French island in a sea of English influence. Four years later France was defeated and under terms signed in Paris agreed to withdraw from North America. When word reached Toulouse, the troops spiked the cannons and threw them into the river. Then the soldiers, along with residents, red and white, from the town around the fort, marched south to join the evacuation from Mobile. When the English arrived to take charge of the city, they decided not to occupy Toulouse. The "key to the country" was left to rot on the bluff.

For the next decade or so English traders and their Indian allies controlled the Alabama interior. The Muskogee, or Creeks as the English called them, may have gained the most from the situation. Aggressively expanding from their towns along the Coosa and Tallapoosa, the Upper Creeks moved west and planted villages, colonial outposts really, crowding against the lands of the Choctaws, who were their neighbors and their enemies. The Lower Creeks, based in towns along the Chattahoochee, Flint, and Apalachicola Rivers, also spread their influence, and soon this confederation controlled millions of acres and the animals that roamed them. It was, in reality, an Indian empire, governed from more than sixty towns by a people who planted, gathered, and hunted as effectively as any Native Americans on the continent. If there was a golden age of the Creeks, it was during this decade after the British victory over the French.

But even as things were going so well for the Indians, problems were beginning to appear. As professional hunters for the British traders, they were an essential element in the colonial economy, but in return they became increasingly dependent on what the English provided—wool blankets, metal pots and pans, knives and other utensils, and especially guns and skilled gunsmiths. As such goods and services became more widely available, dependence on the British grew, until the traders knew that by supplying or withdrawing such favors, they could manipulate the tribes to their advantage. Of course, the Indians could manipulate in return, for they had the deerskins, without which there would be no trade. Yet the impact on the Creeks was far greater, for the more they relied on European goods, the less they relied on traditional means and methods. Over the years the old ways, the old crafts, the old traditions were slowly abandoned and forgotten. The Indians would not realize the significance of their loss until it was almost too late.

BRITISH ALABAMA

Meanwhile, down in Mobile, the British major Robert Farmar took charge of the town, a rotting, humid, musty, muddy hamlet of some 350 souls, guarded by a tumble-down fort the French had named Conde and the victors renamed Fort Charlotte. Applying common sense whenever possible to bring order to the chaos of transition, Farmar untwisted tangled land claims, allowed Roman Catholics to practice their religion, and gave French citizens time to decide whether they should swear allegiance or leave. But Mobile was not a happy place. Almost every disease common to swamps was common to Mobile, and when George Johnstone, governor of West Florida, arrived to take charge he was appalled by the "filth [and] nastiness" he found.

Johnstone and Farmar were at odds almost from the start, and in time the governor also alienated remaining French residents, whom he called "the refuse of the Jails of great Citys, and the overflowing Scum of the Empire." Nor did he do much to further relations with the Indians. With the help of John Stuart, the superintendent for Indian affairs, Governor Johnstone was able to hold some meetings with the Creeks. But those relations soured, and before Johnstone left he was advocating war of annihilation against the natives, a proposal London greeted with horror. Few expressed regret when Governor Johnsone departed in 1767, nor were they upset when his fortune-hunting successor, Montfort Browne, lasted just over a year. Browne's successor proved no better. Although there was "great joy and satisfaction" when the third governor, John Eliot, arrived in April 1769, after only a month on the job, Governor Eliot went into his study and hanged himself. He was followed by Elias Durnford, who blundered along for a few months, and then Peter Chester arrived.

Governor Chester administered British West Florida for eleven years, and considering what came before, you could call him a success—up to a point. He healed (or was able to gloss over) divisions within the colony, worked to entice immigrants to come and settle, and allowed residents a significant measure of self-government. When the American Revolution broke out, Chester offered refuge to fleeing Loyalists, and though his own colonists had their grievances, and once even protested the way he exercised "unwarrantable powers," West Floridians did not join the rebellion.

The rebellion, however, came to them. As the conflict on the east coast expanded, London sent assurances that Mobile would be protected, but in 1779, when Spain entered the war against England, it became apparent that those assurances counted for little. The Spanish governor in New Orleans, Bernardo de Galvez, now saw an opportunity to bring British West Florida under Spanish control. The British commander, Gen. John Campbell, aware of these intentions, decided to concentrate on defending Pensacola. Mobile was left to its own devices. In January of 1780, Galvez, with eleven ships and some twenty-five hundred men, sailed for Mobile. Winter storms and a difficult passage into the bay slowed the expedition, but the force finally got ashore below the city. Confusion reigned, and the commander even considered calling the whole thing off, but when the attack was finally launched the Spanish discovered that the British were in even greater disarray. What followed was a fourteen-day siege, the last stages of which were watched by a British relief column from Pensacola that could not cross the bay to help. Finally the Spanish flag, the third flag to fly over Mobile, was raised at Fort Charlotte.

Residents of Mobile, most of them at least, swore allegiance to their new masters, took Catholic communion, and went about their business. A few houses had been destroyed in the fighting, but on the whole the city emerged from the American Revolution with scant scars to show for it. The same might be said for the rest of Alabama.

Although the British had hoped that the Scottish traders who re-mained loyal would be able to rally the Indians to the Crown, American victories on the frontier, combined with a policy of paci-fication candidly (and accurately) described by Indian Commis-sioner George Galphin as "rum and good words," kept most of the Indians neutral or ineffective. Those "good words" left the Indi-ans, the Creeks especially, believing that once the war was over and American independence won, the woods, fields, and streams they claimed would still be theirs. But with the peace in 1783 that made independence a reality, it became apparent that Americans and Spaniards would also claim the land. This set the stage for a new phase in the ongoing struggle to control what would be Alabama.

But this new contest would be different. William Bartram re-corded the change. In the summer of 1775 the Philadelphia natural-ist was in the Southeast studying flora and fauna when he met "a company of emigrants from Georgia; a man, his wife, a young woman, several young children, and three stout young men, with about a dozen horses loaded with their property." Inquiring as to their destination, Bartram learned that "their design was to settle on the Alabama." This was not a military expedition out to build a fort and raise a standard. Nor were they traders seeking new markets. These were farmers, drovers, family folks. They were the wave of the future.

2

Frontier Alabama

The treaty that gave the United States its independence in 1783 left both the new nation and her Spanish neighbor in Florida claiming land that would one day be the southern half of Alabama and Mississippi. The resulting conflict between Americans and Spaniards would take over a decade to resolve, and in the confusion the Indians who also claimed the land saw their opportunity. They seized it.

Of course the Creeks had been seizing opportunities for some time, and despite their recent alliance with the defeated British, their influence remained considerable. Leading them, or so it seemed to whites, was Alexander McGillivray, who claimed to be "King and Head Warrior of all the Nation." Son of prominent Scottish trader Lachlan McGillivray and a Creek woman named Sehoy, Alexander was raised as an Indian for some fourteen years, then sent to Charleston to learn to be an Englishman, a lesson he learned well. As a result, he was part of both worlds, though some believed he was more comfortable as a white man. When his and his father's loyalty to the Crown put the family on the losing side in the American Revolution, the thirty-three-year-old Alexander decided his future lay with his mother's people. Above the forks of the Coosa and Tallapoosa, in the heart of the Upper Creeks, he built a home and plantation near the ancient town of Little Talassee and there assumed the role of the frontier gentleman that he was. Once situated, he began looking for ways to frustrate American designs and advance his own.

This hope lay with the Spanish. Before the British withdrew, friends among them told McGillivray to form an alliance with the new masters of Florida, who were "jealous in the extreme of the encroachments of the Americans" and from whom the Indians could obtain "a supply of such arms and ammunition as would enable them to defend their territories." He did that, and more. Realizing that he was dealing with two sets of Americans—Georgians, whom he rightly distrusted, and federal authorities, which he rightly figured were not much better—McGillivray spent the next decade playing the various interests against each other. He was an ally when it suited the situation, an enemy when that would serve him best, and an enigma to friend and foe alike. Under his guidance the Creeks remained an important force in the region, and in the process he shaped the future of the tribe as much as any man of his time.

McGillivray believed that the Creeks would never be independent if they were a dependent ally of another, no matter how friendly and reassuring that other might be. So he devised a plan, a scheme he believed would benefit those natives who supported it and would naturally benefit him. McGillivray proposed to turn his plantation into a center for the "Peltry-Trade" and take that lucrative commerce from American merchants whom he thought, with good reason, were corrupting the Indians with rum and cheating them with inferior goods. More important, perhaps, he planned to encourage "Corn, Hemp and Tobacco-Makers" to carve out farms between the rivers and expand the already extensive agricultural lands being cultivated there. This idea was particularly popular among the region's mestizos—"Scots-Creeks," "people of ethnically diverse ancestry," or as they were called in less sensitive times, "half-breeds." Like McGillivray, the blood of both races flowed in their veins, and in most cases they were less devoted to what whites called "the wild Indian mode of living" than their full-blooded counterparts. Anglo-American style farming, a plantation economy, even African slavery appealed to them. They listened to McGillivray and liked what they heard.

Other Creeks were not so pleased. They understood that McGillivray's plan would require the Creeks to live more like whites than like Indians. They sensed too that they were being asked to emulate Alexander McGillivray for the benefit of Alexander McGillivray, and they did not like that idea either. But at the time this opposition was disorganized and unfocused, so McGillivray forged ahead. His goal was to make Little Talassee a regional market center, from which goods would flow down the Alabama River to Mobile, which John Pope, Virginia visitor, predicted, would "'ere long surpass *Pensacola,* in Population, Trade and Buildings." Spain would have to reorganize her priorities to accommodate this situation, and the Americans would have no choice but to accept it. The Creek nation would be a nation indeed, and Alexander McGillivray would be its leader.

But things didn't work out that way. Seldom a well man, McGillivray ignored "an habitual Head-Ache and Cholic" to continue his intrigues against the Americans, and that move proved his undoing. It was cold and raining in early 1793, when he went to Pensacola to discuss American encroachments. McGillivray was already sick, and his condition worsened. Shortly after he arrived, he died.

That was just fine as far as the Americans, Georgians mostly, were concerned. Already they were settling on Indian land, clearing plots among those farmed by natives living there. They were fiercely independent, these new arrivals, individualistic, jealous of their liberties, and not easily bent to the will of others. So it seems unlikely, looking back, that McGillivray could have controlled them, bound their interests to his, and created a free Creek state in and among the ever-expanding whites. However, McGillivray's plan to bring the Creeks into the agricultural market economy that was emerging on the frontier and in the process to integrate them into white culture, as he himself had been integrated, did not die with him. Instead, it was taken up by Americans and by their allies, allies who were themselves as white as they were Creek.

THE UNITED STATES AND ALABAMA

The task of clarifying and expanding McGillivray's plan fell to Benjamin Hawkins. A respected North Carolina political figure and experienced frontiersman, he came to the Creek country late in 1796, as the newly appointed United States Indian commissioner. His plan for the Indians was based on the assumption, widely held back East, that both the Indians and the Americans would be better off if the natives would adopt white agricultural practices and live as part of "civilized" society. To get the Creeks to agree, Hawkins came with assurances that the United States would provide the tools, technology, livestock, and instruction to transform warrior-hunters into self-sufficient frontier farmers. The Indians, for their part, were expected to settle down and live like white men with red skins. The advantages, from the American perspective, were considerable. The Creeks would hold title to the land they farmed, could live unmolested among the settlers, and could enjoy all the benefits of Christian civilization. In this the Indians would be protected by the laws of the United States. All they had to do in return was give up claim to the millions of acres they hunted—land that, in American eyes, was already vacant and wasted and that now, under this arrangement, would no longer be needed.

The Creeks, many of them, saw things differently. Opponents of the arrangement argued that if they gave up their vast hunting grounds to earn their living on farms, more land would be open for white settlement, and soon the Creeks would be a minority in what had been their country. These critics warned that if they abandoned their tribal laws to follow rules laid down by the United States, there would be no recourse, for federal land law would take precedent over their customs and traditions. They might still be Indians, but they would be Americans as well. More important, dissenting Creeks realized that behind such an offer was a general prejudice against them and their civilization. Whites could not understand that from the Indians' perspective, those acres did not lie unused. The land was not just hunted, it was managed. Controlled burning eliminated undergrowth and allowed grazing game to thrive; woodland plants, nuts, and berries were used for food and medicine; and Indian folklore focused on forest animals and spirits. To the Indians the woods were a cultural as well as an economic resource. Giving up the land would be giving up some of themselves.

Nor did whites appreciate the fact that Indian laws and traditions were as important an expression of their way of life as American laws and traditions were to Americans. To ask a warrior to settle down and farm was asking a man to assume a role once played by women while at the same time asking women to give up critical functions they had always performed for their families and their clan. This change was no small matter to those affected. Yet either whites did not understand the degree to which their schemes unsettled and altered Native American culture, or, if they did, they didn't care.

Now it was Benjamin Hawkins who forged ahead, and who was surprised (or so he claimed) when many Indians proved skeptical, if not downright hostile, to the plan. However, his surprise seems to have been genuine when he discovered that some white settlers also opposed the scheme. Although whites liked the idea of more land, the thought of Indians remaining in large numbers among them, living with them as equals, was not their idea of what "civilization" was all about. So Hawkins had problems from the start. And things were going to get worse.

As Benjamin Hawkins worked to find a way to transform Indians into yeoman farmers, other forces were working to transform farmers into planters. Cotton had been in the Alabama region as early as 1772, but it was not until the 1790s, when Eli Whitney's gin made its appearance, that the future of cotton became the future of Alabama. By 1796 a Rhode Island "treadle-gin" operated in the Creek country. Hawkins reported how its owner, Robert Grierson, set up "a manufactory of cotton cloth" and hired "an active girl of Georgia . . . to superintend the establishment." With "11 hands, red, white and black, [employed] in spinning and weaving" and others "raising and preparing the cotton for them," in a few years Grierson had established himself as both a planter and an entrepreneur. Others would soon follow suit.

And like Grierson they would own slaves. Reports from the cotton frontier revealed the increased reliance that emerging planters were placing on slave labor. Blacks in bondage had been part of the scene for a century or more, but it was only after the gin arrived that their numbers began to swell. With the plantation system still in its infancy, and the demands on the peculiar institution as yet ill defined, at times bondsmen seemed able to dictate their own routines, especially when they "belonged" to Indians whose attitude toward the institution was decidedly different from that of whites. Alexander McGillivray's sister, Sophia Durand, and half-sister, Sehoy Weatherford, were two of the largest slaveholders in the Creek nation, a situation that speaks volumes about the role women played in the tribal economy. Though part of the mestizos elite and though married to white men Charles Weatherford and Alexander Durand, these women's treatment of their chattel reflected more the Indians' relaxed attitude toward bondage than the repressive way of American slaveholders. In December of 1796 Hawkins reported that Durand slaves and others celebrated Christmas with "a proper frolic of rum drinking and dancing." But such liberty would not last. Cotton soon brought a seasonal cycle to the region, one that would imprint Alabama and Alabamians for a century and more.

Cotton also brought people, and what had been a slow, disorderly trickle into the region now became a "brisk migration." Some settlers reached the Tennessee River Valley and squatted, hoping that when the land came up for sale possession would count for something. Others wandered in from the west and settled along the Tombigbee above the line that separated American and Spanish possessions. In 1795 the two nations had agreed that the Yazoo Strip did belong to the United States, and that 31° latitude would be the boundary. Two years later the surveyor general Andrew Ellicott marked the line, and the next year, 1798, the Mississippi Territory was created, wedged in between Spanish Florida to the south, Tennessee to the north, Georgia to the east, and Spanish Louisiana to the west.

Things moved quickly then. In 1803 the United States bought Louisiana, and the American domain doubled. Meanwhile, the federal government, concerned with communication between Washington and New Orleans, ordered a horse path cut across Creek country so the mail could go through. Some Indians resisted, refused to let the trail pass through their land, but others agreed, so the route was arranged. Cut at different times and from different directions, the path when finally completed entered the territory at Fort Mitchell on the Chattahoochee, then snaked west nearly to touch the Alabama River at the forks. From there the trail swung south to cross the Tensaw River near where Samuel Mims had built a ferry, and went on to Fort Stoddert where it picked up the Spanish boundary, which it followed to New Orleans. The route would not remain a horse path long. Soon settlers took over the trail, and to accommodate them the path became the Federal Road. For decades this would be the main migration route taken by those who populated central and south Alabama, and many families in the region today, black and white, have ancestors who came this way.

They were a rough, rowdy, and not altogether proper group, these folks who early settled what was then called the Great Southwest. Strung out along the Tombigbee River, with St. Stephens the only site that could be called a town, squeezed in between Creeks, Choctaws, and Chickasaws, and with the Spanish to the south blocking access to the gulf, they seemed a people under siege, and maybe they were. In 1801 the population stood at 500 whites and about half that many blacks. By 1810, the number of white residents had increased to 733, slaves had doubled to more than 500, and the region had a name—Washington County. Two years later the population on the eastern side of the river had grown to the point that Clarke County was created. But the number of slaves should not suggest that a plantation economy was in the making. Most of the people were cattle drovers and would continue to be well after statehood.

Still, cotton was being planted there, and in time cotton would be king.

Leadership says something about a people, and the leading citizen of this southwest frontier was Harry Toulmin, a Scottish freethinker who, it has been said, sought a place "so far from civilization that he could be safe from Presbyterians" and found it there. Though in time the state would become one of the buckles of the Bible Belt, along the Tombigbee churches were few and not that well attended. Ministers were so scarce that older settlers recalled how "young people were accustomed to marry themselves, that is they paired off, like birds, and lived together as husband and wife." Toulmin made this home, prospered, and was eventually appointed a territorial judge, probably because he was one of the few citizens who could read the laws.

Settlement began in much the same manner up in the Tennessee Valley. First came the squatters, mostly from Tennessee, who clustered along the river and around the Big Spring homestead of John Hunt, who was as illegally settled as the rest of them. But in 1809, when what had been made Madison County was open for purchase, it was not the squatters but a bevy of wealthy Georgians, the so-called Broad River Group, who got the best land. Clannish, often related, supremely confident of their abilities, and convinced of their right to govern lesser men, the Georgians had money, slaves, and tastes that set them apart from residents already there. And when this Broad River bunch displaced poorer folk from their homes and farms, bitter rivalries were inevitable.

One case makes the point. In 1810 Leroy Pope, a wealthy Georgian, appeared to claim the land he had purchased around what locals had taken to call "Hunt Springs." Hunt and his fellow squatters were evicted. The new possessor christened the location "Twickenham," after the home of British poet Alexander Pope, whom the pompous planter claimed was his kinsman. The result was Alabama's first "rebellion of the rustics"; for the next year when Madison County chose its delegates to the Mississippi Territorial Legislature, the squatters rallied behind two of their own, Hugh McVay and Gabriel Moore, and overwhelmed their aristocratic opposition. When McVay and Moore arrived to take their seats, the first thing they did was introduce legislation changing the name of the settlement to Huntsville. Alabama's political history begins on that character note.

THE CREEK WAR

Even as Tennessee Valley settlers were sorting out their situation and Washington County folks were trying to decide just what their situation was, Indians from the Gulf to the Great Lakes were coming to the realization that if something was not done to stop white expansion, the land would be overrun and the tribes would be no more. What they saw coming was a cultural clash that would determine just who would live as free men on their own terms and who would live under terms set by others. That this struggle between Native Americans and other Americans became part of a larger conflict between Great Britain and the United States, the so-called War of 1812, has caused some to consider it a side show, something incidental to the more important events occurring elsewhere. But in Alabama at the time that was not the case. The Creek War, as the wider war was locally known, was more than a contest for territorial sovereignty, though that was surely part of it. It was even more than a war for independence, though that too was the victor's reward. It was a war for survival, physical and cultural survival. The winner would seek total victory and demand unconditional surrender. The losers would be left with little to justify their being there. This is why both sides fought with desperate, brutal courage, why so little quarter was given, and why, between August of 1813 and March of 1814, the future of what would be Alabama was decided.

Tribesmen, less than enthusiastic over Hawkins's plan to "civilize," became increasingly alarmed with developments that followed. Talk of another federal road from Tennessee to Mobile unsettled them, and an 1805 treaty under which Georgia Creeks gave up more than 2 million acres of their land seemed to foreshadow things to come. Increasingly these Indians spoke out against future cessions, for as one of them told Pres. Thomas Jefferson, their land "is become very small" and "when a thing began to grow scarce it is natural to love it." But more a concern than roads and treaties was the growing conviction among certain elements of the tribe that their leaders were compromising Indian values. The changes in landholding, subsistence, and governance that Hawkins proposed promised to change some of the most fundamental aspects of tribal culture. If Hawkins and his allies succeeded, the world these Creeks had known, the world of their ancestors, would be abandoned, forsaken for the illusion of American protection and prosperity.

In desperate times people naturally seek spiritual help, and for these Creeks, times were desperate. As the details and implications of Hawkins's plan became clear, uneasy Indians increasingly turned to their own religious leaders—mystical men, shamen, or as they were best known, prophets. These men communed with spirits, foresaw the future, and advised. In ways that whites could not understand, this religious revival was another part of the Creek's cultural defense, for with American "civilization" came Christianity, and Hawkins naturally assumed that to become good Americans the Creeks would have to give up their pagan ways. Thus the prophets became symbols of the threatened order and agents of resistance.

Around the prophets rallied the "Red Sticks," a Creek faction that took their name from the red war clubs that identified them. Assistant Indian Agent Alexander Cornells described them as "enemies of the plan of civilization" who preferred instead to live "wild." Their influence spread, and soon Hawkins was complaining that even "the most industrious and best behaved of all our Indians" had succumbed to what he called "fanaticism." Before long the Americans concluded that they could count on only the older chiefs and on those natives who had made the most of the market-economy arrangements that Hawkins called "the new order of things." This latter group was heavy with mestizos, the people who had supported

McGillivray and who now supported Hawkins. To the Red Sticks, the mestizos were as much the enemy as Hawkins and the Americans.

The Red Sticks would have been a problem for Hawkins under any circumstances, but in 1811 and early 1812, two events occurred that turned Creek resistance into a force with which to be reckoned. The first was the arrival of Tecumseh, a Shawnee leader who came into Alabama in the summer of 1811 to build an alliance of tribes, stretching from Mobile Bay to Lake Michigan, that combined could stop America's westward movement in its tracks. Arriving at Tucka-batchee, the town that served as the capital of the Upper Creeks, he met with the Indians assembled and urged them to resist alien influences that were polluting their way of life. Using a common language of mysticism and spirituality, Tecumseh promised the Creeks that if they would "sing the song of the northern lakes, and dance their dance," this would "frighten the Americans, their arms will drop from their hands, the ground will become a bog, and mire them, and you may knock them on the head with your war clubs." The call was clear. The Creeks heard it. So did the Americans.

Rumors soon spread that Tecumseh had promised the Creeks that the British in Canada and the Spanish in Pensacola would come to their aid. So when the United States, angered over insults to its sovereignty, declared war on Great Britain the following summer, frontier settlers quickly concluded that the Indians were in league with their nation's enemy. Thus the coming Creek War became part of the larger conflict, with white Alabamians fighting not just the Indians but also that familiar foe, the British, as well.

To tell the truth, many Americans welcomed the wider conflict. Having settled illegally on Creek land, squatters feared, as one militia officer put it, that "they would receive no support from the U.S. troops" if the Indians came against them. Now if the Creeks attacked it would not be as injured parties defending their land but as allies of Great Britain. That alliance would change everything—or so the squatters hoped, but just in case they began to build forts along and between the lower Alabama and Tombigbee. One of these, down near where the rivers met, was the fortified home of ferryman

Samuel Mims. Another, located near the center of Clarke County, was Fort Sinquefield.

As this building was happening, a second event occurred that, following hard upon Tecumseh's visit, gave the prophets the spiritual assurance they needed to lead the Red Sticks into battle. Late in 1811 a series of earthquakes rattled the Mississippi Valley with shocks that ran through Alabama and into Georgia. The so-called New Madrid quakes, some of the most powerful tremors ever felt in the southeast, were seen as a sign that the earth was unhappy with what was taking place, and, according to the prophets, it was the Red Sticks' responsibility to set things right. When rumors spread that Tecumseh had actually predicted these quakes, the link between natural phenomena and Indian mysticism was forged. As one of them put it, "White people have the old book from God. We Indians do not have it and are unable to read it. The Indians know it without the book; they dream much of God, and therefore they know it." The trembling earth was the stuff from which dreams were made.

An uneasy calm settled on Alabama, and for the rest of 1812 wary settlers built more forts, while the Red Sticks recruited loyal warriors and prepared for the coming conflict. Now the Indians' arts of peaceful persuasion failed them, and Creeks turned on themselves. Red Stick recruiting opened old divisions within the nation, and as each side sought to suppress the other, recrimination followed recrimination, assault followed assault, and murder followed murder. What had begun as a cultural war against the white man now became a civil war, Creek against Creek.

Meanwhile the larger war, the war in which whites fought whites, took some strange turns of its own. In early 1813 word reached the interior that Gen. James Wilkinson, who was both U.S. garrison commander in New Orleans and a paid agent of Spain, landed some six hundred men below Mobile. He marched his army to the city, told the Spanish commander that the "post was within the legitimate limits of [the United] States" and demanded surrender. With little choice in the matter, the commander complied. That the United States and Spain were not at war and that Madrid's claim to Mobile was as least as good as, if not better than, Washington's made little difference to Wilkinson, to upriver settlers, and to American officials. Mobile was an American city now, and Alabama had its outlet to the gulf.

Spain was hardly happy with this turn of events, and in the months that followed officials in Pensacola began to take a greater interest in the disposition of the Creeks. Sensing this, the Red Sticks reportedly told Spanish and British merchants that as soon as Native Americans got the arms and ammunition they needed, they would begin attacking white settlements along the Alabama River. Though it is unclear just how much aid and encouragement they actually got, Creek parties did visit Pensacola and that, to Americans, was all the evidence they needed.

So a company of militia under Col. James Caller set out to ambush a Creek pack train returning from Florida supposedly loaded with supplies for the tribe. Caller, whom contemporaries recalled as a dashing figure in "a calico hunting shirt, a high bell-crowned hat and top boots," marched his force to Burnt Corn Creek, on the Pensacola road, and waited. The Indians arrived on schedule, and surprise was complete. The Red Sticks fled in disarray, but instead of following them, Caller's men stopped and began looting the horses. Seeing this, the Indians regrouped and counterattacked. Most Americans took to their heels. In what was described as "a disgraceful rout," Caller escaped wearing only "his shirt and drawers"—we can only wonder what happened to the rest of his attire. It was a humiliating defeat, and for years afterward no American would admit ever being at Burnt Corn.

As news of the battle spread, settlers began making their way to neighborhood forts. By mid-August Mims's stockade was crammed with more than three hundred refugees, and smaller outposts were just as crowded. But Mims's commander, Maj. Daniel Beasley, was confident that the Indians would not attack so large a garrison, so he reportedly "turned a deaf ear to all idea of danger" and ignored warnings from experienced woodsmen that there were Red Sticks in the area. On 30 August 1813 Beasley assured his superior,

Gen. Ferdinand L. Claiborne, that the fort could hold out "against any number of Indians" and then, according to eyewitnesses, he got roaring drunk. He was in that condition when he got his last warning. James Cornells, a frontiersman who knew the Indians well, rode up to the gate and called out that the Red Sticks were approaching. Outraged, and full of whiskey, Beasley roared back that the scout had only seen "a gang of red cattle." Cornells retreated, but as he left he shouted that those cattle would "give him a h——ll of a kick before night." The Creeks were already in place, and when the drum called the garrison to its noon meal, they attacked.

Leading the charge was a man the Indians called Red Eagle and the settlers addressed as William Weatherford. The son of Charles and Sehoy Weatherford, Red Eagle was known and respected through the region. Since his brother, half-brother, and a number of other relatives sided with the Americans, whites expected him to do the same, so they were confused and angered when he did not. Weatherford, according to his aunt who was in the fort and survived to tell the tale, "came in the gate at full run, at the head of his warriors." Behind him came the Red Sticks. The fighting was fierce, but the outcome was never in doubt. Ten days later a burial party arrived to find bodies of "Indians, negroes, white men, women and children [lying] in one promiscuous ruin." The party buried 247 in two large pits. Then, according to the commander's report, "the soldiers and officers, with one voice, called on Divine Providence to revenge the death of [their] murdered friends."

News of the fall of Fort Mims created panic in South Alabama. Settlers who had hesitated earlier now rushed to neighborhood stockades, leaving farms and fields just as the harvest was coming in. At one fort they raised a tall pole in the middle of the stockade, built a scaffold on top, and burned "fat pine" at night—a primitive but effective searchlight for frontiersmen who were used to finding deer in the dark by firelight reflecting in their eyes. Now their skill at "fire hunting" was used against another prey.

Then things got quiet, so quiet that some settlers felt safe enough to leave the stockades. Over at Fort Sinquefield members of the

James and Kimbell families decided to return to the Kimbell home, about a mile away. It was a fatal mistake. Shortly after they arrived the Indians attacked, killing and scalping everyone who was there—or so the attackers believed. Sarah Merrill, one of the Jameses' daughters, was knocked unconscious, scalped, and left for dead. That night it rained and, as early historian T. H. Ball described it, "cool tear-drops from heaven fell upon her bloody head" and revived her. Still dazed, she began frantically searching for her baby, a boy barely a year old. Fearing the worst, she fumbled in the dark and found him, identifiable by the buttons on his dress; the other children's clothes were bound up with string. To her surprise he was alive. His hair had been too short to make a decent scalp.

Carrying the boy, she struck out for the fort, but she was soon exhausted. So she hid him in a hollow log and staggered on to Sinquefield to tell her story. A party was soon dispatched to find the child and bury the dead. They did both. There were no other survivors. Sarah Merrill and her son both lived long lives, and it is told how she would sit with her grandchildren, tell them of the massacre, and if they asked, pull back her bonnet to show them the scar.

Then the Americans struck back. In October General Claiborne, coming from the west, crossed the Tombigbee at St. Stephens with an army raised to punish the Red Sticks. With him was Sam Dale. Forty-one years old, "Big Sam," according to contemporaries, stood above six feet, his 190 pounds spread over "a large, muscular frame . . . [with] no superfluous flesh." After fighting in Georgia's Indian wars, Dale, with that frontiersman's disregard for inconvenient laws, got involved in a scheme to smuggle coffee and slaves from Spanish Pensacola. When the plan was uncovered and a warrant issued for his arrest, Dale decided it was time to move. So he left Georgia and ended up in the western part of the Mississippi Territory, where he was when Claiborne signed him on as a scout.

Once the army was over the Tombigbee, Dale was sent ahead with a small party to find the best place to cross the Alabama River. Arriving at Weatherford's Ferry, named after Red Eagle's brother John, they camped, and on the morning of 12 November 1813, Big Sam and three companions took a confiscated canoe and set out to reconnoiter the other side. They were hardly out into the river before they looked upstream to see a large canoe with eleven warriors paddling toward them.

With Dale was Jeremiah Austill, nineteen years old, tall, "very sinewy," and despite his youth considered "a much more than ordinary man." There were also the "stout and finely proportioned" James Smith and an "Indian negro" slave named Caesar. Though badly outnumbered, there was no thought of retreat, as the Americans turned their canoe into the current and moved into position. The river swings wide at Weatherford's Ferry, and in the fall the water usually is low and slow. Still, the Alabama's current is strong, so it was critical to maneuver into place and hold steady. As the two canoes came together Caesar grabbed the other boat and held it fast. Then they fought. Guns and war clubs, knives and hatchets, hand to hand, to the cheers of comrades on the shore, Dale, Austill, and Smith bludgeoned their way to victory. For future generations of Alabama students, this was the famous "canoe fight."

For whites the victory was more important in symbol than substance. Defeating one canoe loaded with Indians cleared the crossing only for the moment. It took Claiborne's army to secure the spot. But what Dale and his comrades did that day was a potent tonic for settlers demoralized by Burnt Corn and Fort Mims. Though the Indians were still a formidable foe, the canoe fight was taken as proof then and by later historians that natives were "not a match even handed for the bold and hardy pioneer white man," Caesar's contribution notwithstanding.

Four days later Claiborne's army arrived, crossed the river, and on a high bluff on the eastern side of the stream built a fort, which the general named for himself. Humility was not his strong point. From that strategic spot Claiborne reasoned that they could "cut the savages off from the river and from their growing crops . . . [and] render their communication with Pensacola more hazardous." Fort

Claiborne also could serve as a supply depot for the next phase of the operation.

THE CREEKS INVADED

Five armies were poised to crush the Red Stick rebellion. Claiborne was ready in the south. In Georgia Gen. John Floyd was prepared to attack from the east. And in Tennessee Gen. Andrew Jackson was in command of a force eager to teach Indians in Alabama and elsewhere the consequences of opposing white settlement. But there also were Indians ready for revenge against the Creeks. A Choctaw force under Chief Pushmataha joined to settle old scores and regain land taken from them by expanding enemies. And from the north, marching with Jackson, came Cherokees, wearing white plumes to identify them as friend not foe. For those Creeks who feared the worst, the worst was coming.

What followed was a campaign of unparalleled brutality. Filled with stories of atrocities at Fort Mims, of men, women, and children dismembered, disemboweled, and burned alive, American soldiers sought revenge and retribution. Coming out of the Tennessee Valley and into Coosa country, Jackson's forces destroyed villages, burned storehouses, and left the people who survived dispirited and desperate. One Creek town, Hillabee, realized the futility of resistance and tried to surrender, but to no avail. What followed was, one historian noted, "a massacre and not a battle." It was not the only one. Talladega, Tallussahatchee, Autossee, and a host of other villages felt the wrath of the invaders. The Creeks had risked everything to preserve their culture, their way of life. And they were about to lose.

As Jackson moved relentlessly south, Claiborne's army and their Choctaw allies marched toward Ikanatchaka, an Indian town on the south bank of the Alabama in modern Lowndes County. This was the Holy Ground, seat of the tribe's most powerful prophets. Located on a peninsula formed by a creek and the river, the site was protected by ravines and by a line of finely split fat pine, a barrier that the prophets claimed, when burning, could not be crossed by their enemies. The prophets were wrong.

The battle took place two days before Christmas 1813. Claiborne's army advanced and broke the magic line; the Indians withdrew in panic. Only Weatherford and a small force that reportedly put no stock in prophets' promises held their ground. They were not enough. The Indians left behind twenty-one dead; only one American was killed.

Weatherford and his men were the last to withdraw, and from his flight comes one of those heroic episodes that enabled future Alabamians to make an epic out of what was in reality a dirty, vengeful war. Later it was told how the Creek leader mounted his horse, Arrow, and made his escape by jumping off a twelve-foot bluff into the stream and swimming to the other side. There, in full view of his foe, Red Eagle "dismounted, unsaddled his horse, wrung the water out of his blanket and other articles, then again resaddling, he mounted and rode off." Some who were there said it never happened, that there was no heroic leap and unvanquished retreat, but most Alabamians believed it was all true—and still do.

Then Claiborne marched away, leaving to Pushmataha's men the spoils. The Choctaws took their revenge and reward, and soon Creek scalps were displayed in villages throughout the Choctaw nation. The Americans got their reward as well. Arriving in St. Stephens, the victorious army was greeted with a celebration and a parade featuring a tune, "Claiborne's Victory," written just for the occasion. All across lower Alabama settlers came out of their forts and returned to their farms. Claiborne had beaten the Creeks in the south. Now, they wondered, could Jackson do the same in the north?

News from the Coosa-Tallapoosa Valley soon confirmed that the Tennessee troops were doing their work with brutal efficiency. Moving south, keeping pressure on the enemy despite fierce resistance and supply problems, Jackson slowly approached the heart of what remained of the Red Stick rebellion. Meanwhile, the Creek nation was collapsing. One army defeated, the Holy Ground defiled, towns in ashes, people dead and dying, facing the hardest winter months without food and shelter, they must have thought that the world, their world, was coming to an end—which of course it was. So it is little wonder that so many of those who could sought sanctuary with what was left of their people, a rag-tag band digging in for a last stand at a place called Horseshoe Bend.

Deep in the river's curve, with the Tallapoosa on three sides and breastworks to their front, the Red Sticks waited. In late March the enemy arrived, war-hardened Tennessee troops and their Cherokee allies, led by a man from whom they expected no quarter. On 27 March 1814 the battle began. It ended that same day.

Fewer than half, maybe no more than a third, of the Indians had firearms. It was the age of steel and powder against the age of stone. Steel and powder won. The Red Sticks fought hard. So did the Americans, but the outcome was never in doubt. And once that was settled, there was the awful aftermath. Drawing little distinction between the warriors who resisted and the women and children refugees who did not, Jackson's soldiers did to the Indians what they believed the Indians had done to settlers at Mims. One trooper, arriving on the scene after Red Stick resistance was crushed, reportedly shot an elderly native so "he might be able to report when he went home that he had killed an Indian." Another soldier told of how, after the battle, an American killed a "little Indian boy" with the butt of his musket, and "when reproached by an officer for barbarity in killing so young a child," his excuse was simply "that the boy would have become an Indian some day." Later one of Jackson's men wrote his wife that "the Tallapoosa might truly be called the River of blood," and for hours after the fighting the stream still ran so red "that it could not be used." As many as a thousand Creeks may have fallen at Horseshoe Bend, and with them perished the Red Stick cause.

After the battle the Tennessee general took his army south to the forks of the Coosa and Tallapoosa, where the French had built Toulouse. There he raised a new fort and, being no less vain than Claiborne, named it Fort Jackson. Then he sent out word for the defeated Creeks to come and learn their fate. That was when William Weatherford appeared.

The hated and feared Red Eagle had, by his own admission, "done the white people all the harm I could," so settlers and soldiers alike wanted revenge. But rather than try to escape when his cause was lost, Weatherford boldly rode into Jackson's camp to surrender. It was all the general could do to keep his men from killing their enemy on the spot. "Awed and impressed" by such courage, Jackson took Red Eagle to his tent, where the warrior expressed regret that he was not able to prevent the massacre of women and children at Mims but showed no remorse for the men who fell in battle—war was war. General Jackson heard him out and let him go.

Weatherford did not return to the Creeks. He settled instead on family land in south Monroe County, not far from the site of Fort Mims. Years later he explained this decision with cryptic simplicity: "[My] old comrades, the hostiles, ate [my] cattle from starvation; the peace party ate them from revenge; and the squatters because [I] was a d——d Red-skin. So I have come to live among gentlemen." Choosing class over race, he became one of them—a frontier aristocrat with a river plantation worked by scores of slaves. In time, forgiven for his trespasses and praised for his "bravery, honor, and strong native sense," William Weatherford, the Red Eagle, was enshrined as Alabama's good Indian. The feared warrior lived out his days in a manner almost indistinguishable from other frontier planters, an example, some surely thought, of how things might have been if the Creeks had listened to Hawkins. But to his white neighbors, Red Eagle was something else. He was one of the spoils of war, and as such, he and his exploits belonged to the victors.

Sam Dale was Alabama's Creek War hero, and his reputation was equal in its place and time to that of Boone in Kentucky. He also settled in Monroe County, which he represented in the legislature. He and Weatherford became friends, and when Red Eagle was married, Dale stood as a groomsman. Eventually a grateful state awarded Big Sam the rank of brigadier general. He later moved to Mississippi, where he died in 1841. But despite an active life and outstanding career, Dale's place in history remains tied to that November day on the Alabama River, when white men in a canoe fought red men in a canoe, while Caesar, a black man, held the two together. Of such, much-needed heroes are made. And for the sake of heroes we should appreciate all the more the strength of Caesar's grip.

3

Becoming a State

In August of 1814 representatives of the defeated Creeks gathered at Fort Jackson to learn their fate. It was all they feared, and more. The treaty forced on them took away over half the Creeks' Alabama land. Then, in a move applauded by frontiersmen, Jackson stripped his Indian allies of much of their land as well. Nearly three-fifths of the future state was soon open for settlement.

Not long after the treaty was signed, Jackson ordered Howell Tatum, his topographical engineer, to descend the Alabama River and "ascertain the courses and distance" down to Mobile. The journey took the engineer through what would be the heart of Alabama's plantation district, the famous, in some cases infamous, Black Belt. Tatum saw the future. "The rich lands on the sides of the river," he recorded in his journal, "are far superior to any I have ever seen in any country, and I have no doubt will prove a source of immence wealth to those who may hereafter be doomed the cultivators." The man was a prophet.

All along the route Tatum noted abandoned farms—"improvements" made by dispossessed Indians and evidence that the country was "capable of producing, in great abundance, every article necessary to the sustenance of man, or beast." All that was needed were the people, and they were coming. Some were veterans of the war who had seen and considered the land as they marched with Jackson and Claiborne, and coveted it. With them were others who had heard stories and wanted to see for themselves. They were followed (sometimes accompanied) by merchants and peddlers, who set up shop and served the limited needs of frontier people and frontier communities. Speculators arrived as soon or sooner, with land to sell and credit to offer; and of course there were professional men, a breed that ran high in lawyers, for there were deeds to record, suits to file, and adversaries (many adversaries) to defend or prosecute. To all these people, this was the land of opportunity, and the able, energetic, lucky, and (perhaps above all else) shifty among them made the most of it.

They were a disorderly lot, and despite government plans for regulated settlement, they imposed their disorder on the land. Even before the war squatters had moved into Creek territory, cleared farms, and settled down to frontier life. So imagine the intruders' surprise when in 1816 federal officials ordered them to leave. The interlopers refused. Pointing instead to what they considered a higher authority, some of them protested that "general Jackson encouraged us to Settle on the allebarmer," which they seemed to think was authorization enough for anyone. On Jackson's word they had "sold there Carages[,] waggons & &" and they were stranded—"how to get back god only knows." Not that they intended to leave. Convinced, perhaps rightly, that speculators were behind efforts to remove them, they protested that if they were not allowed to keep their property, groups like "the Yazoo Company will Purchase all the good land." How, they asked, can it be that people who "fought Brave to obtain this Cuntry . . . Now Cannot Injoy it."

Congress, sensitive to popular opinion on this issue, stopped the evictions and made adjustments that would allow pre-1816 settlers to purchase their claims. But one wonders how many actually did. Most frontier squatters, according to historian Thomas P. Abernethy, were "improvident by nature, [and] did not come to seek wealth but merely to gain a subsistence or to enjoy the freedom of the forest." And being that way, they soon sold their land, if they had actually bought it, and moved on. There was a ready group to replace them. As word of the Alabama land drifted back east, the effect was both excitement and uneasiness. In Hillsborough, North Carolina, James Graham complained that "the *Alabama Feaver* rages here with great violence and has *carried off* vast numbers of our citizens." Graham lamented how "some of our oldest and most wealthy men are offering their possessions for sale and are desirous of removing to this new country." This was a different breed of settler, the sort who, in time, would turn farms into plantations, villages into towns, and towns into cities.

ENTER SARAH CHOTARD

Despite Graham's lament, "men" were not the only adventurers seeking their fortunes in the new country. Around 1820 Mrs. Sarah F. Williams Willis Chotard, whom legend describes as a "glamorous Frenchwoman," appeared in the region. Through a series of circumstances, including two marriages (the second to a San Domingo refugee), Mrs. Chotard (who was actually a Virginian) was granted some fifteen hundred acres in either Alabama or Mississippi—the choice was hers. First she looked at Claiborne, but when it was ruled that her grant was for rural land, not town lots, she shifted her attention to the falls of the Cahaba River, where a major east-west migration route crossed the stream. Here, with water power and transportation, she believed she could build a commercial and manufacturing complex. She named her creation Centerville. In 1821 she convinced the government to give the site a post office, and the next year she arrived on the scene with a surveyor to lay off lots and evict squatters.

As much the promoter as any speculator in the region, Mrs. Chotard made a "liberal offer" of town lots to General Jackson (whom she apparently knew) in hopes that he would endorse her scheme. The general declined the offer, though he softened the blow with the wish that her "town will grow and prosper like the rose." She took the refusal in stride and continued on, but things did not go as she had hoped. Though the surveyor laid out an appealing village with broad streets, large lots, and connecting alleys, buyers did not come, and by the end of 1823 only 23 of the 265 plots were sold. It was a grand failure.

Mrs. Chotard never knew. In 1824 she died downstream at Cahawba, still hoping, believing, that her dream would become reality. Centerville continued without her, but it never became the metropolis she hoped it would be. In later years uncertainty about her background fed legends of how she had met the man she married at a ball after the Battle of New Orleans, how he was one of Jackson's officers, and how she had been Jackson's French interpreter when he was in Louisiana. None of these stories could be verified, but the telling added to the mystery that surrounded the woman who wanted to build a city of her own.

SOCIETY TAKES SHAPE

So it was that the populating process, begun so well before the war, continued apace after it. Madison County, up in the bend of the Tennessee, kept growing and at one point may have contained half the population of the Mississippi Territory. Carpenters in Huntsville were busy, and by the end of the century's second decade that market and political center boasted some sixty commercial buildings around its town square. Out in the countryside other folks were setting up, and the prewar tension between farmer and planter, "haves" and "have-nots," seems to have abated a bit. Times were good. High cotton prices drove up land prices, credit was easy, speculation was normal, and the Alabama portion of the territory boomed. Little wonder *Alabama Feaver* was such a contagious disease.

Yet there were immigrants who did not come voluntarily. Planters, and some who hoped to be planters, brought slaves, so from the beginning the South's peculiar institution helped shape Alabama's character. Early on and for decades thereafter, they came with their masters, "tramping [according to English visitor George Featherstonhaugh] through the waxy ground on foot . . . wet with fording the streams . . . [and] shivering with cold." There were so many of the driven and the drivers that "but for the very decided style of cussing and swearing," another traveler said he would have mistaken them for the biblical Exodus. And when yet another visitor, Harriet Martineau, asked some she met where they were going they called back, "Into Yellibama."

Like almost everything in this agricultural world, the migration conformed to the seasons. After the harvest the wagons were packed, teams were hitched, and the trek began. So it was winter, wet and dreary, when they arrived in Alabama. Then shelter was built and land was cleared for the spring crop—or maybe it was the other way round, for planting was the priority, and a tent or lean-to could, and often did, serve well enough, especially for the slaves, who had little or no choice in the matter. Oh, there were some planters, those with money and credit, who seemed to do everything all at once—clear, cultivate, and build a big house with little houses out back for the laborers. But they were the exception. Plantation culture was for the most part an evolutionary culture. But it evolved quickly. Between statehood and Civil War, Alabama's planter came to power, moved from the cabin to the columned mansion, from courthouse to capitol, but when he crossed these thresholds he still had the mud of the frontier on his boots.

Many, of course, did not even get to the door. They remained where they had started, frontier farmers to the end. Often forgotten in our rose-tinted reflections on this antebellum era is the fact that most white Alabamians did not live in stately mansions with Grecian entablature. Theirs were simple houses, usually log, with rooms built on both sides of an open-ended hall in the famous "dog-trot" design, which gave the inhabitants a place to sit on warm summer evenings, catch a breeze, smell the honeysuckle, rest from the day, and talk. From these homes they would go out to plow, hunt, herd, trap, fish, and make whiskey, which, of course, they tested, just to confirm the quality. Call them yeomen, plain folk, middling sort, or crackers, they were a cut above what would later be termed "white trash" and a notch or two below the gentry whom they envied, admired, liked, disliked, and tolerated, each in their time and in their turn. They were a fluid class, if class is the proper word, with different levels occupied at different times by different people. Some even escaped, got out, moved up. More land and a few slaves and they were planters. That was when they closed in the dogtrots, clapboarded the logs, put columns on the front, painted the whole thing white, bought mahogany and Haviland, and became gentlemen and ladies. But often as not, it was an awkward transition and an uneasy segregation. With lines of demarcation so faintly drawn, with upper and middle and even lower classes sharing so many similar experiences and circumstances (and in some cases even kinship), Alabamians were much closer to each other than even they would have wanted to believe, or some of them would have been willing to admit.

Put simply, which is frequently dangerous and often misleading, all white Alabamians, except (occasionally) those at the extreme ends of the social scale, shared in varying degrees a set of characteristics, values, and habits of action that were shared by frontier folk throughout the South. They were an independent lot and as such feared and distrusted anything or anyone who threatened to take their independence from them. This is why they opposed efforts and institutions that concentrated power and wealth in the hands of a few. In short, they were Jacksonian Democrats even before Jackson and in time became his constituency, though they would surely have rejected the term if they heard it. Their independence, and their determination to preserve it, was reinforced by the presence of slaves, whose very existence reminded free men of what freedom was and made it all the more dear. So it followed that they, the free men, saw nothing wrong, and much right, with shedding blood to defend liberty and liberty's handmaiden, honor. In this culture, according to Englishman Philip Henry Gosse, who tutored children of Black Belt planters in the 1830s, "the abiding thought that 'the people' [were] the source of law" convinced many that "'every man is his own law-maker and law-breaker, judge, jury, and executioner.'" And believing such, a Montgomery lawyer explained to a visitor, everyone carries "arms under his clothes [and] at the slightest quarrel, knife or pistol comes to hand."

Yet these Alabamians were not a dark and vengeful people, brooding their way into bloody action. Among the gentry, and even among yeomen, visitors observed "a bold and gallant bearing," a "frank and free cordiality," and a "generous, almost boundless hospitality" that made outsiders welcome. Even so, the inclination toward violence was always there in the antebellum period, and often accentuated, if moralists are to be believed, by the near universal use of whiskey and the absence of social, legal, and religious controls on the practice. In 1832 the Selma town council tried to regulate matters with a law that subjected those caught drinking on Sunday to arrest and a fine. But when fellow townsmen pointed out that, apart from the council, only two adult males in Selma did not "visit McKeagg's saloon every Sunday," the city fathers decided not to enforce the law. Hardly mattered. Next election they were voted out.

Churches might have helped more with municipal reform, but they had problems of their own. Providence Church in Dallas County spent nine months dealing with Brother Thomas McGill who was charged with "getting drunk and fighting," pleasures that often went hand in hand in antebellum Alabama. During that time McGill was "excluded," repented, and was "restored," only to get drunk again. Exclusion this time was permanent. But alcohol was not the only "pleasure" that threatened church and community decorum. In 1837 one Methodist circuit reported that fourteen members had been expelled for such practices as "dram drinking, attending the race ground, going to dancing parties, or suffering our children to do so, attending circuses, theatres, . . . breaking the Sabbath, the neglect of class meetings, and the indulgence of superfluous ornaments." In another case a minister noted how in his town "Jockey Clubs were better supported than churches, and more appreciated than religion."

This is not to suggest that Alabamians were not a believing people, but rather to acknowledge that early on religion was not the top priority of most. Frequently churches were among the last public buildings erected in a town—houses served the faithful well enough—while out in the countryside frontier folk had to search a bit to find a place to worship. For its first twenty-five years, Montgomery, the future capital, was an "open and shamelessly immoral" city where, according to nineteenth-century church historian Anson West, only a handful of residents were considered "professors of religion." But recall, antebellum Alabama was an evolving social landscape, and religion evolved with it. In time churches multiplied, congregations grew, and variations flourished. Some of these distressed more conservative churchgoers who were taken aback by the "crying, shouting, and groaning" that punctuated "a real Methodist meeting" attended by country folk, but at least they were meeting, and that seemed a step in the right direction. As the ranks of the guardians of public decency grew, they were willing to accept any ally, even "a real Methodist," who would help them reform a people whose "moral status," it was said, suggested "apathy, lethargy, and even things worse."

POLITICS IN ANTEBELLUM ALABAMA

The drama of antebellum politics was played out on this social stage. Down in St. Stephens, a squat jumble of buildings spilling off a high ridge at the first shoals of the Tombigbee, the Washington County district court had been meeting since 1804, a tenure that made the town, for all intents and purposes, the capital of the eastern Mississippi Territory. Aaron Burr, fleeing from his failed expedition, was captured nearby, a source of pride for settlers who, from their accounts, seem to have had more sympathy for the pursued than his pursuers—perhaps because many of them were fleeing from something themselves. These residents were described by Ephraim Kirby (a territorial judge down from Connecticut) as generally being "an illiterate, wild and savage" bunch, a people "of depraved morals, unworthy of public confidence or private esteems." They were "litigious, disunited, and knowing each, universally distrustful of each other"—hardly the stuff from which a great state, or even a stable society, might be made. Better folks soon arrived, the town was incorporated, and in 1811 the Territorial Legislature authorized citizens to hold a lottery to generate $5,000 for an academy there—a fund-raising precedent rejected later by modern Alabamians. The future looked bright.

From St. Stephens traders went into the Choctaw nation and squatters went into Creek lands. It was out of St. Stephens that soldiers under General Claiborne and Indians under Pushmataha marched to put down the Red Sticks, and to St. Stephens they returned to celebrate their victory. Mobile's "fall" to American forces enhanced the importance of the upriver town as a market center, and more people arrived to take advantage of opportunities there. The year after the war more than thirty new houses were built, and the population of the town nearly tripled. Access to the gulf gave settlers up and down the Tombigbee and Alabama Rivers a north-south orientation that led them naturally to support dividing the territory longitudinally, which Congress did. Mississippi became a state in 1817, leaving Alabama a territory and St. Stephens its seat of government.

There was a newspaper there by then, and its editor wrote of how "an air of ease and comfort prevails at St. Stephens and recommends it as a pleasant residence." New settlers continued to come, many, the writer noted, from North Carolina, which he seemed to think was a point in their favor. The town also could boast of professional people—lawyers, naturally, and doctors—plus a local theater company, a hotel, and an English blacksmith, whose claim to fame was the introduction of cowbells to the region, fame being what you make of it, I suppose. There was even a shipyard of sorts, and in May of 1820, "amid the shouts and huzzas of a large concourse of spectators," it launched the *Tombeckbee,* one of the first steamboats built in the territory. On the face of it, St. Stephens was thriving.

But by then the seeds of St. Stephens's downfall were already sown. When the first Territorial Legislature met there in 1818, a committee was formed to determine "the most eligible scite for the

Seat of Territorial Government." Quickly champions of different locations came forward to make their case. No one made a case for St. Stephens. Located far from either the physical or population center of the territory, all but inaccessible to many, it was never a serious candidate. Instead two factions emerged. One wanted to locate the capital on the Warrior River, where Tuscaloosa was a rising town. Another wanted an even more central location, near the confluence of the Alabama and Cahaba Rivers, in the heart of the rapidly growing Black Belt.

The committee favored Tuscaloosa. The territorial governor, William Wyatt Bibb, wanted otherwise. Bibb, another Georgian with Broad River connections, had left that state for Alabama to revitalize his sagging political career and make his fortune—two goals shared by many of his class and connections. Having been a U.S. senator, he had friends in Washington who got him appointed territorial chief executive. His future, as he saw it, was to be governor when Alabama became a state and a rich planter in the Black Belt, near the capital, when he retired. So when the legislature met again in St. Stephens, Bibb preempted the committee report with one of his own that not only recommended the central Alabama location but also proposed to sell state lands to pay for it. Rallied by the governor, supporters of his site—Cahawba they called it— carried the day.

Meanwhile, the decline of the territorial capital had begun. At its core St. Stephens had always been a frontier town, and like frontier towns everywhere, its citizens were transients, speculators, always ready to sell out and move on. As a result most buildings, except for the "elegant" few, had a temporary character to them, a makeshift appearance that quickly showed the effects on any slump in the economy. And that slump was not long in coming. Deprived of the customers who visited to do a little business with the government, hotel rooms sat empty and shops closed early. To make matters worse, yellow fever, the scourge of the river region, struck frequently and hard. And then there was the steamboat. By the mid 1820s those shallow-draft monsters were moving upstream, sliding over the shoals, and steaming on. St. Stephens no longer was needed as a port of deposit for goods coming through by land or by water. That purpose gone, there was little left for citizens to do. So they sought opportunities elsewhere, and St. Stephens faded away. By mid century all that was left were ruts and washes where the streets had been, a crumbling foundation here and there, some spring flowers pushing up where once a frontier wife had put down a bit of beauty, and the graveyard.

Cahawba, on the other hand, flourished fair. Lots were sold, important people invested, and construction began. But the government buildings were not ready in March of 1819, when Congress directed the territory to elect a convention to draw up a constitution under which Alabama could be admitted to the Union, so forty-four delegates from what were by then twenty-two counties gathered in Huntsville. It was an appropriate site, for the town of some "260 houses, principally of brick," with stores, a bank, warehouses, and a courthouse, could provide the best Alabama had to offer. Its citizens, according to a lady from Virginia, were "gay, polite, and hospitable, and live in great splendor." That description, of course, was of men like Leroy Pope, who was among those who set the standard for wealth and influence. Had the visitor ventured out into the countryside, she would have found a few wealthy planters scattered among a host of frontier farmers of decidedly plainer interests and inclinations. The elements of the class conflict that turned Twickenham into Huntsville were still there.

The convention may have been only the second most exciting event in Huntsville that year. The day before the delegates were scheduled to assemble, a federal officer rode into town with the "unexpected" news that Pres. James Monroe, on his grand tour of the nation he governed, was on the outskirts of the city. No one seems to have even known that Monroe was in the area, so they hastily formed a welcoming committee and went out to meet the president and his party. The greeting was effusive, and it delayed the guests long enough for word to go out that food, drink, and tableware were needed for a banquet. Townsfolk pitched in, and that evening "more than one hundred of the most respected citizens of Madison County" sat down with the president to dine—on their own food, perhaps, and even on their own plates. Then came the toasts, twenty-one of them, including one to Andrew Jackson, hero of the Creek War and considered a candidate to follow Monroe. It was a prophetic bit of partisanship.

Then the president left and the convention got down to business. And what a business they did. Although the delegates ran high in men of wealth and status, what they wrote, by measures of that day and this, was one of the most liberal—they would have said popular—constitutions of the era. Provisions such as white manhood suffrage, without property or other qualifications, would have been enough to recommend the constitution as a democratic document, but Alabama's fundamental law went further. The governor and both houses of the legislature served short terms, so the people could reaffirm or remove their representatives frequently. A bill of rights granted citizens the freedom to hold whatever religion they wanted, or none at all. Slaves were given protections that included the right to humane treatment, and there was even an effort by two prominent members of the body to give the legislature the power to enfranchise free blacks. The attempt failed, but that it was made is something to consider.

Perhaps the most progressive part of the constitution dealt with apportionment. Representation in the legislature was to be based on white residents. In other southern states planters had seen to it that the federal constitution's so-called "3/5th Clause," which allows three slaves to be counted for every five when apportioning congressional seats, was adopted for apportioning state legislative seats as well. Once in place the counting solidified slaveholder control of those state governments. But not in Alabama. In Alabama it was the yeoman farmer whose count determined legislative seats, and though planters would later try to change the constitution, farmers would hold them off. This innovation, white-only apportionment, politically pitted farmers against planters and made the hill country of the north and the Wiregrass of the southeast rivals of Black Belt and Tennessee Valley plantations. Such divisions are what make Alabama politics complicated, interesting, and, according to many, fun.

But why would delegates who were plainly elites, men who felt confidently superior to most of their fellow citizens, write a constitution that gave those same citizens control of the government? Hard to say, but it has been suggested that coming from a tradition where common folk regularly elected their betters to govern them, Alabama aristocrats expected the same to happen here. Or it is possible that since Alabama's aristocrats had successfully championed the most popular issue of the day—statehood—they assumed that the people would reward them for services rendered. Or perhaps it was because so many of them had not long left the ranks of plain folks and so believed that a remembered class solidarity would keep them in office. Whatever the case, the aristocrats would be wrong.

The constitution was never submitted to the people, but considering the document's popular features, to do so would probably have been a waste of time. So it was approved there in Huntsville, then sent to Congress, approved again, and in 1819 Alabama was admitted to the Union. Then, to no one's surprise, William Wyatt Bibb was elected governor, and the scene shifted to Cahawba.

Antebellum Alabama

William Wyatt Bibb did not live to see his creation, Cahawba, "vie with the largest inland towns in the country," as he predicted it would. He was already ill, and a fall from his horse in July of 1820 aggravated his condition; a few days later he died. His brother, Thomas Bibb of Limestone County in the Tennessee Valley, president of the senate, was next in line and became governor. But if Cahawba noticed the difference it was only for a moment. Everything seemed to be in the town's favor. Broad streets laid out in a grid pattern commanded the bluff, where large lots were surveyed for sale. But for investors studying the plat, the feature that set the plan apart and made the city just a little more grand, a little more special, was Arch Street. Drawn along the palisade line of an ancient Indian town that today some speculate might have been Mabila, the thoroughfare rose from the river's edge and curved gently up the bank so wagons could reach the top with ease. At the crest it began a similar curved, gentle descent back down to the Alabama. Lots inside the arch, closest to the river, were set aside for warehouses, to hold the bounty of the Black Belt. In time some were built, but Arch Street did not work out quite as planned; but then, neither did Cahawba.

Attracted by its political importance and its economic promise, visitors crowded into the capital. Ferries operated on both rivers to handle the flow, hotels opened, courts began to hold sessions, and the business of government was conducted. Soon there were stores and shops, the *Cahawba Press* appeared, and land sales continued brisk. But even as things seemed to be going so well, trouble appeared, trouble from which even prosperous Cahawba was not immune.

The long arm of economic panic reached the Alabama frontier late in 1819, and conditions quickly worsened. Cotton prices hit bottom, land lost its value, speculators suffered, and up in Huntsville Leroy Pope's Planters and Merchants Bank, arguably the most powerful financial institution in the state, could not pay its depositors. Hundreds, many of them yeomen farmers and aspiring merchants, lost all they had, and in the face of what was understated as "pecuniary embarrassment," they looked for help and for answers.

Financial failure, we must understand, was more than a loss of money to frontier Alabamians. It diminished the failed, be he farmer or merchant, in the eyes of his fellows, some of whom might have suffered because of him—interconnections in the economy being what they were. It was, in that sense, a loss of honor, for the hallmark of an independent man was his ability to care for his own, govern his property, without interference or help from others—unless, of course, that help was returned in kind. A man who lost his farm or his store lost not only his livelihood but also his status in the community, his reputation. He was reduced to dependence, which was, to himself and others, tantamount to slavery. So he, the failed, did what any honorable man would do. He resolved to punish whoever was responsible for his plight, if the responsible could be found.

AND THAT IS WHERE ISRAEL PICKENS COMES IN

Israel Pickens was one of those North Carolinians who settled in St. Stephens and gave the frontier town a more civilized veneer. A three-term congressman from his home state before moving to Alabama, he became registrar of the land office, helped organize and run the local bank, and gained a reputation as a "bold" yet "principled" man of business. Moving into the political vacuum created by Bibb's death, he stood for governor in 1821 and won largely on the force of personality. That campaign, however, confirmed what he surely suspected all along, that under Alabama's democratic constitution, the candidate who could excite and engage the people, who could put himself forth as one of them and as their champion, could and would carry the day.

This discovery soon made Israel Pickens the most powerful politician in the state, but more than that, he set the precedent for successful politicians right up to the present. What Pickens realized was that Alabamians, rich and poor, were fearful of an imminent loss of freedom—or as historian J. Mills Thornton put it, early Alabamians were "obsessed with the idea of slavery." "Slavery" in this sense did not mean black chattel, though whites were hardly unconcerned about that institution. No, the slavery Alabamians feared was the slavery based on dependence, the slavery that followed when free men were no longer able to control their own affairs, the slavery of being told what to do and having to do it. In other words, the slavery into which so many sank during the Panic of 1819.

That fear realized, the aspiring politician had to identify the cause of the condition. Who, or what, threatened the liberty of free men? And if the cause could be cornered, then the candidate had to present his claim that he could conquer it—could bay the bear in its den, could slay the dragon. If the people, the fearful people, believed him, his election was assured.

Israel Pickens found his dragon: the Planters and Merchants Bank. To farmers who lost their money, Planters and Merchants was more than a bank, it was an extension of aristocrats like Pope, men who, despite claims that they had lost their fortunes as well, seemed to live as they always had. The "Royal Party," Tennessee Valley yeomen called them—and when they did, farmers in South Alabama understood, for they had men of the same sorts in their midst. So it followed that Pickens rallied countrymen, rallied failed merchants, rallied anyone who had reason to resent, then explained in simple terms how wealth concentrated in the hands of a few, how the economy engineered to the advantage of bankers and their allies, threatened common folk. And the common folk understood, for they had seen it—or thought they had.

So what was his solution? It may come as a shock to modern Alabamians whose conservatism is rooted in a deep distrust of government, but Pickens proposed that the state go into the banking business to protect the public, and the public liked the idea. And so the stage was set for a complicated controversy over banks, state versus private, which would punctuate politics for decades. That debate notwithstanding, what really happened was that a style of politics emerged, one that would excite the yeoman voter and terrify his more aristocratic neighbor.

And if you wanted to see the excitement, and the terror, the best place to go was to a Madison County barbecue.

PULLING THE GANDER'S NECK

Now Alabamians have always been serious about barbecue and today still debate the merits of the meat, the sauce, and the method. But in the 1820s barbecues—the meeting, not the meat—became a matter of controversy up in the Tennessee Valley. In and around Huntsville, barbecues were political events, where voters mingled with candidates, got pledges from them, and made promises in return. To the more democratically inclined, this was democracy in action, politics as politics should be. But to members of the Royal Party, barbecues were where self-serving candidates seduced the people with food, drink, games of chance, blood sports, and promises. If freedom was the issue, critics argued that the people's liberty was surely in as much danger from such politicians as it was from any bank.

Newspapers took sides, and in one a local scoffer who wrote under the name "Barbacuensis" warned the people of the danger they faced. Such electioneering, he claimed, drove good men from the field and left only the bad because "the question now, is not, what is his mental capacity? But, what are the dimensions of his stomach? Not, does he read and think? But, does he eat and digest? Not, if he will enact wholesome laws and promote and preserve the peace, happiness and prosperity of the state, but if he will drink raw whiskey,

eat rawer shote, dance bare foot on a puncheon floor, . . . and pull at
a gander's neck"—a contest that challenged a horseman to pull the
head off a well-greased gander hung by its feet from the limb of
a tree.

Country folk, the ones who enjoyed what the Royal Party found
reprehensible, saw things differently. Insulted that royalists believed
their vote could be bought with pork and promises, they rallied to
their candidates, and in the end references to them being "a poor
ignorant sett, easily gulled by fine speeches" only made their loyalty stronger. Over time this affection for barbecues and barbecuers
would fade, but hardly because of the Royal Party. Post-panic prosperity would narrow (though not erase) some class differences, while
evangelical Protestantism would rise to condemn many of the pleasures found at the gatherings without condemning the democratic
urges of those who attended. But until times got better and reformers came to power, barbecues remained a place where those inclined
could, as "Barbacuensis" versed it, see and be seen by

A gander-pulling mob that's common here,
Of candidates and sovereigns stowed compactly, —
Of harlequins and clowns with feats gymnastical
In hunting-shirts and shirt-sleeves—things fantastical; —
With fiddling, feasting, dancing, drinking, masquing
And other things which may be had for asking.

THE MARQUIS COMES A'CALLING

This is not to suggest that Alabama's upper crust was not capable of
pitching a party when called upon to do so, which is just what they
did in 1825, when the state was visited by the sixty-eight-year-old
Marquis de Lafayette, who was making a grand tour of the nation
he helped free from colonial rule. Everyone wanted to honor the
hero of the Revolution, in part because he was truly loved and respected, but also because this social event promised to be the most
important one in the life of the young state. It was an opportunity

for towns and citizens along his route to put on a reception that would reflect, if not magnify, their importance, and in the climate of boosterism that warmed Alabama, this was serious stuff indeed.

With a retinue that included his dog Quiz, Lafayette followed the Federal Road out of Georgia and west to Montgomery, which is what promoters finally agreed to call the struggling little village on the Alabama River, just down from where the Coosa and Tallapoosa met. There he was greeted by Gov. Israel Pickens, up from Cahawba with what one of the party described as "a large concourse of citizens, who had assembled from great distances to accompany him." Montgomery's finest house was stocked with French wine and food and given over to the general. In the evening a "grand ball" was held on the second floor of a large brick building, above the prying eyes of the masses not invited. A band brought up from New Orleans provided music, and a good time was had by all. Among the revelers was Samuel Dale, in full uniform, who claimed to have ridden 250 miles to see the show and be part of it.

Not long after midnight Lafayette left the party and, escorted by "all the ladies of Montgomery," went to the river, boarded a steamboat, and, to the salute of artillery from a bonfire-illuminated shore, headed downstream. The next day he passed the frontier town of Selma, which was just beginning to show the growth that would in time make it the "Queen City of the Black Belt," and arrived at Cahawba. Citizens of Alabama's capital were determined "not to be outdone by the capital of Georgia," which reportedly spared no expense to entertain the general, but they could not agree on how to do it. The "gentlemen" of the city wanted an invitation-only dinner for their guest, but this did not sit well with the common folks who also wanted to dine with the great man and believed they had every right to do so. Meanwhile, the "ladies" of Cahawba wanted more than a meal with speeches and toasts. They wanted a ball, which would "give them the opportunity to pay their respects to him"—and show off like everyone else. What Lafayette wanted was probably a good night's sleep, but no one, at least no Alabamian, seems to have asked him.

So they decided to do all three. There would be a public barbecue for those who could not pay five dollars for the dinner—a sum that comfortably drew the line between the haves and have-nots and made invitations unnecessary. Lafayette would first attend the formal affair. After "a few toasts" he would leave to mingle with the people and eat a little pork. Apparently "gander pulling" was not part of the entertainment, and if "raw whiskey" was on (or under) the table, no one was reported the worse for it. After toasting the yeomen, with what they did not say, he would return to the gentry and their ladies for the grand ball. It was a tight schedule, but it worked. Lafayette's secretary recorded that Cahawba's arrangements were "remarkable for their elegance and good taste," and everyone seemed to have a fine time. At eleven o'clock the exhausted general took his leave, boarded the steamboat, and headed south and to bed.

There was one more stop, Claiborne, the Creek War fort that had grown into the principal town on the lower Alabama. Then it was on to Mobile and from there to New Orleans, leaving Alabamians with fond memories, a few headaches, and a bill for over $15,000. It had been a grand affair and a marvelous diversion, but it was over.

SHIFTING PEOPLE AND POWER

Back in Cahawba politicians were debating the capital's fate. When the town was created and designated the seat of government, opponents who hoped another capital would be chosen added wording to the act that required permanence to be confirmed later. Later had arrived, and legislators whose interests lay outside the Alabama River region rallied for removal. Luck was on their side. Almost yearly since construction began, heavy rains had brought floods, which critics exaggerated to the point that later generations would believe that the town had been entirely cut off from the outside world. Claims that the site was unhealthy as well as inconvenient were difficult to refute, and with no William Wyatt Bibb to twist arms and make promises, removal carried the day. On 13 December

1825, by a single vote, Tuscaloosa was declared the capital of Alabama.

Moving the capital did not disappoint Israel Pickens, who had relocated to Greene County, in the heart of the western Black Belt not far from the new seat of government. But unfortunately, he did not live to see Tuscaloosa in its glory. In poor health by the time his second term as governor ended, he accepted appointment to the U.S. Senate when that seat fell vacant, but by then tuberculosis had been diagnosed. His condition worsened, he resigned the office, and he left for Cuba, where he hoped warm weather would bring relief. It didn't. He died there on 24 April 1827.

Pickens's death also prevented him from seeing his democratic disciples, and some who had actually been his enemies, carry his strategy to victory on issues he might never have anticipated, much less championed. Nevertheless, during his administration Pickens was able to get a state bank chartered, and though the bank would eventually fail during a second national depression, it represented a major accomplishment for those who believed the people's freedom was better protected by the state than by corporate interests, an idea later abandoned when corporate interests got control of the legislature. Until that time, however, yeoman farmers and their allies, some from the planter class, would dominate the government. On the whole they opposed state aid for internal improvements (roads, bridges, canals, and eventually railroads) and of course the chartering of private banks. These yeomen became Democrats, when that party emerged, and Andrew Jackson was their hero. And as good Jacksonians, they stood against concentrated power, which at times made them appear antibusiness, when more often than not it was the size and influence of the interests that they opposed.

Competing with them was the faction eventually called the Whigs. More inclined to support state paternalism for business, education, and other "worthy" undertakings, no small number of them were what they were because they feared the masses more than they did the gentry. Usually involved in commercial agriculture rather than subsistence farming, the Whigs were considered a more aristocratic, more elitist group. However, within their ranks were many who might have been Democrats had not some personal matter between themselves and a member of that party caused them to seek a new political home. Or to put it another way, some people were Democrats because they disliked Whigs, and some were Whigs because they could not stand Democrats. That was all, but that was enough.

As a result of these divisions Alabama voters witnessed and took part in their share of partisan rivalries, and though the Democrats won most of the time, the vote was often close, and the result was anything but a mandate. There was, however, a consensus on one particular issue—taxes. Adhering to a principle that, like popular government, would get lost in later years, Alabama's majority concluded that taxes, when they were necessary, should fall heaviest on those who could most afford to pay them. As a result, during the antebellum era two taxes—on land and on slaves—brought in some 70 percent of the state's revenue. The rest came from taxes on luxuries—carriages, race horses, expensive watches, private libraries, and the like, those things that set the planter apart from the common herd—and on capital, both investment and income. It was a system, quite simply, that required the wealthiest Alabamians to support the state that made them so.

Faced with an electorate determined to place the burden on them, Alabama's elites could only hope to keep levies low, which they were able to do because yeomen disliked taxes as much as the gentry. So the wealthy were taxed, but the weight was light, and most carried it without complaining. To keep it that way, many planters allied themselves with the yeomen, arguing that regardless of their higher station in life, they were one of the people and one with them. Some actually were. Those who had risen to the gentry, rather than arrived as part of it, could and often did keep their common-man credentials and sometimes were elected to protect popular interests. But their selection did not mean that class no longer mattered. It did, and it would.

WHAT DO THE LADIES SAY?

It is not an easy question to answer. There were many ladies in antebellum Alabama. There were belles like Octavia Walton Le Vert, the grande dame of Mobile, indeed, of Alabama, culture and society, who traveled widely and wrote of it, and who gathered in her salon what intellectuals and celebrities she could find to discuss what intellectuals and celebrities of the age felt like discussing. But she was one of a few, maybe one of a kind.

And there were farm women who today appear, when they do appear, more often in census records and tax digests, just numbers, with their children, also numbers, unless as widows they came to court to settle what little there might have been of what the law called an estate. In the field and in the home they worked as hard as, maybe harder than, their yeoman husbands, endured the pain and danger of childbirth, lived, loved, died, and were buried, often in unmarked graves, usually near a son or daughter who had died before them. Today historians try to resurrect these women from faded records but find, when the work is finished, only shadows.

Then there were slave women, a few almost belles in their own right, black matriarchs presiding over households (slave and free) who became the prototypes for an endless stream of "mammies" in southern plantation novels. But more, maybe most, must have lived like Jenny Proctor, who years later told a WPA interviewer how, when only "a little gal" herself, she was put to cleaning house and tending babies. She tried to do "just like Old Miss [told] me to," and did, until one day "Old Master" decided she was big enough and "he say, 'Git this here nigger to that cotton patch,'" and that was where she went. She was ten years old. Childhood, what there was of it, was over for Jenny Proctor.

In the field Proctor could have been much like one of those slave women whom Englishman Philip Henry Gosse saw ploughing when he arrived in Dallas County, late in the spring of 1838, women "whose clothing—if the sordid rags which fluttered about them deserve the name—was barely sufficient for the claims of decency." "Poor wretches," he wrote, "whose lot is harder than that of their brute companions in labour! For they have to perform an equal amount of toil, with the additional hardship of more whipping and less food."

Jenny Proctor could have told him a thing about whipping and food, could have told him of how, one day, she recalled, "I finds a biscuit, and I's so hungry I et it," and how "Old Miss" found out and began beating her with a broom. She fought back—"I guess I just clean lost my head 'cause I knowed better than to fight her if I knowed anything 't all"—and had to be subdued by the "driver," who whipped her with a "cat-'o-nine-tails" until she fell to the floor "nearly dead." Her back was "cut to pieces," and she carried the scars "right on to the grave." "Lord, Lord, honey!" she reflected years later and far from Alabama, "them was awful days."

And there was Sarah Haynsworth Gayle. Born in South Carolina upcountry in 1804, she came at the age of six with her family to the Alabama frontier, a journey filled with adventures she later recounted with delight. Though a slaveholding planter, her father was hardly in the same class as the Carolina coastal elites. In Alabama, however, his property and chattel put him above most others. After the Creek War the Haynsworths joined the cream of Alabama society, and Sarah met John Gayle. She was fifteen. He was thirteen years her senior. Also from a slaveholding family, Gayle was more interested in legal and political matters than in planting. By the time he and Sarah were introduced, he had already served in the Territorial Legislature and would go on to be a judge, the Speaker of the Alabama House of Representatives, and governor. Sarah would be with him, for not long after they met they married.

Sarah Gayle seemed the stuff from which belles were made. Described by a contemporary as "very beautiful" with "classic" features and "noble bearing," her "fascinating manners" won for her "universal admiration." Her looks, her social graces, and her love for literature, especially poetry and romances, might have inspired her to create a salon of her own, but Greensboro, where she, her husband, and their two small children settled in 1826, was not Mobile. It was not even Tuscaloosa, the new state capital, only thirty-five miles away.

Greensboro was like many Alabama villages of the era. In the heart of the western Black Belt, with a population of hardly a hundred, its citizens came from the network of slaveholding families of the region. The business district consisted of a hotel, six stores (including a tailor's shop), and some law offices, one of which was John Gayle's. Residents, many of them relatives, lived close in, which allowed Sarah the routine but pleasant life of the gentry—"a chance visit, the going to Church, shopping, an odd volume read, an odd page written—and when the long list of seams and hems and gatherings added," she wrote, "my life is given, [or] at least the mode of spending it."

While some might have found in this a numbing sameness, Sarah apparently did not. That "odd page written" was her diary, a journal filled with observations of the time and place, which she prepared more for her children than herself, but which gave her a creative outlet. Graced with what Elizabeth Fox-Genovese described as "an immediacy of voice, a charm of style, and a poignancy of narrative," her diary, along with "lovely poems" she also wrote, revealed "an extraordinary, if gentle and muted, perspective on her self" that sets her apart from most of her peers. Despite "minimal schooling," and "undisciplined, . . . untutored reading," Sarah Gayle was a writer of promise, maybe great promise, which unfortunately for us, and maybe even for her, was never fulfilled.

What was fulfilled was her duty to her children, on whom she doted, to her husband, whom she adored, and to her religion. She attended Baptist and Methodist meetings but seems to have been more comfortable with Presbyterians. These responsibilities she carried out with the help of her servants, who occasionally appear in her letters and journals. Like other women of her class, her way of life depended on their labor, and she seems to have had no doubts about the arrangement that made them her slaves and her their mistress. She was deeply concerned, however, over moral improprieties that found their way into the system, and recoiled with horror and disgust when she heard of a man whose "children and his son's children are their slaves" and whose "child and his grand-child have one mother." Still, to her the problem was not slavery but the unchristian character of the slaveholder.

Worrying Sarah Gayle as much as anything in that small world of hers were her health and the health of those close to her. Two of her children died young, and though six survived, their well-being was constantly on her mind. As for her own condition, her curse was the dentist. Toothache was not an uncommon complaint of the age, and contemporary descriptions of Alabamians of almost every class mentioned rot, gaps, diseased gums, and slack jaws. By the time she was in her twenties, cavities in her front teeth had been painfully filled, and her dentist wanted to pull the rear ones. As she approached her thirtieth birthday she saw in the mirror a child-bride who now looked older than her husband and wondered how long she could, for him, "preserve some trace of youth." It was one of her few moments of vanity.

SARAH GAYLE, ALABAMA'S FIRST LADY

John Gayle was elected governor in August of 1831, and Sarah began dividing her time between Tuscaloosa and Greensboro. It is hard to say just how interested she was in politics. Not long after she arrived at her new residence, she visited the capitol and told a friend that she "intend[ed] to stay there a great deal this year." If she did, however, she made little mention of it until months later when she recorded how "the State House was crowded with ladies" there to hear "what is call'd the Lady's bill" discussed. Since 1828 some in the chamber had been trying to separate married women's estates from those of their husbands. There was strong opposition; legislators arguing that the bill altered "human and divine laws . . . [that] God had vested in Adam and Moses" blocked it time and again. Finally it passed, but opponents did not give up, and soon they amended the measure to make it almost meaningless.

Like most women of her time and condition, however, Sarah Gayle was more comfortable in social situations, where she reportedly "dispensed hospitality . . . with dignity and grace never surpassed." If her teeth, or lack of them, were a disability, no one mentioned it. Yet in her role as hostess Mrs. Gayle may have helped her husband more than was or still is generally acknowledged, especially in 1833 when Gov. John Gayle challenged Pres. Andrew Jackson over federal Indian policy.

By the 1830s white Alabamians had given up on the idea that Native Americans could be successfully integrated into "civilized" society. And so, either to put into production land that whites claimed was going to waste or to protect the Indians from rapacious settlers—some argued one, some argued the other, some argued both—it was decided that the natives had to be removed. On that point Alabamians agreed. The only question was how to bring it about.

In 1832 the Creeks ceded the rest of their Alabama lands to the state, with assurances that the federal government would protect the individual holdings left to the tribesmen. But the squatters, the exploiters, spilled into the land, hoping to lay a claim then and confirm it later, when the cession was subdivided for sale. Soon federal authorities began to hear complaints from Indians abused and cheated by the intruders, so President Jackson ordered troops to remove all whites from the cession until the official survey was completed. Governor Gayle joined the squatters in protesting the eviction, and with this encouragement, some resolved to resist. One of these was Hardeman Owens.

Owens, a member of the Russell County Commission and a man respected by his neighbors, had taken up some one hundred acres of Indian land and was not about to return it. Knowing federal troops were coming to turn him out, he mined his house with gunpowder, and when the soldiers arrived he tried to lure their commander to his death. The plot failed. Owens fled, was overtaken, and in the struggle was killed by one of the soldiers. Hardeman Owens was now a martyr.

The Owens incident provided Governor Gayle with what every

Alabama politician needs—an enemy. Quickly the chief executive announced that the federal government's efforts on behalf of the Indians were an insult to Alabama and a violation of her rights. Claiming that the state had jurisdiction over the land in question, Gayle argued that state courts should have been allowed to deal with the matter. To do otherwise suggested that Alabama could not handle her own affairs.

Up in Washington President Jackson considered the situation serious enough to send a mediator to settle the matter. The man he selected was Frances Scott Key, a leading District of Columbia attorney and the author of "The Star Spangled Banner."

MRS. GAYLE AND MR. KEY

When Key reached Tuscaloosa in December of 1833, he was greeted by the governor and his family, and over the next few weeks, while negotiations were going on, he visited frequently in their home. "Mr. Key . . . interests me greatly," Sarah confided in her journal, and not just because he was "a man of much intelligence, a lawyer of high standing, [and] a man of honor," though those traits were important. Key was also "a poet and a Christian," and in those two characteristics Sarah Gayle found a friend. In the evenings after a hard day of meetings and talk, Key relaxed with the first lady and her children, listening while she read to him and reading in turn to her, talking with piety and simplicity of religion and its poetry, its hymns and psalms. He admired her, and she admired him in return.

During this interlude Key and Sarah exchanged poems—his written to her daughter, also a Sarah, and to a niece; hers written entreating him to favor the children with some verse. Mrs. Gayle's was clearly the better of the bunch, for Key's efforts (one critic "candidly confessed") "add nothing to [his] reputation as a poet." Employing almost every word found to rhyme with Gayle, the visitor dedicated a lengthy poem to the nine-year-old. A few verses are enough to prove the critic right.

Light the task to lovers pale
To sing of lovely Sarah Gayle
Ne'er shall words of numbers fail
To sound the praises of Sarah Gayle

See, from distant hills and dales
They come to gaze on Sarah Gayle
And teach the Alabama vale
To echo the name of Sarah Gayle.

See, I told you.

THE INDIANS REMOVED

The negotiations went well, made easier perhaps by the congenial surroundings in which the federal commissioner found himself. After some discussion Key agreed that the soldier accused of the crime would be brought to justice, which was what the Alabamians wanted. Then news arrived that the man had deserted and could not be found, which was just as well, and maybe even planned, for with no criminal to punish, passions quickly cooled. Key tarried while the land was surveyed and oversaw the confirming of Indian claims; then he left, and the squatters poured in again. Though Jackson could announce that the law was enforced, it was clear that Gayle had won. It was also clear that, once again, the Indians had lost.

While all of this was going on, the stars fell. It was one of the most spectacular meteor showers ever recorded in the region. Many who saw thought it was a warning from God that the end of the world was at hand. For the Creeks, it was.

During the months that followed whites and Indians clashed repeatedly in the cession, and these incidents escalated into the Second Creek War. It was also the last. Hardly a war, really, for by the end of 1836 it was over. Indians who survived either fled to Florida and joined the Seminoles to fight another day or agreed to be transported to the west. There was no place for them in Alabama. "It was a melancholy spectacle," one observer wrote, "as these proud monarchs of the soil were marched off from their native land to a distant country, which to their anticipations presented all the horrors of the infernal regions." Soon, except for a few stragglers hiding out in the hills and swamps and a few of mixed blood trying to assimilate, they were gone. Before there had been an Alabama there had been the Indians. Now, for all practical purposes, only the names remained.

Sarah Gayle did not witness the removal. In the summer of 1835, while her husband was in the Indian cession looking to speculate in the land being opened to settlement, problems with her remaining teeth forced her back to the dentist. It was a horrible experience. The pain was excruciating, and soon after the doctor was finished, tetanus set in. Death was slow but certain, and before her beloved John could return, Sarah Gayle passed away. She was thirty-one years old.

While no single individual can serve to explain the people of an era, the life of Sarah Haynsworth Gayle does shed light on certain aspects of the world of women in antebellum Alabama. On one hand one can see in her the "might-have-beens," can reflect on how, with more education and opportunity, Sarah Gayle might have emerged a major writer, or how, with better health care, she might have lived to a ripe old age. But those things were beyond her capacity to change. She was what she was—a wife, mother, friend— and apparently was happy with it.

For all her life Sarah Gayle lived in or near frontier conditions, and her outlook, like that of most of her contemporaries, was shaped by the situation. She was also born a woman and never seemed to doubt the role her gender required of her. Though she frequently took on management duties when her husband was away, and revealed real skills when she did, she never thought of herself as the head of the household. Sarah was also a southerner, and as such took much of southern life for granted. This attitude was particularly true when it came to slavery. Though she was quick to criticize masters who abused their servants, she never questioned the relationships on which slavery was based. Though she might mourn the death of her children's nurse "as if she had been white as snow," she nonetheless understood that the nurse was not white, and believed that color made a difference. In this belief, as in so much else, Sarah Gayle was a woman of her time.

And she was religious. Of all the many things that appear in her journals, her Christianity stands equal in importance to her family. Indeed, the two are often inseparable. The dangers of the frontier, the loss of children, the death of her beloved parents, and her own declining health turned her naturally to her family for support and to that other refuge available to all. Her faith, simple yet thoughtful, romantic yet rational, sustained her time and again, as indeed, faith sustained other Alabamians.

Yet Sarah Gayle was an individual. Though her experiences reflected those of many other women of her time and place, she was unique, was able to do things other women did not do, and accomplished things other women did not accomplish. Still, like many of her contemporaries confined by conditions and circumstances, her most lasting legacy may have been her children. Those who survived her went on to make their contributions to the state. She would have liked that.

5

Stumbling toward Secession

By the end of the 1820s political Alabama looked a lot like Israel Pickens and his supporters wanted it to look. The state bank was in place, the Royal Party was in disarray, and popular government seemed assured. Success, however, bred uncertainty. Pickens had taught politicians that success depended on a candidate's ability to convince the people that he would and could defend them against their enemies. Problem was, there were no enemies to speak of. So aspiring politicians were faced with the task of divining popular prejudices to discover what was feared or desired, then putting themselves forth as credible champions. Thus began what historian Mills Thornton has called a "desperate search for issues with which to authenticate democratic credentials," credentials on which could be built a political career. But where earlier politicians who catered to the masses could admit to themselves (though not to the people) that it was all, or mostly, a way to get elected, a strategy, a ruse, later politicians, the ones who would lead Alabama and the South into secession and Civil War, could make no such admission. For to them popular prejudice was principle. They were true believers, zealots; some called them "fire-eaters."

But issue-finding was not easy.

CONSIDER THE CASE OF DIXON HALL LEWIS

Dixon Lewis came to Alabama from Georgia around 1820, a bright young man with good connections. He studied law, a common course for the ambitious, married well, then set up his practice in Montgomery and prospered. In 1826 he was elected to the legislature. His views, shaped by his maternal uncle, Bolling Hall, a staunch Jeffersonian who had once represented Georgia in Congress, led young Lewis to become an advocate of low taxes and tight budgets—positions that endeared him to planter and yeoman alike. Then, believing he had established himself as a popular spokesman, in 1829 Dixon Lewis ran for Congress.

The issue he chose to exploit was federally funded internal improvements, which he opposed because (he claimed) they would open the door to tyranny by making people dependent on Washington instead of on themselves and their states. It did not seem a particularly promising platform. The Alabama River ran through his district, and most of the men of property and influence who were his constituents lived on or near the stream. They wanted federal funds to improve navigation. Rather than modify his views to suit the circumstances, Lewis decided to seek votes where the steamboats didn't run. Reinforcing a wagon with springs and braces—a necessity since he weighed around 350 pounds and was growing—Lewis took to the back roads. In speeches that provided as much entertainment as enlightenment, he convinced the electorate that he would defend them from a federal government by which few, if any, felt threatened. It is hard to say whether they voted for the man or the message or some combination thereof, but they voted, and Dixon Lewis went to Washington.

States' rights, the philosophy that was the foundation of Lewis's campaign, was neither popular nor unpopular at the time—it simply was not an issue. During the nullification agitation of the early 1830s, when South Carolina attempted to void a tariff Carolinians claimed threatened their sovereignty, Alabamians sat comfortably on the sidelines. Lewis and other states' rights supporters tried to raise the alarm, but it was no use. President Jackson was against nullification, and Alabamians, being Jacksonians, were against it as well.

Yet if nullification was a distant and abstract issue, Indians were not. Governor Gayle's claim that Alabama, not the federal government, had authority over the Creek cession was a state right Alabamians could appreciate, so they rallied to the governor. For many the confrontation proved a learning experience. State leaders learned they could successfully stand against the federal behemoth. Jackson learned that loyalty had its limits, even for Jacksonians. Lewis and his allies learned that states' rights was a powerful force, if the "right" was right.

They were out of relevant rights, however, at least out of those rights that got the public into a state of acute political indigestion. Gayle had won, the Indians were leaving, and Alabamians were enjoying the "flush times" of easy credit, cheap land, and high cotton prices. So Lewis planted himself in the center of the states' rights movement and played the various issues as they came and went. He continued to denounce federal intrusions into state affairs, and as different groups at different times became upset over the national bank, internal improvements, and the protective tariff, Lewis was there to speak to and for their concerns. In the process Dixon Hall Lewis became one of the inner circle that advised John C. Calhoun, the most important spokesman for the states' rights position. These accomplishments, plus his skill as a campaigner, were enough to keep Lewis in office, but they did not generate the excitement of Indian removal. States' rights had its place in Alabama politics, and Dixon Lewis was its spokesman, but there were other options that, for the time being, some Alabamians were taking.

DIXON HALL LEWIS AND WILLIAM RUFUS KING

While Dixon Hall Lewis was making a name for himself as an advocate of state sovereignty within a weakened Union, another Alabamian, William Rufus King, was carving out a career as a southern unionist devoted to using federal power to improve his state and enhance the lives of its people. While not the mirror image of Lewis, William Rufus King did not see demons at every turn nor fear Washington's designs. Together King and Lewis represent the bipolar nature of Alabama politics along with the tension that existed, and still exists, among Alabamians and their leaders. This was the issue: Should the state divorce itself, as much as possible, from the central government and go its own way even though such philosophical purity demanded that it give up advantages that come from collective action within the Union? Or should the state accept federal aid, with accompanying regulations and restrictions, so that its people could have the same advantage enjoyed by other states? It was a dilemma, and efforts to solve it have made up much of Alabama's history.

So while Dixon Hall Lewis denounced federal intrusions and suggested that states had the constitutional authority and moral responsibility to oppose laws that infringed on their sovereignty, William Rufus King offered a more moderate course. And Alabamians rallied to both. Understand that, and you are at the heart of the matter.

WILLIAN RUFUS KING

King came from a prominent North Carolina family. Well educated, he read law, got into politics, rose fast, and in 1810 was elected to Congress. One of the young nationalists of the era, he supported the tariff, voted to declare war on Britain in 1812, and championed a strong government in war and in peace. In 1818 he left Carolina and Congress to settle in the Alabama Black Belt near Selma on a large plantation, which he worked with some eighty slaves—the second-largest labor force in Dallas County. Immediately active in politics, he helped write the state constitution and was chosen by the legislature as one of Alabama's first U.S. senators.

A staunch Jacksonian and loyal Democrat, King spent his long career vigorously supporting popular causes, such as liberal land policies that favored the farmer over the speculator. He could join Lewis in denouncing the national bank, then oppose his Alabama colleague on the question of nullification and present himself as a moderate on the tariff issue. In short, he was a reasoned and reasonable alternative to what was, at the time, Lewis's more extreme position, and the skill with which he was able to advance planter interests without losing popular support is a testimony to his ability as both a politician and a statesman.

Helping shape King's national outlook was his "close and affectionate relationship" with fellow senator and future president James Buchanan of Pennsylvania. Both lifelong bachelors, the two men agreed on most political questions and were known to hold each other in the highest esteem. Today their association would be a source of tabloid speculation, but back then it was merely gossip among a small group of men. More important, the friendship seems to have helped convince them both that northerners and southerners had much in common and that extremists—Lewis and Calhoun on one side and increasingly vocal abolitionists on the other—did not reflect popular sentiment.

FINDING THE ISSUE

Yet it was the extremists whose voices were being heard, and the issue that was on their minds was slavery. Here, to put it simply, was the "right" to be defended. It was not a new one. Slavery had been attacked and defended since the early days of the Republic, and southern sensitivity on the subject was well established. But in the 1830s the right to own slaves became part of a larger debate over southern equality within the Union and as such could be and was discussed in broad constitutional terms without actually mentioning that the real issue was human bondage. As a result it has become possible for modern defenders of what will come to be known as the "lost cause" to claim that slavery was only incidental to the larger conflict over the nature of the Union and the rights of states within it.

They are wrong. Alabama's own experience bears this out. In the mid 1830s Texas rebelled against Mexico, won its independence, and asked to join the Union as a slave state. The request was rejected, not so much because northern congressmen opposed slavery as because they and their constituents had come to see slavery as central to and symbolic of a frame of mind not just different from theirs, but incompatible with what they thought of as American. More to the point, if another slave state came in, that incompatibility would be all the stronger in Congress. If southerners wanted to own slaves, that was their business, but northern opponents did not want slaveholders to determine what America was and would become.

Some Alabamians saw the question of Texas in much the same light but from a different perspective. To them keeping Texas out of the Union was part of a larger scheme to limit southern influence. This, they concluded, was something that the South must resist or all would be lost. Thomas Gaillard, a Monroe County planter and prominent politician, understood things that way. He wrote to his brother just before Christmas 1837:

> on the annexation of Texas to the United States . . . This I
> think should be the determined policy of the South—I
> had almost said—at all hazards. The movement of the Aboli-
> tionists at the North, should urge us to an early union and
> co-operation of Slave Interests. Let us extend our General
> Government over as wide and extended a slave labor Terri-
> tory as possible. In our strength at last shall be our safety. . . .
> In my opinion, there is no Constitutional Question, whether
> touching the subjects of Internal Improvement, the U.S.
> Bank or the Tariff, so vitally important to the South, as this
> one, of the annexation of Texas.

Most Alabamians weren't thinking about moving to Texas. A few headed there in the wake of the Panic of 1837, nailed "GTT" ("gone to Texas") to the door, and took off to escape their creditors, but not many. Alabama's legislature, ever sensitive to a popular cause, heard the debtors' cry and, with the best of intentions, did something thoroughly stupid. It ordered the state bank to put more money in circulation and suspend foreclosures, a move that so weakened the institution that collapse was all but inevitable. But for the time it made staying home an attractive alternative. The people were happy, so what the heck.

What really troubled Alabamians was this: By telling Texans they were not worthy to be part of the Union because some of them were slaveholders, the northern-controlled Congress was sending the message that it considered anyone who owned slaves, or might own slaves, or hoped to own slaves, to be tainted. It was a slight, a cut, a slap in the face, an insult that no honorable man could tolerate. But whom to call out? From whom to demand satisfaction? Who needed a whipping? Alabamians weren't sure.

SLAVERY AND POLITICS

This is as good a time as any to try to explain why non-slaveholding Alabamians, the majority of the population at any given time, rallied to defend the rights of the masters. The explanation is important, for later, after the cause was lost and even up until today, some people look at the enthusiasm of non-slaveholders for secession and Civil War and conclude that slavery must not have been the issue—"My granddaddy didn't own any slaves in '61 and he fought. How do you explain that?"

Well, I don't, can't, for the explanation varies from person to person. What I can say is that while granddaddy and his kind may not have owned slaves, they probably wanted to, for that species of property was the key to prosperity in antebellum Alabama, and Alabamians wanted to prosper. But even if they did not want to own slaves, there is little to suggest that they opposed others' owning them. Although there surely were some Alabamians who thought slavery was not a good thing economically or morally or socially or didn't like it because it brought black folks into the neighborhood or gave planters advantages they didn't deserve, there was no anti-slavery agitation to speak of. White Alabamians accepted their peculiar institution, whether they had a piece of it or not.

One must also keep in mind that though slaveholders were in the minority, their class and category were in flux. People moved in and out of them with consistent regularity. A man counted in 1850 as owning no slaves might have two in 1853, four by 1855, and none again in 1860, so when he marched off to war he was listed among those believed to be fighting for a cause other than slavery—but was he? And even if he never owned slaves, did that matter? There are countless cases, opportunities, where contact between the slaveless and the slave was anything but casual: the yeoman whose cousin, or uncle, or best friend, owned slaves, and the children who lived to adulthood and beyond in a slaveholding household, and many, many others. Except for the hill country of North Alabama and some pockets of population scattered in poorer sections of the state, white Alabamians lived with and among slaves. Whether they owned them or not, slavery was part of the vaunted "Southern Way of Life," and no one would deny that granddaddy fought for that.

SLAVERY IN ALABAMA

But what was slavery? Once again, opinions are mixed. Scholars and lay people, black and white, still debate the nature of the institution. They try to fathom the impact it had on the slave. They talk of planter paternalism and black intransigence. They marvel at the way people in bondage maintained their dignity, held families together, created a culture that would carry over into freedom. They decry the abuses, the physical pain, the emotional distress brought on by circumstances and conditions that to the modern mind are all but incomprehensible. And they wonder, how could free folk have thought there was any justice in it?

Slavery offers us the opportunity to see how far the human mind will go to justify, rationalize the exploitation of others. Antebellum Alabamians tried to explain to their northern counterparts that a slave on a Black Belt plantation was better off than a worker in a New England factory. They argued that slaves were constitutionally recognized property and thus should be protected, not threatened, by the federal government. They enlisted preachers to cite biblical chapter and verse to support the institution. They concocted elaborate racial theories to put African Americans into a category fit for slavery and little else. And (perhaps the ultimate irony, some would say hypocrisy) slaveholders claimed they were doing God's will by rescuing blacks from pagan Africa and bringing them into the Christian South, thus making slavery an evangelical exercise.

That today most, if not all, of these pro-slavery arguments have been discredited is not the point. Back then they were believed, accepted, and acted upon. To question them was to question the foundation upon which was erected the elaborate edifice that was Antebellum Alabama. We may wish that our ancestors had been more critical of the system, had themselves taken the hard stands others were taking, but they didn't, perhaps couldn't, because the alternative to slavery was, for the time at least, unacceptable if not incomprehensible. And Alabamians have never been much good accepting the unacceptable or comprehending the incomprehensible.

SLAVERY SECESSION, AND WILLIAM LOWNDES YANCEY

What white Alabamians needed was someone to explain it to them. Someone to tell them why Texas got them so upset. Or if they weren't upset, why they should be. Someone to give voice to their uneasiness, stir it into anger, then show them how to make it right. The man who would do this was William Lowndes Yancey.

He was no Dixon Lewis, scion of solid political stock, or a William Rufus King, Black Belt gentry of unimpeachable character. No, Yancey was the Georgia-born child of a dysfunctional family dominated by a Yankee-evangelical-Presbyterian stepfather who took them to live in New York where he brutalized the mother and convinced the son that northerners were, as a breed, heartless hypocrites. Young Yancey did get a good education in the bargain, but it was not enough to keep him home. In 1833, at the age of twenty-one, he moved to the South Carolina upcountry where he read law and under the influence of his maternal uncle became a staunch unionist. He married well (the dowry included thirty-five slaves), but before he could fully enjoy his new wealth, he got into an argument with his wife's uncle and, revealing an inclination to violence that would be a character note, attacked the man and killed him. Convicted of manslaughter, he spent three months in prison, and when he was released in January of 1839, he, his wife, and the slaves moved to Alabama and settled on a plantation near Cahawba.

Texas was still on the minds of many Alabamians when Yancey arrived. Unannexed, it had gone its own way and become the Lone-Star Republic, but Alabama folks were still bitter over the loss of so rich a country, so sure an ally. Other things also occupied the thoughts of his new neighbors—debt relief, state aid for internal improvements, and a bill "more effectually to restrain the sale of liquor" (which failed by a two-to-one vote)—and Yancey found himself in a land of Lilliputian legislators guided by popular prejudices and little else.

In the years since Israel Pickens, local politicians, legislators, and a governor or two had learned to give voice to popular causes that rose from the general gut—taxes, reapportionment, squatters' rights, whether or not to charter a railroad, and such. In the process they created a constituency that expected, indeed demanded, that their views be listened to and acted upon. So the smart, successful politician was the one who felt the issues rumbling even before the fissures appeared, raised the issues before the people knew they were issues at all, then led the electorate to the polls and victory. During the Texas debate the ground began to tremble. Alabamians needed someone to tell them why. And when William Rufus King couldn't tell them, and Dixon Hall Lewis wouldn't tell them, they turned to William Lowndes Yancey. He would and he did.

Arrived in Alabama, Yancey was already undergoing his metamorphosis from anti-Calhoun unionist to "fire-eating" secessionist, a transformation in which personal demons played no small role. When his hated stepfather, now an ardent abolitionist, turned out Yancey's southern mother to eventually die propertyless, living on the charity of her children, Yancey saw the act as an example of relations between the North and South writ small. Convinced that the South must protect itself from such fanatics, must defend its own, William Lowndes Yancey completed his conversion to the states' rights cause and with the zeal of a convert launched his political career.

Still, it took Yancey a little time to find his focus. Elected to the legislature in 1841 and to the state senate in 1843, he championed causes his constituents wanted championed, some of which, like property rights for married women, were dear to him as well. He was, by most measures, a loyal Democrat. Then in 1845 he ran for Congress, barely beat his Whig opponent, and headed for Washington. It was a good time to be a states' rights-leaning freshman representative from Alabama. Unionist and conciliator William R. King had resigned his senate seat to become minister to France, Dixon Lewis was appointed to replace him, and the Lewis faction was eager for new allies. But Yancey quickly became disillusioned with the party squabbling and clandestine compromises that, so it seemed to him, promised to sell southern rights for a mess of porridge. Northern Democrats, like northerners in general, came across as an unprincipled lot, ready to surrender all, including honor, to gain an advantage, hold an office, make a dollar. So Yancey said his piece, voted his increasingly intransigent conscience, and in 1846 resigned his seat and returned to Alabama.

But what was the piece he said? In Congress Yancey first allied himself with Calhoun's followers, spoke and voted against protective tariffs and internal improvements, and on these issues acted just as a good states' rights Democrat would and should have. Then the question of Texas came up again, and the Alabamian found his cause. In Yancey's mind opposition to annexation was part of a northern conspiracy to deny southerners an equal role in governing the Union, for without additional slave states and their votes in Congress, the South would be reduced to a permanent minority. He was outraged that some of his fellow southerners failed to see this, and his volatile temper got the better of him. He orally attacked a North Carolina congressional colleague who responded with a challenge that Yancey quickly accepted. It looked like the end of a promising career: He would either be killed or return to prison, for Alabama law prohibited dueling by office holders. But admirers at home, realizing that Yancey cared not one whit for either consequence, came to his rescue and pushed through legislation exempting their friend from the law. Thus freed from legal restraints, he faced his foe on the field of honor; both fired, both missed, both felt vindicated, and neither mentioned the matter again.

Yet in the incident the point comes clear. William Lowndes Yancey was no ambitious politician bent on using states' rights to further his career. He was a true believer. For him the issue, both in the duel and in the Congress, was honor, southern honor, which was the one thing free men could not surrender and remain free. Northerners harbored, he believed, "a deeply seated hostility to the South" which for some time had manifested itself in a perverse desire to prevent southern influence from expanding and a willingness to violate constitutional principles to do so. Keeping Texas out of the Union was one way to accomplish this. Prohibiting slaveholders from taking their property into federally controlled territory was another. In either case southern freedom was threatened, and if the threat was not challenged and overcome, southern honor was lost. So Yancey met the enemy head on. Denying abolitionist assertions that the South's peculiar institution was an abomination in the sight of man and God, he replied that "African slavery, as it exists in the Southern States of this Union, is both politically and morally right, and that the history of the world furnishes no proof that slavery is either evil or sinful." Therefore, he reasoned, the abolitionists' attacks on slavery were part of a Yankee plot to reduce the white South to servitude. Or to put it another way, the independence, the freedom of southerners depended on the preservation of black slavery. Thus convinced, he returned to Alabama to press his point.

But did Alabamians believe him? Sure they did. Some may have even believed before he did. In 1840 the popular governor Arthur Pendleton Bagby, in his annual address to the legislature, had defended slavery as a "positive good" and an honorable institution in keeping with God's divine will. Others were predisposed to believe and were easily convinced. A few took a little longer but eventually came around. And they did so because it was already part of their political culture to believe that liberty was always in danger. Israel Pickens alerted them. Dixon Lewis warned them. And John Gayle revealed that even their beloved Andrew Jackson could be a threat, unwittingly perhaps but threat nonetheless. So when William Lowndes Yancey told them that Yankee abolitionists were going to use the federal government to free southern blacks and enslave southern whites, they listened and believed.

Yancey planted the seed, predicted the future, and in his brilliant, sometime tortured mind, things began falling into place. Though a Yankee plan to prohibit slavery in territory taken in the Mexican War failed, in no small part because of Dixon Lewis, the effort was seen as more evidence of the suspected northern design against southern liberties. Responding from his new home near Montgomery, the latest and last capital of the state, Yancey coauthored a series of resolutions to be presented at the 1848 Democratic convention. This Alabama Platform pledged the party's candidate to protect the right of citizens to own slaves in federal territory. And when the platform was rejected, Yancey walked out. One other delegate joined him. The rest remained.

The incident is significant, for on one hand it reveals that Yancey was coming to the conclusion, as he would put it later, that there was no longer any "middle ground between *submission* and *secession*." But on the other hand what happened underscores the fact that many, perhaps even most, Alabamians did not agree, not yet. No small number of them felt secession could and should be avoided. Yancey, of course, rejected their position. Continuing the course he had set, the Alabama "fire-eater" denounced the Compromise of 1850, under which southern congressmen, led by Alabama's own William Rufus King, gave away California as a free state and got, according to Yancey, little in return. So he rallied a group of young Democrats to his cause, created a southern rights faction within the party, and set his sights on separating Alabama from the Union.

Increasingly the field was Yancey's to command. Dixon Hall Lewis, grown to 450 pounds, died in 1848. Though a passionate advocate of states' rights and a staunch defender of southern liberty, Lewis was a reluctant secessionist at best, and he might have offered Alabamians an alternative to the path Yancey wanted them to follow. Five years later William Rufus King, recently sworn in as vice president, returned from Cuba to die on his Dallas County plantation. He was antebellum Alabama's last great, national figure. Without King politics fell to lesser lights, and leading them was William Lowndes Yancey.

Or was he? During the 1850s events seemed to take control of people. The creation of the Republican Party, which promised to elect a president and a congressional majority with or without the South, and then close the territories to slavery, whether the South liked it or not, seemed to confirm Yancey's warnings. Events in Kansas appeared a harbinger of bloody conflicts yet to come. Republican resolve to overturn the Supreme Court's decision that Congress could not prohibit slavery in the territories convinced many southerners that constitutional protections were worth little. And finally John Brown's attempt to raise slaves against their masters and "purge the land with blood" foretold the abolitionists' ultimate design to abolish slavery, one way or another. All these things, when seen as Alabamians had learned to see them, led to an inescapable conclusion. Freedom was impossible in a Union dominated by the North.

And so it was that by 1861, it became hard to tell whether men such as William Lowndes Yancey were inspiring the people or were themselves being inspired. Either way the result was the same. It was no longer a question of whether or not to secede, but when and how to do it.

6

Secession and Civil War

How to explain it? How to tell the tale of Yancey leading the Alabama delegation to the Democratic convention in 1860, introducing the Alabama Platform once again, to have it rejected once again, and walking out once again—but this time taking with him delegates from seven southern states? And then to tell of the Democrats, divided, with northern members nominating Stephen A. Douglas of Illinois who was committed to union and southern delegates nominating Kentucky's John C. Breckinridge who was committed to . . . what? Add to the confusion the Whigs imploding, collapsing around John Bell declaring his loyalty to "the union and the law" and the Republicans running Abraham Lincoln committed to stopping the expansion of slavery but promising to protect it where it was (and no one south of Tennessee believing him) and you have a mess to untangle.

Everyone in Alabama, everyone paying attention a least, knew that a vote for Breckinridge was a vote to leave, at least if Lincoln won, for as Mills Thornton has pointed out, "Breckinridge speakers repeatedly proclaimed that, though existing wrongs were not adequate to justify secession, the election of Lincoln would be sufficient cause." And Lincoln won. So they knew what came next. The Montgomery *Confederation,* conservative, Democratic, made it plain: "The issue—though we regretted it—was made this summer that the election of Lincoln was a good cause for secession. The black

Republicans knew this. They were told so by our friends who were battling throughout the North for the rights of our section. The issue, we may say again, has been made and we must stand up to it. We shall and we must resist Lincoln."

So we can say, with some certainty, that Alabamians who voted for Breckinridge were Alabamians ready to leave the Union if Lincoln was elected. Yet who were they? Slaveholders in the Black Belt, certainly, but they also voted for Douglas and Bell, as did commercial counterparts in cities. The true believers, the hard core, the fed up and ready to get out were concentrated in other quarters. Of the statewide vote 54 percent went to Breckinridge, and in fifteen counties he polled more than 65 percent of the votes. But only four of those landslide counties were plantation counties, and none were what you could call commercial. No, Breckinridge ran strongest in the eastern and western hill country of North Alabama and down in the southeast, the wiregrass. Breckinridge got his votes from yeoman farmers whose granddaddies had listened to Pickens, whose daddies had listened to Lewis, and who, when local politicians no longer seemed to understand their anxieties, themselves listened to Yancey, all telling them that liberty was theirs to lose if they were not vigilant. These were folks who felt Yankee arrogance most keenly and believed they had the most to lose if the South was relegated to permanent inequality. They knew their enemy and in their frontier simplicity wanted to strike out against it. Here was their chance.

But lest someone should say, "See, it wasn't slavery after all. Those folks didn't own slaves and they were for secession," understand this. These yeomen, slaveholders and non-slaveholders alike, wanted to preserve slavery, were willing to leave the Union to preserve slavery, and ultimately were willing to fight and die to preserve slavery, not because they owned slaves (though some did) or because they wanted to own slaves (though most did) but because they believed that limiting slavery's expansion, then abolishing it altogether, would confirm both a northern victory and their own bondage. And not incidental to this was the fact, as Yancey often reminded them, that abolishing slavery meant abolishing the tax on slave property, and if that tax was abolished, non-slaveholders would be called on to take up the slack, pay more to the state, and have less to freely use themselves. The issue, therefore, was not slavery but freedom, the freedom of white Alabamians. And white Alabamians knew, or at least by then believed, that there could be no freedom without black slavery.

So what next?

Lincoln was elected. The secession convention was called. Then the delegates met, and the secessionist majority (a slim majority, but a majority nonetheless) drew up the ordinance that made plain their belief that because the Republican candidate was elected "upon the avowed principle that the Constitution of the United States does not recognize property in slaves and that the Government should prevent its extension into the common Territories of the United States and that the power of the Government should be so exercised that slavery, in time, should be exterminated," they were justified in leaving the Union. Then it was just a question of how to do it—act individually, immediately, or wait for other states to make up their minds and act in concert.

In Alabama, where frontier individualism so often spoke collectively and emotionally, the issue wasn't long in doubt. Years later Walter Calloway, who had been a slave on a plantation near the capital, told a WPA interviewer what he heard, which the interviewer transcribed in dialect:

> When de war started 'most all I know 'bout it was all de white mens go to Montgomery an' jine e army. My brudder, he 'bout fifteen year ole, so he go 'long wid de ration wagon to Montgomery 'mos 'ebry week. One day he come back from Montgomery an' he say, "Hell done broke loose in Gawy." He coundn't tell us much 'bout what done happen, but de slaves dey get all 'cited 'caze dey didn' know what to 'spect. Purty soon we fin' out dat some of de big mens call a meetin' at de capitol on Goat Hill in Montgomery. Day

'selected Mista Jeff Davis president and done busted de
Nunited States Wide open.

On 7 January 1861 Alabama's "big men" gathered in what a critic
called their "Athenian yankeeized" capitol in Montgomery. Four
days later they voted for secession. Then the ceremonies of congratu-
lation began. In a letter to his wife the Reverend W. H. Mitchell
described how, "amid the most deafening cheers" the doors of the
legislative chamber were thrown open. Then, with "the galleries . . .
crowded with ladies and gentlemen, . . . the noble-hearted, pure and
patriotic women of Montgomery" presented the assembly a banner "to wave over the Capitol of our new Republic." It was accepted amid "peal after peal of applause," while outside "bells were
ringing—cannons [were] firing[, and] a steam boat [was] whistling."
For Mitchell, it was "one of the most stirring-enthusiastic & thrill-
ing scenes [he had] ever witnessed."

It would not have been so for Nicholas Hamner Cobbs, Alabama's
Episcopal bishop. An opponent of secession, which he was convinced
would lead to war, Cobbs openly prayed that "if it was God's will,"
he would be spared the sight of his beloved state setting itself on the
road to disaster. Just before the vote was taken, God's will was apparently done. Within sight of the capitol, Bishop Cobbs died.

PREPARING FOR WAR

One by one the rest of the deep South states seceded. Montgomery
was declared the capital of the new Confederacy. Jefferson Davis
arrived to take the oath of office. A government was created. So was
an army. Throughout the state "gallant young men" rallied round.
Selma raised five companies whose membership reflected both the
diversity of the growing town and its dedication to the cause. John
Hardy, an early historian, watched and recorded the organization of
the socially prominent Magnolia Cadets, in whose ranks were "the
first young men of the place," the Selma Blues made up of "the
more sober, settled men of the city," and the Phoenix Reds "com-

posed almost entirely of working men." Before the year was out, the Queen City of the Black Belt had contributed more than six hundred soldiers to the cause.

Contrary to legend, Cahawba, the former capital, had flourished fair in the years after the seat of government was moved, and there, in a ceremony reenacted in towns and villages throughout Alabama, "Dallas County's bravest and most gallant sons" met and formed the Cahaba Rifles and waited for word of war. It came soon enough, and in April, just before they departed "for the scene of conflict," their commander, Capt. Christopher C. Pegues, accepted a company banner from a local belle and swore to bear it to "victory or to death." "Right royally," recalled Anna M. Gayle Fry, a local girl who witnessed it all and wrote it down, "was that oath fulfilled." Pegues proved an able officer, became a colonel, and might have been a general and later a governor or a senator had he not fallen leading his men at Gaines's Mill in the summer of '62.

But that day the war still lay ahead for them, still lay ahead for the "wealthy cultured, young gentlemen [who] voluntarily turn[ed] their backs upon the luxuries and endearments of affluent homes," still ahead for the "working men" who left jobs and families to join the cause, and still ahead for the "more sober, settled men" who probably should have known better but joined anyway.

It also lay ahead for the hundreds of farm boys from a state of farm boys, whose families counted their acres in tens, not thousands, who owned no slaves, and who had never seen a Yankee until they shot at one. They enlisted (and were later conscripted) without ceremony. No flags were consecrated for them, no bands played, no belles gave them flowers and kisses.

And it lay ahead for John Pelham, scion of a prominent Calhoun County family, already at West Point, where he was making a name for himself as more a scamp than a scholar. Like many others of his class he would give up that appointment and join the Confederate Army. Young, handsome to the point of beauty, blond, blue-eyed, fair, and firm in the saddle, smiling with an innocence that revealed no trace of the talent that would make him one of Robert E. Lee's finest field commanders, he rode away the symbol of what Alabama was sending to fight and what Alabama was fighting for. It was fitting, those left behind surely thought, for a cause so pure, so untainted by self-interest, so favored by God, to be defended by such as he.

Montgomery was capital of the Confederacy for fewer than five months. When Virginia seceded Confederate officials agreed to move the seat of government to Richmond, to assure doubters that the first colony would be defended to the end. Alabama was left with memories of its fleeting importance, with a house that would become a memorial to the president who briefly lived there, and with a sacred spot at the entrance to the capitol where the oath of office was taken. But Montgomery, for all its political significance, soon took a backseat to its downstream neighbor, Selma, where Gen. Josiah Gorgas, chief of ordnance, moved the Confederate arsenal in the spring of 1862. In time the town would become a military-industrial complex that produced nearly half the cannon and two-thirds of the ammunition used by Southern armies, along with guns, swords, bayonets, and other military hardware. Other Southern cities—Atlanta, Charleston, Mobile, for example—might seem of more strategic importance to Union planners, but to the soldiers in blue, who had to dodge rebel shot and shell, Selma was as important as any.

Moving the Confederate arsenal and Confederate hopes to Selma told a tale of a war already going badly for Alabama. In early April of 1862 citizens of Huntsville heard the news that "the turnpike is black with Yankees," and a short time later the enemy came down on them with "such a clatter [as] never before woke the echoes among those Alabama hills." Union forces that had been relentlessly moving along the Tennessee River and into the heart of Dixie took the former capital, then began spreading out into the valley. In most cases Union soldiers acted like soldiers, but in one incident, an attack on the quiet farming community of Athens, some turned into what locals called "lawless vagabonds." The Federal commander, Col. John Basil Turchin, a Russian immigrant and former soldier of the tsar, was found guilty by a court-martial, but that news did little to blunt the impact the atrocity had on Southerners. His eventual pardon by President Lincoln only added salt to the open wound.

RALLYING THE HOME FRONT

Although the Tennessee Valley was, in effect, Union territory, Confederate Alabamians continued firm in their belief that they would win in the end. Among the committed, none were more zealous than the women. A Union officer in recently occupied Huntsville was amazed at what he called the "foolish, yet absolute devotion of the women to the Southern cause," which did "much to keep it alive." It seemed to him that women "encourage[d], nay force[d], the young to enter the army, and compel[led] them to continue what the more sensible Southerners know to be a hopeless struggle." He wrote in May of 1862. That very devotion would keep the war going for nearly four years.

Women were doing more than encouraging and compelling. Before the capital was moved, word reached Montgomery that a thousand sandbags were needed to protect the batteries at Pensacola. Howell Cobb, then president of the Confederate Congress, told an Atlanta assembly of how "someone suggested that the ladies be made acquainted with our wants," which they were, and in a matter of hours "the money had been raised, the cloth purchased, and the lovely women of that city, with their own delicate hands, at their homes and in the sanctuary of the living God, were making bags." The next day the job was done and on its way. "Talk about *subjugating* us!" Cobb thundered. "Why, we might lay aside the men, and all Abolitiondom *couldn't run down the women even!*"

Meanwhile, in the south the Federal blockade closed Mobile Bay to all but the most daring smugglers. It was more than a severe blow, for if the South was going to finance its freedom with cotton, much of that necessary commodity would have to flow through the city by the bay. By 1860 Mobile was second only to New Orleans as a cotton exporter. At the mouth of two of the state's major river systems, the terminus for road and rail, Mobile was the commercial capital of Alabama. Yet with its diverse population (50 percent foreign born), moderate politics, religious pluralism, and tolerant sensibilities, it was unlike the rest of the state—and would continue to be for almost a century.

Still, Mobile was Alabama, and with Union forces threatening the city, insular Alabamians hunkered down to defend what was left. And many marched away to do just that. How many? Hard to say. By the end of 1861 more than twenty-seven thousand Alabama boys were in the army, and the number grew to more than ninety thousand before the war was done. But after that first rush of patriotism, the pool of volunteers shrank, and the urgent need for men to stop the seeming endless hoards of Federals moved the Confederate government to order that able-bodied men between the ages of eighteen and thirty-five be conscripted, drafted, in short, forced to serve. The order was a blow to Southern sensibilities, for it violated one of the most cherished principles of states' rights—that the central government should not impose its authority directly on the people of a state without that state's permission. If Alabamians, and other southerners, were in this war, fighting, first and foremost for the right to be left alone, then conscription surely left them wondering if what they were creating was any better than what they were out to destroy. Add to this the belief that the measure of a cause was the willingness of people to support it without coercion, and we are left with another reason for Alabamians to ask if this was a country worth fighting and dying for. One wonders today how many "neo-Confederates" who proudly hail their ancestors' sacrifice would find, if they could find, that great-granddaddy volunteered one step ahead of draft or was actually forced into the ranks. Either way, circumstances suggest that Alabama had more than its share of reluctant rebels.

Alabama also had more than its share of the brave and gallant who went without coercion and served faithfully. Again, the question of numbers is difficult to answer, but some have estimated that the state led the Confederacy in the percentage of its population that wore the gray. Add to that number those who wore Union blue—some three thousand from the northwest counties, the "Tories of the Hills" they were called—and figure in the over ten thousand black Alabamians from occupied areas who also joined the fight to make them free, and the total was impressive. So, as we shall see, were the casualties. And as those reports began to come back from the front, reports of the dead from battle and disease, and as the wounded, the maimed, returned, Alabama and Alabamians began to consider and reconsider what it was all about.

LOSING

Reconsidering the cause came then, and comes today, in different guises. Some were unsettled when the Conscription Act was amended to exempt anyone who owned or oversaw twenty or more slaves, which led to charges that the struggle was becoming "a rich man's war and a poor man's fight"—but records indicate that slaveholders volunteered more often and served longer than their yeoman counterparts, and one suspects that most yeomen knew it. True enough, there were those who agreed with the Winston County father who at the outset of the war warned his son, a staunch Confederate, that he was about to "go to fight for [the planters'] infurnal negroes, and after you do there fighting, you may kiss there hine parts for o they care," but most other Alabamians appear more concerned with being forced to kiss Yankee "hine parts" than those of their more prosperous fellow citizens. No, while such class tensions may have contributed to the growing discontent, there were reasons more real and more immediate.

There were the casualties. Companies were raised from communities and were composed of men who might be kin by birth or marriage. And even if they weren't related, they had lived together, worked together, been together at weddings, births, and funerals. So they marched off together, fought together, and, so many of them, died together. Little Mount Pinson in Jefferson County raised a hundred men in 1861. By 1865 only nine were left. And there were few to replace them. Only fifteen recruits were raised to replenish the ranks. So we can also count among the casualties the maids never married, the children never born, and the leaders who never led. The news in most cases came slowly, name by name on the lists sent down from Virginia and Tennessee, until, by the sheer weight of them, they overwhelmed and crushed those left behind.

But occasionally the news arrived with sad suddenness, as it did in of March of 1863 when Jacksonville learned that "the noble, the chivalric, the gallant" Maj. John Pelham had fallen in Virginia. He was only twenty-four. In less than two years Pelham had gathered admirers including none other than General Lee himself, who watched him in battle and wrote how it was "glorious to see such courage in one so young." A gifted artillery officer, a favorite of the men he commanded and those who commanded him, in death Pelham reminded them all that war took the best and gave back sorrow. Three (or was it six?) Virginia girls dressed in mourning for the dashing boy. His comrades put his body in an iron coffin with a window through which the face, unblemished in dying, could be seen, piled it with floral tributes, and sent it home. He was buried in Jacksonville, where today some say that in the spring flowers bloom, rooted from cuttings that came from Virginia with the bier.

Then it was summer, and it was the numbers again. News came from Gettysburg that in three days 1,750 Alabamians had fallen, with scores of others wounded and captured. It was a long way from home to die. And there was word from Vicksburg too, and more casualties.

There were bright spots, of course; how else could they have gone on two more years without something, sometime, that was at least like victory. In the fall of 1863 Gen. Nathan Bedford Forrest and five hundred rebels followed seventeen hundred Federals under Col. Abel D. Streight across North Alabama, harassed them into thinking five hundred rebels were ten times that many, and finally ran them to ground just before they crossed into Georgia. There Streight handed Forrest his sword and then, learning of the ruse, demanded it back. Forrest refused. It made a cracking good story and elevated a young girl named Emma Sansom to secular saint-hood for showing Confederates a ford that allowed them to avoid a burned bridge and keep pressure on the Yankees. But it was victory by stealth and luck, and the South was running short of both.

Confederate Alabama seemed to be running short of just about everything else as well. In September of 1863 reports came out of Mobile that hundreds of local women, "rendered desperate by their sufferings," marched on the city "with banners on which were printed . . . 'Bread or Blood' on one side, and 'Bread or Peace' on the other, and armed with knives and hatchets, marched down Dauphin Street, breaking open the stores in their progress, and taking for their use such articles of food or clothing as they were in urgent need of."

Things were just as bad in the rest of the state. By the end of 1863 food for man and beast was hard to find, especially in the hill country. Salt, necessary for preserving meat, also was in short supply. Drought coupled with a lack of manpower, literally, compounded the situation, for on many of the state's small farms, only women and children were left to plow, plant, cultivate, and harvest. Women, whose role in Alabama's society and home economy has often been underestimated and underappreciated, took on a heavier burden. From the planter's wife, trying to manage increasingly restive slaves, to the farmer's wife, struggling to hold body and soul together on land from which they could barely scratch a living before her husband marched, or was marched, away, the effort was heroic and, as often as not, futile. In Shelby, a county where over thirteen hundred of its sixteen hundred men went into the army, by 1864 over 66 percent of the families were destitute. That was the worst. Things were better down in the Black Belt, but inadequate transportation made it difficult for a surplus in one region to help sufferers in another. Before the conflict ended, fully 25 percent of the state's white population was receiving some form of relief, precious little though it was. Back at the beginning of the war, a widow living with her children on a Cherokee County farm considered the future and wrote in her diary, "I fear our happy days are all gone." She was a prophet.

So they wrote their husbands, told them of shortages, or the mule dying, or a harness breaking and no way to fix it, or of children hungry and sick, and the husbands, many of them, considered the cause that was failing and how they could do nothing about it, and thought of home and how they could do something about that, and made the choice, and began trudging south. Some believe these men were deserting their country, maybe even told them so; but the men, many of them, believed their country had deserted them. When we lump their numbers together with those who avoided the draft, fled to the hills, even joined the enemy, or went out with others like themselves to raid friend and foe alike, we begin to get a feeling for the slow but steady collapse of the home front that paralleled and complemented the slow but steady collapse of Confederate armies. The war was being lost by degrees. The cause was dying, as it was said, "by the graduals."

And the people, as they had done so often in the past, went to the polls and let their leaders know. Voting their fears and apprehensions, as well as their hopes and desires, in 1863 they replaced a governor who had ordered slaves pressed into state service, enforced conscription, rationed salt, and told them to stop making whiskey because it wasted (*wasted,* mind you) grain, replaced him with a former unionist who, if not actually expected to bring peace to the land, at least was expected to make things better—which of course he could not. Other elections went much the same way as "Reconstructionists" were swept into office. These were men who believed the war was lost and the sooner peace was made and the Union restored the better. Their movement was especially strong in North Alabama, where occupation had made disillusion more acute, and in the hill counties, where once-ardent secessionists had begun to conclude that their less-than-enthusiastic friends and neighbors may have been right all along. Years later Confederate memorialists would try to convince history that the South supported the cause, united to the end. And some, wanting, needing to believe, would believe. Some still do. But they were, and are, wrong.

The enemy knew that dissent and disillusionment no more meant surrender than did a lost battle that left the defeated army intact to fight another day. They also knew that the war had taken a turn, as wars tend to do, and what Northerners fought for at the outset—Union—was no longer the cause that sent them into battle. With the Emancipation Proclamation, President Lincoln had made the issue what Southerners believed it was from the beginning—slavery. Thus, though the Federal officers who planned the final invasion may not have understood that white Southerners were fighting for their freedom as surely as they were fighting to keep black Southerners in bondage, the planners understood that whatever motivated the Confederates had to be crushed where it was.

ALABAMA INVADED

In the spring of 1864 a Union army under Gen. William Tecumseh Sherman began moving south from Chattanooga, heading for Atlanta. To protect his western flank and disrupt Confederate supply lines, Sherman ordered Gen. Lovell H. Rousseau and a force of three thousand to move south from Decatur to a point near Opelika, where they could cut the Montgomery & West Point Railroad and deprive Atlanta of needed supplies. Moving quickly and encountering little or no opposition, they made it to the Coosa River and crossed near where Andrew Jackson's Tennessee troops had crossed years ago. It was, according to one report, "a beautiful sight," with "the long array of horsemen winding between the green islands and taking a serpentine course across the ford—their arms flashing back the rays of the burning sun, and guidons gaily fluttering along the column."

But it was not a "beautiful sight" to residents of the valley, who watched helplessly as the invaders marched south, missing by a few miles the town where Pelham's body lay but finding Talladega, where they destroyed what they could not eat and carry, then on to Loachapoka and Opelika, tearing up track, burning cross-ties, and twisting rails. The line of march marked by black smoke, they turned east to report the mission accomplished with little opposition and almost no casualties.

The news of setbacks came faster now. Not long after Rousseau's troops left, word arrived that the CSS *Alabama,* the South's most feared commerce raider, had been sunk by the USS *Kearsarge,* off the coast of France. Commanded by Mobile's Raphael Semmes, the *Alabama* fought bravely against a superior vessel and went to the bottom rather than surrender. To the bitter disappointment of the Federals, Semmes was rescued by an English yachtsman who had come out to see the battle.

In Mobile news of Semmes's defeat was made all the more bitter when, a short time later, a Federal fleet ran the guns of Fort Morgan and Fort Gaines, captured the mighty but fatally flawed ironclad CSS *Tennessee,* and anchored in Mobile Bay. The last significant Southern port was closed, and, Mobilians realized with horror, the Bon Secour oyster beds were now in enemy hands. It was one thing to be losing the war, but if we are to believe letters and journals of the day, to lose that staple of their cuisine compounded the tragedy.

Now news came that Atlanta had fallen and Sherman was marching to the sea as easily as Rousseau rode through Alabama. Then it was '65, and they knew the last blow would soon be struck; the only question was where. Word came out from Montgomery that sixteen- and seventeen-year-old boys could enlist, should enlist. Some did, but not many. Mothers who had earlier proudly sent their sons to a war they were told could be won would not, if they could help it, suffer their children to go into what they knew, now, was the slogging horror of defeat.

But the decision was soon made for them. On 22 March 1865, Maj. Gen. James Harrison Wilson with three divisions of Federal cavalry, more than thirteen thousand well armed, well horsed, well seasoned soldiers, crossed the Tennessee River. Facing him was Forrest, with a force less than a third in size and smaller still in supplies and experience. It would take more than stealth and luck this time, and Forrest did not have it. Swiftly the Federals moved south. Tus-caloosa, Elyton, and Montevallo were all taken, Confederate iron works were destroyed, but these were incidentals along the way. Selma, the last great enemy arsenal, was the goal, and on April 2 the invaders were on the outskirts of the city. By dark it was over.

Then the victors rounded up the vanquished, some twenty-seven hundred prisoners, put them in a stockade that once held Union captives, and began the paperwork that would eventually put them out on parole. Confederate officers were invited to share the Union officers' mess, and some probably got the best meal they had eaten in months. Complaints were few, though one of the prisoners re-called later how a Yankee band played "Dixie" late into the night, which kept him awake and depressed.

Stories were later told of how Union soldiers had sacked the town, brutalized its people, and left Selma a smoldering shell of a place, but what else could you expect from men who (so it was claimed) were recruited when "prison and penitentiary doors had been opened to swell the columns of the invading hosts." Truth was, most of the invaders behaved well enough, but some did discover a liquor store and began "making very free" with the contents. A ser-geant found them at work, and before he could stop the looters they invited him to join the party. "No soldier," he remembered, "needs a second invitation of that nature at the end of a campaign." So there were drunken soldiers, just as the stories tell, and robbing in the bargain. But General Wilson moved quickly to post guards to protect people and property. As for the fire, retreating Confederates torched some thirty-five thousand bales of cotton and most of the warehouses in the commercial district. This fire spread to other buildings but did not consume the entire city, as Selma's famous antebellum architecture testifies today. Still, many businesses along downtown streets were lost, and as far away as Cahawba refugees could see the red glow on the horizon. In Selma the bitterness would last long after the fires burned out.

Now the word spread. "Yankees at Selma," shouted the head-lines of the *Clarke County Journal*. But they were not there for long. Crossing the river, Wilson's army headed east through the Black Belt, a course as demoralizing to Alabama as Sherman's was to Georgia. Through the heart of the plantation district they marched unopposed. When they arrived at Lowndesboro just after midnight, "no living creature appeared in the town, not a light was seen, not a sound was heard except the subdued rattle of arms in the column." According to one of them, "It was a dream world, through which the war-worn soldiers marched silently in the deep shadows of the oaks." And from behind shuttered windows, those who did not flee watched unmolested, as the victors passed in review.

They were more like tourists than an invading army. And when they could, they talked to residents—often to black Alabamians who until recently had been slaves. When they asked one freedman what had happened to his former owner, he replied that "old massa headed down to Big Swamp, crying all done gone, Selma gone, Richmond gone too." Selma the Federals knew about, but Richmond? The Union soldier assumed the reference was just another example of the southern flair for the dramatic overstatement. But "old massa" was right. Before they reached their destination they learned that the day Selma fell, Jefferson Davis fled his capital. Richmond was, indeed, "gone too." So was the Confederacy.

It was fitting, therefore, that Montgomery, where it all began, would be one of the places where it ended. But what was launched amid "deafening cheers" was about to end with the silence of surrender. With orders to abandon the city Confederate soldiers began destroying anything that might be of use to the invaders. Syrup, it was said, ran "ankle deep" outside the commissary, and Walter Calloway "heard tell dey burn up piles an' piles of cotton an' lots of steamboats . . . an' lef' de ole town jes 'bout ruint"—just about.

Then reason (or resignation) won the day. At three on the morning of April 12, the Montgomery mayor, W. L. Coleman, and a party of prominent citizens rode out to Union lines under a flag of truce. There, to the delight of Wilson and his men, they gave up the city. When residents awoke they found guards posted at key streets and buildings and a new flag, the old, familiar one, flying above the capitol. Then the army, with its band leading the way, rode in four abreast. On they came, a resident recorded, "host upon host of blue coats . . . fine looking men—handsomely dressed . . . brass buttons, brilliant epaulets, sabers drawn and clashing . . . mak[ing] their entrance at full gallop." Anyone who had seen the ragged Confederates who had burned the cotton and fled understood how Wilson had won, and why.

Four years to the day after the South fired on Fort Sumter, the first capital of the Southern Union was occupied by Federal troops. Few, however, made the connection. Surrender was everywhere. Though some felt "humiliated" and wondered if "the good Lord will allow us long to be so downtrodden by such people" as Yankees, soon they learned that even Robert E. Lee had given up the fight, proof enough that there was no disgrace in defeat. Many in the city and around the state became "Union Men of the 11th hour," and the ladies of Montgomery were so friendly that victorious soldiers were disappointed that they would only stay a few days. But they were no army of occupation. That would come later.

Meanwhile, on distant fields, soldiers in tattered gray—men who had fought to the end—stacked their weapons, furled their flags, and turned South toward home, toward Alabama.

7

After the War That Never Ended

Now they came home, those who could. While there is no general agreement on the casualties Alabama suffered, all agree the sacrifice was great. The often-quoted figures, thirty-four thousand killed out of ninety thousand who served, with another thirty-five thousand disabled, are probably too high, but whatever the numbers were, they were high enough. Then there were the other casualties—the fields that would not be planted and families not fed because a father fell, the labor lost (or at least readjusted) with the emancipation of nearly half the population. Worthless currency, unredeemable bonds, and some $200 million in capital transferred from the masters who once owned them to the slaves who now owned themselves. Then there was the uncertainty of it all. On whom or what could anyone depend?

One of his former slaves told how "Massa Cal" returned to his Lower Peachtree plantation "all wore out and ragged." He called his hands together in the front yard and told them, "you are today as free as I am. You are free to do as you like, 'cause the damned Yankees done 'creed you are." He promised that any that wished could stay and "work and eat to the end of his days, as long as this old place will raise peas and goobers," but those who wanted to leave could. Some stayed, but others did as George Taylor and his father did. Taylor, who had been a lad on a plantation a little farther south, recalled how his "Old Master" called his former slaves out into the yard and told them that those who wanted to remain should stand over on one side and those who wanted to go should move to the other. Father and son moved to the other. Then they left the place and, Taylor said with simple eloquence, we "paddled down the river in a paddlin' boat."

T. H. Ball, a Baptist minister from Indiana, had lived in the south-west part of the state before the war, had left, and then returned afterward and witnessed the system's collapse. Describing what must have been more the rule than the exception, Ball told of how "the colored people remained, for the most part, on the plantations and at their old homes as usual and worked regularly till the close of that year [1865]." But "when the usual Christmas holiday came they went out, many of them never to return." Each seemed to depart in his or her own way. "At some homes they would leave in the night, to avoid any special painful sensations. Some however would leave in the daytime, apparently in order to make an impression on the white family. Some made arrangements immediately at their old homes to work the coming year. Some sought new places. Some went from their old owners sorrowfully; and some refused to go at all."

Most white Alabamians seemed to accept emancipation as a logi-cal outcome of the war, and there was more resignation than anger in the loss of property and the end of the peculiar institution. "The negro is free whether we choose to admit the fact or not" was how one of them put it. What whites did not accept, could not accept, was the end of the racial code that had defined master and retainer, superior and inferior. They could not believe that the order of things had really changed. Anna M. Gayle Fry, a girl at the end of the war, told of how most of the former slaves left her family's Dallas County plantation and got as far as Selma, where her father went in the fall of '65 to find workers to help him harvest what passed for a crop. Arriving in town, Mr. Gayle saw his old servant Patty, who in the past was "the one of all others who expressed the greatest devo-tion to her 'young master.'" But "freedom had worked a marvelous change" on Patty, for when he called to her "she turned, saw who it was, and flounced [that was the word, "flounced"] off, exclaiming:

'Lord a massie, Chile, I ain't got time to fool wit you now.'" Gayle was stunned. It was "the first time in his life a negro had ever refused to come at his bidding." That refusal, compounded by the "offhanded manner" in which he was answered, "was too much to be borne." Gayle went home, "gave his crop to the Confederate Soldiers," and made "no further overtures" to his former bondsmen.

Whites simply could not understand what freedmen wanted, or why they wanted it. Or if they did understand what and why, could not accept the idea of freedmen having it. Though no poll was taken, no survey made to determine the desires of former slaves, from their requests, and from their enthusiasm and lack of it, a pattern does emerge, a pattern that defines freedom as they wanted it, believed it should be. Black Alabamians saw freedom through the eyes of slavery. Slavery had been work, unremitting and unremitted labor. So it followed that when liberty came in the summer of '65, they did what Patty did, what George Taylor and his father did—they left Massa and the plantation. But it wasn't just the work (many found jobs elsewhere); it was the sort of work—some refused to pick cotton, some women refused to care for white children, others refused jobs with white supervisors. If the jobs smacked of slavery, reminded them of bondage, they "flounced" away to freedom. And to whites, who had never known blacks except as workers, their attitude was insolent, insulting. So whites told each other of how lazy, useless, good for nothing blacks were without slavery to give order to their lives. Some whites even wondered if blacks could survive without whites to tell them what to do. Former slaves saw things differently. They were doing what they did because they were free to do so. That was what freedom was all about.

White Alabamians' confusion over the role they expected black Alabamians to play was compounded by the fact that whites were anything but certain what they could or would do themselves. Word had come down from Washington that if former Confederates pledged loyalty, accepted emancipation, and forgot about trying to collect debts incurred in the rebellion, they could reorganize their government and get on with what was being called Reconstruction.

Some refused, but Isaac Grant, a rural editor in South Alabama, would have none of it. Addressing the community, he urged friends to register and vote for delegates to a constitutional convention— "voting as a good and loyal citizen, and bowing meekly to the stern decree of that fate which, for four long and bloody years, we have vainly striven to set aside," was how he put it. Don't look to the past, he told his readers, but "endeavor, for the future, to control events for the security of our happiness and prosperity under the laws of our State and Federal Government."

Grant was a practical man. To him swearing loyalty was "only taking an oath to do what we have to do whether we take it or not." What really concerned him was that defeated Southerners might withdraw, say "to hell with it," and let the victors run things. So he issued his call to arms, told them that "by taking the oath and voting—governing as far as possible, our own affairs in our own way, we have everything to gain and nothing to lose." It was time, he told them, to "yield to the stern logic of events and make the best of the 'situation.'"

Other Alabamians saw matters much the same way, and over the next decade parties and factions tried to do just that—govern their own affairs in their own way. And because one group's "own way" often threatened others, conflicts were bitter and scars lasted long. Reduced to its essence, what followed was a struggle over who would govern Alabama to their own advantage. It would take the rest of the century to decide the winner.

RECONSTRUCTING ALABAMA: THE WHITE TRADITION

Here is how it once was told among white families and in white schools, and not just in Alabama, or just in the South:

After the war defeated Confederates accepted the outcome and set about to follow the plan laid down by martyred Lincoln, who became, in a bit of historical gymnastics, "the South's best friend." Lincoln wanted to bind up the nation and the nation's wounds quickly, and with as little lasting rancor as possible. But radical Republicans in Congress betrayed the fallen president, and with malice toward many and charity for few, set out to humiliate the downtrodden South—which they did with the help of renegade southerners ("scalawags") who did it for personal and political gain and "'corrigable" Negroes who did it for revenge and restitution. But "good and sensible" men (whites of course), "noble" and "self-sacrificing," stood firm against these evil forces, fought them by whatever means possible (including, "regrettably," violence), and at last, after a decade of struggle, "redeemed" Dixie from black Republican bayonet rule. "Faithful" Negroes and "loyal" whites praised what was done. The rest didn't matter.

This is what the people who would lead Alabama for nearly a century would believe. You need to understand that if anything else is to make sense.

RECONSTRUCTING ALABAMA:
ANOTHER VIEW

Over the years historians have come to see things differently. They note how all concerned wanted to "reconstruct" Alabama in their own way. Planters wanted to restore as much of the old order as possible, which meant holding onto their land and keeping a docile labor force in the fields. The commercial community had no problem with this, so long as it meant that there was cotton to trade, merchandise to market, and people with money to buy. White yeoman farmers, many of whom became deeply disillusioned as the war dragged on, wanted a postwar balance of power much like the one that existed before secession, one that responded to their needs and desires. Yeomen, especially up in the hills of North Alabama, forgot how enthusiastically many of their class and kind had supported secession. Now they talked of how it was all the fault of the slaveholders and how those to blame should not be allowed to make any more disastrous decisions for the state. Planters heard them, of course, and understandably were concerned.

Meanwhile black Alabamians had their own hopes for Reconstruction. They wanted to be free from intimidation, free to form their own associations, free to work where they chose under an arrangement mutually agreed upon. They expected the Freedman's Bureau, created by Congress to ease the transition after emancipation, to help them, help them learn to read and write, purchase land, and gain the right to vote. They understood, close observers that they were, that with those things a man was truly free.

Seen from the white perspective, black efforts often appeared misguided, superficial, and in some cases silly. But whites did not understand. So they pleaded with blacks to stay in the white-dominated churches they had attended as slaves, stay with whites who "understood" them, and they were deeply hurt when, in the first (and the most lasting) act of segregation, blacks left to create churches of their own. Or maybe whites did understand, and feared, that black churches would be the place where leaders, men and women, could learn and lead and pass the experience along. Maybe whites did understand that black churches would be a place of refuge, "a rock in a weary land." Maybe that is why whites ridiculed black churches that seemed to spring up like weeds (or flowers, depending on where you stood to look) and made jokes about black ministers who acted more like politicians than preachers. Maybe it bothered former owners to know that former bondsmen were free to preach on Exodus, sing about Moses, and worship a deity who cared for the poor and suffering. And maybe it worried them that the line between preacher and politician was drawn faintly, so faintly that it might well disappear.

Nor did whites have much good to say about freedmen who seemed to wander about aimlessly, because they, the whites, never bothered to ask why they were wandering and where they were going. Had they asked they might have discovered families being reunited, laborers looking for work, or African Americans doing what Americans on the frontier had always done, moving to improve. In truth, anything that black Alabamians did to distance themselves from slavery and masters was unsettling to whites who wanted things put back the way they had been. So dreams of education were belittled and eventually went unfulfilled, hopes for land were dashed, and the right to vote—they got that, but. . . .

And then there were the carpetbaggers. These were men who, according to tradition, arrived from the North with all they owned stuffed into a carpetbag, Republicans come to exploit white and black alike, steal what they could and make off with the loot one jump ahead of the law. Allied with scalawags and renegade blacks, they descended on the prostrate South like a biblical plague of locusts. Once blacks got the franchise, carpetbaggers stole or bought their votes, got elected, raised taxes, forced the sale of farms and plantations, filled their pockets from the treasury, and drove the state near to bankruptcy. Carpetbaggers, scalawags, and their black allies—Alabama's evil trinity.

Well, not exactly. Northerners did come down, some to exploit, but most to invest. No small number of them were Democrats, and today some of the most prominent families in the state can trace their lineage to these postwar immigrants. As for those who did get into politics as Republicans, their white allies were hardly the degenerates that the name "scalawag" implies. Most native whites who became Republicans did so as an alternative to the Democrats who in those postwar years came increasingly under control of the planter and commercial classes. Where else was a North Alabama farmer to go? Who would champion the cause of the common man? So a Republican party began to rise in Alabama, a party composed of northerners who came for reasons singular and personal, of farmers removed from the plantation districts who wanted a party that would champion their causes, and of freedmen, who by this time could vote—and did.

When Reconstruction began only the most radical Republicans thought it wise to give the franchise to newly freed slaves. But within a year of surrender, news of white attacks on freedmen, stories of former masters intimidating and exploiting former slaves, and examples of southern resistance to congressional policies convinced northerners that the white South had not learned its lesson. Therefore, many northerners concluded, true Reconstruction was possible only through black political participation. Most holding this opinion were Republicans who, not surprisingly, believed grateful blacks would become Republicans and send Republicans to congress. So Alabama got a host of new voters.

THE POLITICS OF RECONSTRUCTION

Despite all that was altered by the war, in one way, at least, Alabama had hardly changed. The state and its people still felt the flow of that prewar political culture that had rallied them to the likes of William Lowndes Yancey because he told them that liberty was threatened, that enemies were abroad on the land, and that he could save them. They believed then, and they were ready to believe again.

And why shouldn't they, for all around were examples of sinister forces working against them. States' right zealots, bloodied but unbowed, claimed that Republicans were bent on increasing federal power and warned that requiring ratification of the Fourteenth Amendment before a state could be restored to the Union was evidence of federal tyranny in the making. When whites turned to violence blacks raised the alarm and warned that the Ku Klux Klan was nothing more than a terrorist band out to intimidate newly enfranchised voters and their Republican friends. Planters feared that blacks and yeoman farmers might unite under the Republican banner and run the state to their advantage. And yeoman farmers feared that planters were out to manipulate black votes and with them get control of the legislature—something their fathers and grandfathers had never been able to accomplish before the war.

The important thing to realize is that they were all correct. Battles based on these beliefs would be fought on many fronts. Race was certainly one, and to deny the influence of that issue is to deny the importance of attitudes that permeated all aspects of life in postwar Alabama. Class too would define and divide the combatants, and though it would prove less important than race in determining who sided with whom, differences between poor, rich, and middle mattered. Geography and demography also cemented alliances. Hill country folks from North Alabama, white yeoman farmers for the most part, opposed Black Belt planters and the former slaves who in time voted (or were voted) as told (or forced). And planters (Black Belt and otherwise) watched poorer whites with a studied distrust handed down to them as a political legacy. Meanwhile, black Alabamians, on or near plantations mostly, looked for dependable allies but found few.

So what thread do we pull to unravel the fabric, separate out the interests and alliances, and make some sense of what follows? Given that choice, I chose taxes.

Let me explain. Who taxes whom reveals where power lies and who is in a position to use that power to their advantage. Before the war power lay mostly in the hands of white male adults, regardless of property or prestige. We know this because their representatives put the tax burden on the wealthy. As we have seen, revenue was raised from levies on slaves, personal property, and other such accouterments that defined the planter class. And since the state spent little on things like internal improvements and education, so long as times were good, there was revenue enough. It doesn't cost much to do nothing.

The war changed all that. The loss of slave property was also the loss of a tax base, so if those governing under the first Reconstruction constitution were aiming to do anything for Alabamians, black and white, a new source of revenue had to be found. But the state's first postwar government, created under liberal terms and filled with former Confederates, was much like its predecessors and thus little disposed to spend money on social services, though the people, black and white, were in need of them. So it followed that few state taxes were collected, and relief for the destitute came from federal sources. (The fact that more white Alabamians than black received this largesse was shortly and conveniently forgotten.)

But riots and resistance in the South enabled Congress to take a more aggressive role in Reconstruction, to set aside Pres. Andrew Johnson's moderate plan, and in early 1867 to divide the South into military districts. Thus began the so-called "bayonet rule," a time, according to white tradition, of occupation and humiliation, of federal troops violating civil liberties, of black rule and misrule, of carpetbagging and scalawagging, and of former Confederates helpless to defend anything save honor, which they did under white hoods and at night. Reality alters the story but does not erase all its elements. There were federal troops, but southerners outside areas where there was violence seldom saw them. Some blacks were elected to the legislature, but they never "ruled" the state, and most black officeholders served as honestly and well as their white predecessors— not necessarily a compliment, but it says a lot about persistent political traditions in the state. The truth is that neither side—Republicans in their various incarnations and Democrats in theirs—had much use for the other, and, given the choice between the two, Republicans in Congress naturally favored the former. So a new state constitution was called for, and over Democratic protests, despite political skullduggery, and with the help of federal legislation that was at best partisan and at worst unconstitutional, in 1868 a new government, a Republican government, came into being.

Then came more violence and more troops, and from election to election the tide swung between Democrats, who were now the party of white southern loyalists, and the Republicans, in whose ranks were other whites and most blacks. Reading what they said, one finds it easy to believe it all revolved around race, since so much was couched in racial terms. Democrats denounced the Constitution of 1868 as a document that "takes all political power from the superior and intelligent race and gives it to the inferior and ignorant race," and as their ranks grew they made their position clear. "There are but two parties now in the field," a North Alabama newspaper declared, "the negro party and the white man's party. There is no middle ground between the two—to one or the other, every man must belong. He that isn't for us is against us. . . . Nigger or no nigger is the question."

But that was not the only question, or even, for many, the most important. As issues of race and Republicanism excited and incited crowds, the state moved closer and closer to bankruptcy. And as it did, deeper problems were revealed. It happened, more or less, this way:

When Republicans came to power in 1868, they began looking for revenue to provide services that past Alabama politicians had avoided or ignored. Like their northern counterparts Alabama Republicans favored state-financed internal improvements—roads, bridges, and the like—and believed the state should fund a school system as well. However, these projects cost money, and since so many prewar sources of revenue were gone, the state's new leaders decided to tax Alabamians' most common and available resource—land. In a state where more than 80 percent of farmers owned their own farms before the war, these new taxes were widely felt and deeply resented, not just because of what they cost the taxed, but because it was generally believed that most of the revenue went to "undeserving" blacks, while carpetbaggers and scalawags made off with the rest. Such suspicions could not be proved then and remain unproved today, but if there was misappropriation and stealing, it was not the first time in Alabama history, nor would it be the last.

Reconstruction folklore is filled with tales of planters unable to pay their taxes and plantations sold at sheriff sales, though in truth it was the yeomen who suffered most. A planter strapped for money might be forced to sell off some of his land, but usually enough remained to carry on. A small farmer in what was often a cashless economy had no such surplus. So it was his farm, more often than not, that went on the block—which goes far toward explaining why, during the years that followed, poor whites so often saw their interests linked to their wealthier brethren and so often sympathized with stories of planter hardship. There was more than racial solidarity at work back then.

Compounding these problems was a national economic recession, the Panic of 1873, which drove down cotton prices and made taxes even more difficult to pay. By then, however, both sides had learned a fundamental lesson: Whoever controlled the black vote won the election. Republicans planned to bring black voters to the polls with promises of protection and patronage. Democrats set out to hold black voters home with threats and intimidation. The results were predictable. In the election of 1870 Klan activity in key Black Belt counties kept African Americans away from the polls and gave the Democrats the victory. Two years later, with federal troops at polling places in those counties, the Republicans won. So with 1874 looming on the horizon, both sides girded for battle.

They got girded for nothing. Even before the campaign began, white and black Republicans clashed bitterly over who would control their party and where they would take it. In the process they destroyed any chance they had of winning. Meanwhile united Democrats watched contentedly from the sidelines, and when the smoke cleared they stood over the wreckage and denounced the "carpetbaggers," "scalawags," and blacks they claimed were conspiring to enslave whites. Thus confirmed as the champions of their race, the Democrats promised that in the future Alabama's government would safeguard property, keep taxes low, reduce state expenditures, and maintain white supremacy. The platform had something for everyone who was not a Republican, and on that platform the Democrats were swept into office.

ALABAMA REDEEMED

It was not a total victory. Republicans still held thirty-three seats in the legislature and one seat in the congressional delegation, but everyone could see the end was near. For whites, at least white Democrats, there was hope for a better day. For Republicans, especially black Republicans, the future looked bleak. Reconstruction had promised freedmen much, and on the national scale much had been accomplished. But black Alabamians soon learned how little that mattered. Before long decisions made in Montgomery, not Washington, governed their lives, and their influence in Montgomery was getting weaker and weaker. Former Confederates saw things differently. For them Reconstruction was a time of trials that they suffered, they endured, and from which they were finally redeemed. It was the biblical "tribulation," and only the faithful survived. For black Alabamians, however, a second "tribulation" was beginning. Some say it was more bitter than the first, more bitter than bondage.

To confirm the redemption of '74, Democrats decided to write a new constitution. Arguing that the 1868 document had opened the door for unfair taxes, corruption, and debt, the victors called for the election of a convention to put things right. The delegates chosen, whose members ran heavily to lawyers and Confederate veterans, created and organized a government that addressed most of the concerns that brought the Democrats into office. Constitutional limits were set on state and county property taxes, the revenue from which would no longer be needed since in the new document state-financed internal improvements were prohibited. "Expensive and unnecessary" state offices were abolished, and the salaries of others were cut, thus reducing state expenditures even more. The less you had to pay for, the less you needed to collect, which, of course, was the point. Just as before the war, there were no educational or property qualifications to vote or hold office, which pleased yeomen and other Jacksonians. The provision might have also pleased blacks, had the constitution not specified that state and federal elections be held at different times, meaning that state offices would be filled without federal officials there to make sure all voters were treated fairly. Blacks still could vote. The Democrats just wanted to make sure that their votes didn't count for much.

Black voting was a dilemma for Democrats. Some surely wanted to take the franchise from African Americans, but the fear of federal intervention was still too great for them to actually do it. Democrats in Black Belt counties worried, however, that voteless blacks would not be counted for representation purposes. That would reduce the size of the planters' legislative delegation and their clout at the capitol. Planters wanted blacks on the voting rolls. They just wanted to control how their votes were cast. Holding separate elections was a step in that direction.

So they wrote it up and announced that the demons of high taxes and corrupt government had been slain. What they did not announce, but what would soon become apparent, was that an under-funded state could do little to educate its people and enhance their lives. That did not matter to the delegates, who were determined that their money would not be spent on anyone other than them-selves. So Alabama was declared redeemed, and Alabamians were told that to stay that way these redeemers, or men like them, must continue to govern. And Alabamians, a lot of them anyway, be-lieved.

POST-RECONSTRUCTION ALABAMA

The last federal troops were soon gone, withdrawn, dribbled out, without fanfare, and in most cases without notice, for they had been only here and there, and you don't miss what you never saw. They were just gone. Now black Alabamians had no one to protect them, though most probably never thought they were protected much anyway. And white Alabamians had no presence to remind them that they were a defeated people, but they knew that without seeing blue coats in the community, if they had ever seen them, which most hadn't. No, that ending, so significant on the national scene, just happened down here. And no one seemed to pay it much mind.

What they did mind was getting by, which in the aftermath of the Panic of 1873 was no easy task. But it wasn't just the planter, the farmer, the tenant, the 'cropper who were struggling. In all the talk about cotton and conditions, it is easy to forget that there was a commercial community abroad in the land, and its contribution to the debate over "whither Alabama" was and would be significant.

Before the war you could find merchants in what passed for cities—Mobile, Montgomery, Tuscaloosa, Huntsville. They were in towns as well, one or two or three of them, and at occasional cross-roads, in stores the entire stock of which could have been, and prob-ably once was, loaded into a single wagon. Plantations often had similar establishments, commissaries some called them, where shirts and shoes and such were distributed to slaves and occasionally sold to neighboring farmers, but planters weren't too keen on this sort of thing, so the transactions were primitive at best. To put it simply, outside cities, towns, and a village or two, you had to go a ways to find a merchant, and the smaller the community, the less the commerce.

After the war that began to change. The Reverend T. H. Ball, down in Clarke County, saw it in his place, and surely others saw it in theirs. When he lived in Alabama in the 1850s, Ball was enamored with the planter class, which was small in his county, and critical of the lower orders "whose homes had very little attractiveness, where the presence of filth, and indications of the excessive use of tobacco and whiskey, were manifest." As for the others? They were there, some were his friends, but he showed little interest in them as a group. Then he went away and returned to record the transformation. "In general," the minister wrote after the war, "neither class of the two extremes of society could adapt themselves to the demands of the new circumstances; but the large middle class, accustomed to some effort, and possessing more energy and physical endurance, pressed bravely and nobly onward amid their trying circumstances." By the mid 1870s this group, with a few admitted exceptions, had become "the prominent, prosperous, useful, influential families" of the community. Leading this group were the merchants.

It is difficult, and often misleading, to generalize about the rise of Alabama's small-town and rural merchants after the war. They were a varied lot, more prominent in some locales than in others, mobile, evolving, rising, and falling with the greater economy. To treat them as something apart from the general scheme of things, as interests separate unto themselves, is to miss an important point: They were as much a part of the cotton culture as those who planted, chopped, picked, and ginned. In some cases they were farmers themselves, for two jobs were always better than one at a time when one often provided less than a living. And also keep in mind that they were equally an element in the larger economic scheme. The goods that stocked their shelves were bought from other merchants higher up a chain of commerce that stretched from small towns to large towns to cities and then to the North, that same North they had rebelled against, that North that did not need an army of occupation to know who had won.

THE LANDSCAPE, CIRCA 1875

Not so long ago one could still ride around the state and see the remains of what emerged back then. And one could, with effort and imagination, piece together elements from different locations to create a single example, one that would serve to explain the post-war, post-Reconstruction order of things that appeared in Alabama. There was no plan to it, no genius at work. It was a reaction, a response, an accommodation, an effort, in the words of editor Isaac Grant, to "make the best of the 'situation.'"

It might have happened like this, and in some cases it did. "Massa Cal" came home, made his offer to what was left of his "hands." (He might have called them his "family" before, but not now; now they were hands, and like hands their purpose was work.) Those who decided to stay went back to the quarters, and "Massa" returned to the big house. And they brought in the crop.

But old ways did not suit. Gang labor and overseers were not for free men, so in the negotiations that followed former slaves moved out of the quarters. They built cabins on land parceled out to them about the place and with their families lived as tenants who paid rent or sharecroppers who farmed in return for part of what they produced. So now the big house was the center of a farming community, far-flung where the plantation was large, tighter-knit where it wasn't. Hands drifted in and out, made a crop, moved on or not as freedom allowed. Landless whites joined blacks in the same circumstance and took up residence on the place. The new labor system settled in on Alabama, a system tied to the soil and governed by the rhythms of the seasons.

The hands had needs: plows and mules to pull them, seed to plant, hoes to chop with, the "furnishings" to make a crop. They also needed to be carried over until harvest; they needed an advance, or "'vance"—meal, meat, molasses, shoes, shirts, shifts, and all the other things families used—so the planter built the store and became a merchant. And he moved. Once the commissary out behind the big house was located well enough, but now, with hands scattered about the place, there was a new center to it all, down close to where the road from the county seat crossed the one that ran from the river, so he put the store there. It was a business decision. He needed access to the town merchants who supplied him, on credit, the goods he supplied, on credit, to the people on the place. So soon, without really planning or even knowing it, he diversified and became part of the larger economy.

There was a railroad in the county now, running from city to city, and then to an outside world little known before the war. Goods unimagined in antebellum times now could be bought at stores in towns. So what if the styles were dated? So what if Yankee suppliers used Dixie as a dumping ground for what had not sold the previous year—a practice acknowledged when they referred to anything no longer of value, consequence, as having "gone south." Now southerners who could pay the price could dress almost in fashion.

But not out at the plantation. Massa's store stocked only the essentials. There the hands would start coming in even before the weather began to warm for planting, coming to get their 'vance, because what was earned with the last crop was used up by then, and children in the cabins were hungry. So the planter-merchant (or merchant-planter) went back to the shelf and took down the cans, filled up the sacks, cut the meat, slid them across the counter, and wrote it down in the big leather-bound ledger he kept back in the little room that passed for an office, the room where only other white men went, men like himself, landowners, not tenants.

And the ledger told the story of cotton promised even before it was in the ground, of debts incurred through the spring and into the summer and finally settled in the fall, paid out. Only usually they weren't.

There was a time, not long ago, when one could stand in the shells of those old stores and imagine how it was. The hand—tenant or 'cropper—bringing in the cotton that he and his wife and his children had sweated from the soil. Taking it to the gin across the road, which also, probably, belonged to "the man." (That's what they called him now, "the man." Not to his face, for there was more than a hint of disrespect in the title. To his face they called him "Mr.," but he and they knew he was more than that. He was "the man.") And the cost of ginning and baling was added to the debt when the hand returned and stood across from the man, the counter between them, as he totaled up what was owed and compared it to what the cotton would bring. Then the man told the tenant how much more was needed to pay out, get free. If the tenant had it, which he seldom did, there usually wasn't enough left to make it to the next harvest. So a new arrangement was made, a new 'vance was given, and the cycle began again.

Challenging it was not an option. Even if the tenant could read and write, which was unlikely, the very thought of questioning the man was absurd. If he did challenge the balance, he would be put off the place, or . . . ? There were rumors of tenants disappearing after altercations with the man, and everyone believed the rumors were true. So there was no alternative but to accept the situation and hope that next year would leave you clear and free to find another man with better terms. Only it seldom did. A little verse, repeated in varying forms and at different locations, told all:

Read and write, figure and figure
Everything for the white man,
Nothing for the nigger.

Only not just the black folks, the freedmen, were caught in this system. Every year there seemed to be more whites, so that by the turn of the century, sharecropping and tenant farming were Alabama's most thoroughly integrated occupations.

It was, no one can deny, a vicious cycle, and even today its legacy is felt in parts of the state. To be fair, on those farms and plantations where the owner kept faith with his tenants, balanced the books honestly, and never forgot that hands were attached to human beings, the system filled a need, "made the best of the situation." Unfortunately, the opportunity for exploitation proved too great for many landlords and merchants, so the system became, in most cases, what its critics claimed it was—another form of slavery. Economically and socially, sharecropping and tenant farming kept alive, indeed spread, relationships that before the war were generally confined to plantations. By the 1870s those relationships had become part of the political fabric of Alabama.

ONE MORE CASUALTY

By the time the redeemer constitution was ratified in 1875, it was apparent that Civil War and Reconstruction had claimed another victim. In the antebellum era most Alabamians, Jacksonians to the core, believed that government was there to serve the people, common folks. For better or worse it usually did, and it followed that in most matters, common folks trusted the government, through their representatives, to do right by them. But during the war popular concerns more often than not got caught up in the greater struggle, and Alabamians became disillusioned with leaders who conscripted, confiscated, and circumvented with what seemed like impunity. Postwar leadership was little better, for no matter who was sent to Montgomery—Republican or Democrat—someone other than the farmer, which is what most Alabamians were, benefited from legislation passed and laws enacted. So by the time Reconstruction ended, run-of-the-mill Alabamians had become convinced that trust put in government was trust misplaced.

Redeemer victory scarcely changed this belief, for redeemer sympathies lay with the planter and the merchant, not with the yeoman, and certainly not with the tenant and 'cropper. The Constitution of 1875, which confirmed the Democratic victory, was equally a victory for the state's propertied elite, especially in the Black Belt, and though it was not apparent initially, that document set the example of how to compose a constitution to keep the lower classes where they were. Gone were the days when the legislature would rush to relieve debtors of their burdens. Although farmers were just as desperate in 1875 as they had been in the 1840s, no help was offered. Alabama's new ruling class had other things on its mind.

The Democrats, the redeemers, were worried about holding on to what they had, the power they had just gained, which meant they were worried about black folks. Despite economic intimidation, despite violence, the black voter remained a potentially potent force in state politics. With the Republican party in shambles, blacks had little hope of electing many of their own, but in critical Democratic contests, black votes could make the difference. White politicians knew this and were not happy about it. They did not relish the idea of going into the black community and asking, appealing, for support. Nor did they like to think about what black voters might ask for in return. The whole process turned relationships upside down, put African Americans in the preferred position, gave them the advantage, which was something no white man could endure. And what would happen if other whites learned a candidate was "making deals" with blacks? More than once a candidate lost because he was accused of catering to black demands. This uncertainty unsettled Democrats as surely as it enhanced and frequently confirmed black political power. But what to do about it? That was the question. Little did they know, these Democrats, that soon black voters would be the least of their worries.

ENTER THE BOURBONS

Names are important. The politicians who wrote the Constitution of 1875, whose ascent to power marked the end of Reconstruction, liked to be called "redeemers," for that is how they saw themselves— men who had redeemed Alabama from Republican misrule. But their opponents, and even some of their friends, soon took to calling them "Bourbons," after the ancient French ruling family whose members tried to restore the Old Regime after revolution and Napoleon.

These new Bourbons, Bourbon Democrats, were accused of wanting to restore an old order that resembled what existed, or at least they believed existed, in the Arcadian days before The War. And if pressed on the matter, most of them would have admitted that it was true. They were seeking to create a social, political, and economic system under which propertied people like themselves would govern for the good of all and those beneath them would see the benefits to be gained and follow willingly. What they would neglect to tell, or gloss over if it came up, was that they would be the principal beneficiaries of such an arrangement. What they also avoided was any mention of the fact that Bourbon power in France had rested on the shoulders of a downtrodden, docile peasant class. Alabama didn't have that. Not yet.

8

A World Made by Bourbons, for Bourbons

So what did they want, these Bourbons? They wanted a lot of things, as one of their number, John S. Graham explained.

Born in 1848, Graham was a teenaged Civil War veteran who came home to clap together an education, become a staunch Democrat, and learn the newspapering trade. Eventually settling in Jackson, a rising river and railroad town, he became reporter, editor, publisher, owner, and just about everything else for the *South Alabamian,* which he used to promote his town, his region, and his party. A businessman and booster, as interested in industry as in agriculture, he was the typical Alabama Bourbon—small town, small minded, and, on the whole, of small influence. At least by himself. But put him with a host of others like him, the bourgeois Bourbons who dominated towns and villages and who, allied with prosperous farmers and planters, created and constituted the "courthouse gangs" that ran each county, consider him with these, and it becomes apparent that by the turn of the century the John Grahams of Alabama ran Alabama. So what they wanted was what Alabama got.

This is what they wanted. Graham explained it in a county history he wrote in 1923, which included a single page titled simply "what the author stands for." Had Alabama's Bourbons wanted a creed, a statement of principles, this would have served.

"The author of this book," Graham wrote, "stands for white supremacy, for United States Americanism; for a government of the people, by the people, for the people; for a government economically administered; for the principles of old-time democracy. He stands for law enforcement, for Christianity, morality, honest and up-right dealings among men. He stands for strict observances of the provisions of our constitution, both state and federal."

Graham went on to pledge his unwavering support for a free press, for free speech, for free public schools, and (good Baptist that he was) for the separation of the church and state. To this he added a ringing denunciation of "bolshevism, socialism, and every other 'ism' which holds itself out as being superior to this government," then closed with a statement of his opposition "to the liquor traffic, to the descration [*sic*] of the Sabbath, and [to] all kinds of rowdyism."

THE POPULIST CHALLENGE

Recall that Graham was writing in 1923, after he and his kind had fought hard, had won, and were comfortably (albeit warily) enjoying the fruits of their victory. But it had not come easily. From the late 1880s until 1901 Bourbon Democrats struggled against a force that threatened their hold on the party and, more important, their control of the state. The enemy they faced went by many names, but sooner or later everyone called them Populists.

The populist movement in Alabama should be seen as the heir to the political tradition begun by Israel Pickens, continued by Dixon Lewis and Williams Lowndes Yancey, and revived by the redeemers, a tradition of popular democracy rising to elect popular politicians dedicated to protecting the people from popular enemies. By the 1880s the people, many of them, had become convinced that the enemy they faced, the enemy bent on taking their liberty, was a new Royal Party, a new elite, a new class of rich and powerful men who intended to stay that way by controlling the state and its resources. They called them Bourbons.

Although elements in this conflict were evident during Reconstruction and redemption, Alabama had been governed a decade under its 1875 constitution before serious splits began to appear in what many thought was a seamless Democratic fabric. On the whole, those few years had been good to Alabama farmers. Cotton prices were sufficient to make debt less an issue, and with taxes low thanks to constitutional limits, landowners from yeoman to planter had little reason to complain. True, sharecroppers and tenants, black and white, saw scant improvement in their lot, but they were still a minority in the system and a powerless one at that, so their complaints made little difference. Then by the end of the '80s things began to change. The economy slowed, and the price of cotton slid downward, while the price of everything associated with it—from plows to processing—seemed to rise. Alabama farmers began looking about for some way to voice their concerns, and they found the Farmers' Alliance.

The alliance began in Texas, entered Alabama in the 1880s, and soon "spread like a marsh fire" across the state. Initially men like John Graham welcomed its arrival, for alliance leaders were mostly middle-class farmers who voted Democratic and who espoused the values of hard work, thrift, moral conduct, and responsibility, values Bourbons wanted adopted by everyone under them. But when alliancemen began denouncing merchants who seemed to profit as the farmers sank deeper into debt, began raising questions about planters who prospered while their tenants suffered, and started criticizing politicians who seemed to care little for the plight of those on the lower end of the economic pecking order—in other words, began attacking Bourbon institutions and Bourbon authority—Alabama's Democratic leaders took notice.

What made alliance attacks particularly unsettling was the fact that, despite redemption and a constitution created by and for themselves, Alabama Bourbons still had an uneasy hold on power. The black vote, usually controlled by planters, could always turn against them, and the poor white voter, whom Bourbons had taken for granted, was becoming increasingly restive. Then there was a new element in the mix—industrial labor. Bourbon boosters praised and promoted a more diversified economy, and with their support new cotton mills began to spring up in the Piedmont. But more important, in Jefferson County coal and iron production increased dramatically, and the little town of Birmingham was on its way to becoming the "Pittsburgh of the South." Although those who toiled in the mines and the mills were not farmers, they had much in common with folk who worked the land. Their lives were governed, their liberty was limited, by similar forces—owners, merchants, and politicians—all of whom could be, and were, lumped together as Bourbons.

So Alabama Bourbons had a lot on their minds. They worried when alliance leaders talked of setting up their own stores, cooperatives, which would bypass merchants and give farmers a better deal on what they bought and sold; they worried when farmers talked of legislation to ease the burden of debt, for no small part of those debts was owed to Bourbons; and they worried when labor talked of organizing to improve their lives on and off the job. But mostly they worried when they heard talk of farmers and workers, black and white, uniting, turning the Farmers' Alliance into a political alliance. They worried about this because they were hearing how a new party, the Populist Party, was growing and challenging the political establishment. If this movement came to Alabama, Bourbons could foresee nothing but trouble.

The Bourbon dilemma was this. Successful redemption made the Democratic Party the most powerful political force in the state, and they ran the Democratic Party. But small farmers, the party's core constituency, were not happy, and Bourbons knew it. They also knew that if politicians rose to give voice to farmer discontent, focus farmer anger on individuals and institutions that could be blamed for their troubles, and offer themselves as the solution to these problems, those politicians might make the party their own. The Bourbons could not let that happen. They had to find a way to dominate without alienating the farmer faction. Put simply, they had to take democracy out of the Democratic Party.

THE BOURBON RESPONSE

Things began to get serious near the end of the 1880s, when farmers found their leader, their champion, Reuben F. Kolb, state commissioner of agriculture. Although a member of the planter class and a wealthy Barbour County agricultural innovator who had gained fame and fortune developing a popular watermelon, the "Kolb Gem," the commissioner understood the plight of the yeoman, and through his office he had become a powerful spokesman for farmer interests. A loyal Democrat like most of the farmers who rallied to him, he hoped to use the network of alliances to elect candidates better attuned to the needs of the struggling instead of the concerns of the secure.

Complicating the picture was the presence of a small but influential Colored Alliance, separate and distinct from its white counterpart but nonetheless available as a political ally if needed. The possibility that black and white alliancemen might form a coalition that could dominate the party and the state seemed real to the Bourbons, and as alliance-endorsed candidates began to get elected, Bourbon concerns grew. Black Belt Bourbons especially feared that white support and promises of protection might embolden black voters to defy planter authority and take control of county governments. And as every good Bourbon knew, in Alabama control of the courthouse was the first step toward control of the statehouse.

Bourbon anxiety increased when, in 1890, Kolb announced as a candidate for governor. The move proved premature, and the commissioner failed to get the party's nomination. So he and his followers loyally supported the nominee, Thomas G. Jones, while they also campaigned for candidates who shared their views. When the new legislature met later that year, observers noted that alliance-endorsed candidates held a majority of seats in the lower house and made up a significant minority in the senate. Reuben Kolb now had a base of power from which to operate. The Bourbons were not happy.

Then Kolb announced that he planned to run for governor again in 1892. Now the Bourbons were mad. It was traditional for a sitting governor to be nominated for a second two-year term, and if nothing else, the Bourbons believed in tradition. So Kolb was not only challenging Jones, the Bourbon governor, he was challenging the customs and arrangements on which and by which Bourbons established and maintained their power. More than that, his announcement confirmed the Bourbon belief that he was a man who would not play by the establishment's rules, a man who could not be trusted. So now the Bourbons had their own enemy. Here was someone they believed would turn tradition on its head, who would excite simple people with wild promises, and who would claim to be championing the cause of the farmer when he was actually rallying the farmer to the cause of Reuben Kolb. Here was the Bourbons' worst nightmare: One of their own turned against them, an apostate, a traitor. He had to be stopped.

The Bourbons were not without resources. They controlled the state convention, which nominated candidates, and in a raw display of power they rejected Kolb's delegates and seated those pledged to Jones. Denied a place at the table, alliance supporters cried foul, demanded that the nomination be put to a popular vote, and threatened to bolt the party if they weren't treated fairly. When their cries fell on deaf ears, they left the party and met as the "Jeffersonian Democrats."

In a rump convention the defectors nominated Kolb, who excited his supporters with an acceptance speech that hit at the heart of the Bourbon program. Promising prison reform, he vowed to end convict leasing, a system that allowed Bourbons to avoid the cost of building penitentiaries by turning prisoners over to employers (mostly mine owners) who paid the state for the privilege of working them long hours on short rations under horrible conditions. This arrangement also had the advantage of reducing the need for Bourbon-paid taxes and underscored the state's determination that whenever possible revenue would be raised from the dispossessed rather than from those who possessed. Kolb also advocated "better schools and better roads" and called for the election of legislators who "would secure a fair ballot and an honest count." Bourbon reaction was expected. Prisons, schools, and roads would improve the lot of common folk (never a Bourbon priority), but more than that, they would cost money, and Bourbons knew who would be expected to foot the bill. They also knew that a legislature elected by a fair ballot and honest count would likely pass the legislation necessary to secure these things. More frightening still was the possibility that such an energized electorate might rewrite the Constitution of 1875, the document which codified the Bourbon way of governing. With this future looming before them, Alabama's Bourbon Democrats resolved to do whatever it took to defeat Reuben F. Kolb.

What followed was one of the most bitterly contested elections in Alabama history. It was also one of the most ironic, for in many ways Jones was not the best man to carry the Bourbon banner. He opposed the convict-lease system and thus enjoyed some labor support. He also denounced lynching, and though he was a white supremacist, his attitude toward African Americans was more benevolent paternalism than racist repression. (Compare this to a fellow Democrat and future governor, William Dorsey Jelks, who praised lynching as "a cure and an effective one" for black outrages and warned that any African American Alabamian who got out of line would have "his neck . . . broken without the benefit of judge, jury, or clergy.") But above all else Thomas Jones was a loyal Democrat, and when it became apparent that Kolb was creating his own political organization, the governor joined those vowing to stop him, even if it meant further corrupting an already corrupt political process.

The Bourbons began their campaign by denouncing Kolb for promising to protect black rights and work for "a better understanding and more satisfactory condition . . . between the races." Calling this the "nigger rights" plank of the Jeffersonian platform, Bourbons reminded those who might stray from the fold that they, the Bourbons, had redeemed the state from black Republican misrule and stressed that "the only place for a white man was in the Democratic Party." But with Kolb's support growing, Bourbons began to fear that this appeal to white racism might not be enough. So in some counties local Democrats clandestinely cut deals with black leaders who considered the odds, figured the Democrats would probably win, and reasoned that an arrangement with the victors would be preferable to one with the losers. Yet even with these agreements, the Bourbons were worried.

So it followed that the white man's party found itself needing

black votes to defeat a challenger whose platform offered black voters at least the hope for a better future. And realizing this, the Democrats fell back on their time-tested strategy; they called on Black
Belt Bourbons to deliver—and they did. Hardly hiding their activities, Black Belt Democrats used fraud and intimidation almost at
will, and when the votes were counted, by those same Democrats,
they proudly announced that in their counties Jones had defeated
Kolb by more than thirty thousand votes. Jones won statewide by
fewer than twelve thousand. The Black Belt had carried the day, and
Kolb, with no legislative or constitutional avenue of appeal, had to
accept the outcome.

Now let's be fair, or at least impartial. True, the election was stolen,
just as elections were stolen in the last days of Reconstruction, and,
so the thieves claimed, for the same reason—to protect the decent
people of Alabama. While we can look back and see the Bourbon
versus Populist conflict as a struggle between a noble assemblage of
common folk, out to use the power of democracy to overthrow the
forces of privilege and greed, to people living then, the populist
threat was more than political. When John S. Graham said he stood
against "all kinds of rowdyism," he was surely recalling an incident
in the early 1890s when in his county, Clarke County, a group of
"countrymen" with alliance sympathies organized a secret society
they named, with a fine feeling for words, "Hell-at-the-Breech" and
set about to terrorize good folks—or so the good folks believed.
What followed was known locally as the Mitcham War, called that
because it occurred in the mostly white backwoods farming community known as Mitcham Beat. In Bourbon lore it was a victory
of law and order over Kolb-supporting rural rowdies who had no
respect for either. Countryfolk, of course, told a different story.

It all began on Christmas night, 1892, when a local fellow (and
member of Hell-at-the-Breech) decided the best way to get even
with the merchant and Democratic Party official who had fore-
closed on his farm was to kill him. So he hired his brother and a
friend (also members), who took shotguns and blew the forecloser
all over his front porch. The news spread quickly through the county

elite, for they saw this as more than a murder. The incident was a direct challenge to the system that protected creditors' money and, according to debtors, kept them in debt—what Graham called, with no hint of irony, "the honest and up-right dealings among men." No one in authority interfered with the merchant's family, which included the sheriff and a justice of the peace, when it extracted its revenge, but when retribution flushed out the gang, the "good people" of the county armed and rode to get the "outlaws." Killing followed killing as the "war" escalated amid rumors that the "Mitchamites" planned to attack the county seat, kill county officials, and make off with public funds. Finally the fighting ended when the sheriff and his posse (folks in Mitcham Beat called it his "mob") rode into the region, killed some of the suspected, drove others into exile, and cowed the remaining families, innocent and otherwise. The rowdies were routed. The Democratic establishment carried the day.

But victory did not calm their concerns. Despite the outcome, news of the "war" struck fear in the hearts of courthouse Bourbons throughout the state, for its causes—overbearing merchants, courts that favored creditors, and small-town elites determined to run things their way—were everywhere. Graham's county was not the only one visited by what the Bourbons considered populist "rowdyism," and each incident seemed to confirm the growing conviction that the lower classes, the *white* lower classes, were a danger to the order and security of society. Despite the fact that many in the populist ranks were men of property, men whose opposition to the Democratic establishment rose from a genuine belief that the sacred authority of the people was being subverted by the selfish and self-seeking, men who were as concerned with "rowdyism" as the most conservative Bourbon, those who ran the state saw something sinister in this opposition and looked for ways to subvert it. In 1892 they were willing to steal an election rather than let such people elect an alliance-endorsed governor. And they were willing to ride down opponents if that was what it took to keep the community at peace and under their control.

We can see, then, why the Bourbon establishment got so upset. What had once been an article of political faith in the state—the conviction that popular virtue rose from popular participation—was now a deep concern that the will of the people was somehow counter to the good of society. And believing that, Bourbon Democrats concluded that "a government of the people, by the people, for the people" was a government that governed the people, and not the other way around.

THE BOURBONS VICTORIOUS

Knowing what they had to do, Alabama Bourbons set out to do it. They had to take the ballot out of the hands of those who threatened Bourbon rule. The year after Kolb's defeat, the year the Mitcham War broke out, Bourbons pushed through an election law that complicated voter registration and increased the power of local officials to determine who was qualified to cast a ballot. Most insidious in the act was the provision that registration would take place only in May, one of the busiest months in a farmer's year. If the weather was good, a farmer was in the field. If the weather was bad, impassable roads (recall Kolb's campaign promise) made it impossible to get to the county seat. The result was just what the Bourbons expected. Throughout the state, voter rolls shrank as poor farmers, white and black, failed to register, and those who didn't register didn't vote. In Graham's county three years later, more than a thousand former voters did not show up at the polls.

But some Bourbons wondered at the wisdom of this. Black Belt planters wanted to keep black voters registered so they could be "counted in or counted out" as needed. Any effort to disfranchise blacks threatened their ability to rescue the party from such as the Kolbites. They also feared that a decline in registered voters might lead to the reapportionment of the legislature and reduce Black Belt influence even further. And there was always the possibility that such efforts would attract federal attention and federal intervention, which Black Belt officials feared more than most, since their offenses were the greatest. So it was hardly surprising that when various interests in the state began talking about a new constitution, Black Belt Bourbons were less than enthusiastic.

Anti-democratic elements were not the only ones wanting a new constitution. Teachers and the sprinkling of folks who believed the state would be better served if its children, at least its white children, were well educated had complained that the 1875 Constitution failed to provide adequate funding for schools. They wanted to remove limitations on taxation and give local governments the flexibility to raise and distribute money as needed. But many Bourbons, some would argue most, liked the constitution just as it was. In the first place it meant that their money would not be used to educate someone else's children. They had the resources to educate their own and, as the sprinkling of excellent primary and secondary schools around the state reveals, Bourbon boys and girls were often educated well. As for the children of the lower orders, the congressman and later governor William C. Oates seems to have summed up the view of his class and circumstances when he argued that "it is not the duty, nor is it to the interest of the State, to educate its entire population beyond the primaries. Universal experience teaches that if a boy, without regard to his color, be educated beyond this point, he declines ever to work another day in the sun."

The fields, the mills, and the mines—these were what the future held for poor children in Bourbon Alabama. More to the point, that was how most Bourbons believed it should be. To do otherwise was to go against the laws of nature, and Alabama Bourbons weren't about to do that, especially when it was not in their interest to do so. Call it selfish. Call it hypocrisy. Call it whatever you like. It made no difference. In the Alabama envisioned by Bourbon Democrats, education would only raise hopes and inspire ambitions that could never be fulfilled; education would only make the masses miserable, and no decent people wanted that—did they?

Nevertheless, there were idealists who wanted the constitution changed so schools could be better funded. And there were other complaints as well, complaints that the state needed to be able to improve the infrastructure and promote the economy, complaints that local governments needed more authority to handle local needs, and complaints that important offices and agencies, abolished or restricted in an effort to save money, needed to be restored. But everyone who was paying attention knew that a new constitution would never be written for these reasons. They knew that the real impetus for change came from Bourbon Democrats who saw a free electorate as a threat to their authority. If a new constitution was written, they would write it and for that reason.

Meanwhile Bourbons outside the Black Belt were at work. Claiming that they were out to reform the system, conservative Democrats argued that "honest elections" (elections they could win) were possible only if "corruptible voters" (those who might someday vote or be voted against them) were removed from the rolls. Untroubled that this argument suggested that the best way to keep the white man from stealing the black man's vote was to take the black man's vote away from him—or to put it another way, whites would stop stealing only when blacks had nothing to steal—they canvassed the state. To make their campaign more attractive to white farmers who might be susceptible to populist promises, the Bourbons noted that under their plan, the white man would always be supreme. On that point they left no doubts.

Still there were obstacles. Black Belt Bourbons had to be assured that their political power would not diminish with black disfranchisement. They wanted guarantees that their seats in the legislature would not be reduced and the new constitution would not allow state officials to interfere with the way they handled local affairs. But on the other hand, many Bourbons inside and outside the Black Belt wanted to find a way to make sure that a county-based popular movement could not take over the courthouse and carry out populist reforms on the local level. They feared that reform forces might get control of a county, raise property taxes, upgrade schools and roads, and so improve the quality of life that other counties would institute reforms of their own. In other words, the Bourbons would be forced to pay for reforms that would create an electorate that would keep the Bourbons out of office. Who could blame them for wanting to nip such reforms in the bud?

So around the state the Bourbons worked the crowds, cut deals, made promises, and garnered allies. Black Belt planters, finally convinced that disfranchised blacks would still be counted for representation, joined the movement. White alliancemen, although promised that a way would be found to take away black votes without endangering whites, remained skeptical, but their resistance was cracking. Hopeful educators, ambitious businessmen, industrial leaders in the rapidly growing Birmingham District of Jefferson County, commercial interests, and cotton-mill operators all got on board. So the legislature ordered the issue put to the people, and on 23 April 1901 Alabamians went to the polls and voted 70,305 to 45,505 for a constitutional convention and for the delegates who would attend it.

Opposition came, as expected, from alliance strongholds in the northern hills and down in the Wiregrass, but this was more than countered by support from the Black Belt, where blacks voted, or were voted, in numbers that surprised even seasoned observers. In Lowndes County, where black voters held a five-to-one majority, 3,226 votes were cast for the convention, and only 338 against it. In Dallas, Green, Perry, Hale, Sumter, and Marengo Counties, the returns were much the same. It looked as though Alabama would have a new constitution.

The convention met in May and went to work. Though some tried to put a fine spin on what they planned to do, stressed "the necessity of relieving the Black Belt of the incubus resting on it," others were more blunt, though no less truthful: "We are here to get rid of the nigger [vote]" was the way they put it. Controlled by a coalition of planters and industrialists, the delegates resolutely moved to guarantee suffrage to "the intelligent and the virtuous voter" and deny it to the rest. Residence restrictions, literacy requirements, the poll tax, and property qualifications were written into the document, as were stipulations that potential voters had to be engaged in a lawful business and could not have been convicted of one of a host of crimes, many of which (such as vagrancy) were frequently charged against blacks. Poor whites who might have been disqualified were allowed to slip through if they or an ancestor had served in the military (the "grandfather clause") or, failing that, if they were of "good character" and understood "the duties of citizenship in a republican form of government"—qualifications that black Alabamians at the whim of white election officials had little hope of meeting. But white exemptions would soon run out, and when they did, poor whites and poor blacks would be in the same situation and with little hope of changing it.

There were some who spoke out against this. Former governor Oates, who had opposed educating most children beyond the primary grades, nevertheless felt that "the disfranchisement of the whole Negro race would be unwise and unjust . . . [for] among them are many honest, industrious, and good citizens, capable of fairly understanding the issues of a campaign." Oates, a paternalistic Bourbon, wanted a system under which "the better class of Negroes," could participate, instructed, of course, by the better class of whites. As for the rest of both races, being incapable of playing a constructive role, they would play no role at all.

Also speaking out against black disfranchisement was Booker T. Washington, the founder of Tuskegee Institute and arguably the nation's most famous African American. Together Washington and his colleague George Washington Carver had turned Tuskegee into a model, not just for black education but for education in general. If whites could have looked beyond race and seen what Washington and Carver had accomplished, they might have profited from the example. But they didn't. So Booker T. Washington was heralded, not as an educator, but as a "Negro Educator," and Dr. Carver, whose work with the lowly peanut would prove the salvation for many a southern farmer, would labor, for a while at least, in undeserved obscurity.

Although Washington was known to favor economic independence and accommodation over social equality and political confrontation, he refused to accept quietly what the Bourbons planned for his race. He led a group that petitioned the convention to grant black Alabamians "some humble share" in selecting who governed them and hinted that blacks denied this right might well become the lazy, shiftless, irresponsible Negros that whites believed they were. But it was no use. The issue already was decided.

Although disfranchisement took up much of the convention's time and has been the focus of most of the discussion since, it was not the only matter resolved that summer. Determined to preserve a status quo under which they had prospered, Bourbons refused to revise the tax ceiling to provide more funds for state and local governments and did not lift restrictions on state support for internal improvements. Counties could use local money to build roads, bridges, and public schools, but the constitutional limits placed on what they could raise or borrow made such projects difficult to carry out. In other words, state and local governments would remain starved for revenue, and the services they provided, especially in education, would be underfunded for the foreseeable future.

Delegates also addressed what critics called "the evils of local legislation." For some time there had been complaints that the legislature spent so much energy on local bills that matters of statewide concern often were neglected. Since 1875 representatives had enacted some twenty times as many local as general laws, and because of the vote-swapping and backroom deals that were part of the process, Bourbon reformers, especially those from urban, commercial areas, considered this issue second only to suffrage. But conservative Bourbons, rural-based and fearful of local majorities, would have none of it. And since they had the votes to write it the way they wanted it, they did. Under the new constitution almost all local bills had to receive legislative approval and, often as not, a constitutional amendment in the bargain.

When they were finished the Bourbons stepped back to admire their handiwork. All that remained was ratification.

Out came the slogan: "White Supremacy, Honest Elections, and the New Constitution, One and Inseparable." But this time the opposition was stronger and better organized. Poor whites, yeoman farmers, alliancemen, and their allies understood what had been

written, understood that once it was the law of the land it was only
a matter of time before many of them would be disfranchised just
like blacks. Then, and they understood this too, Alabama would have
a weak, Bourbon-dominated central government holding sway over
weaker local governments, and common folk would have to "make
the best of the situation," as Isaac Grant advised back in '65.

Opponents also seemed to understand intuitively that no matter
how many votes they cast against it, the Bourbons could deliver
more. So most were not surprised when the results were recorded
and it was announced that the constitution was ratified, 108,613 to
81,734—a majority of 26,879. Nor were they surprised when the
returns showed that outside the Black Belt, the constitution lost.
They had expected this, expected the fraud, intimidation, ballot-box
stuffing, and tombstone voting. What did surprise them was the
sheer magnitude of it all. It was not that there was corruption; it was
the openness, the shamelessness, the blatant disregard for what was
legal and what was right, the casual rejection of any suggestion that
John Graham's treasured "honest and up-right dealings among men"
applied to them in this situation. In Dallas, Hale, and Wilcox Counties alone, 17,475 votes were cast for the constitution and only 508
were recorded against it—figures all the more remarkable when you
consider that the total white male voting population of these counties was 5,623. If you didn't know better, it would seem that nearly
12,000 black Alabamians had gone to the polls, some unseen by anyone, and voted for their own disfranchisement. But everyone knew
better.

And there was nothing the opposition could do about it. Bourbon
lawmakers had refused to pass legislation allowing for election ap-
peals, and now the wisdom of that decision was revealed. Alabama
Bourbons had written and ratified a document that guaranteed that
men like themselves would live rich and secure while the rest of the
population would stay poor. They had done this by turning Alabama
politics on its head. Since the days of Israel Pickens power had resided in the people, the democratic mass. For better, and often for
worse, politicians addressed popular concerns and catered to popular

prejudices. In the fall of 1901 that tradition came to an end. Alabama greeted the new century with a government that could, and generally did, ignore the needs and desires of the people. This was done, so it was explained, because the uneducated, the unskilled, the incapable had to be led by "white men of character," or they would destroy themselves and society with them. No one suggested that with education and training the excluded might just become capable. No, things didn't work that way.

BOURBON HISTORY: THE PAST REWRITTEN

The Bourbon Democrats saw themselves as the product of historical forces, the culmination of a struggle between good and evil, and the saviors of a South that would have descended into corruption and chaos had it not been for them. History, they believed, justified the course of action they had taken, and the future would confirm the rightness of their cause. So it was no accident that even as they were beating back the Populists' challenge, they were writing up their justification, telling themselves why they deserved to govern, and putting together a framework that would serve future generations who might one day find the same forces rallied against them. Many would set down the story. You can find it in Democratic newspapers of the period and in textbooks written to teach Bourbon children the "true history" of the South—no need to teach the others; they were working out their "day in the sun." Politicians built speeches around it; preachers alluded to it; and James Oscar Prude told it as well as anyone could when he addressed the Alabama Historical Society in Tuscaloosa in June of 1895.

Prude was the ideal choice to speak that day. A man of impeccable pedigree, he came from a family that once owned "Green Springs," a plantation in western Jefferson County on which they worked one of the largest slave forces in the area. In 1848 they moved to Tuscaloosa, where James Oscar was born in 1856. His father soon branched out into business, got into local politics, and during the war "rendered great aid to the Confederate cause as a manufacturer of clothing and shoes for the soldiers." Though not yet in his teens when the conflict ended, James Oscar nevertheless saw enough of war and Reconstruction, and heard enough of the talking, to make rebels and redeemers his heroes. Educated as one of his class and circumstance at Pleasant Hill Academy and the University of Alabama, Prude settled in Tuscaloosa, married a belle from the Mississippi Delta, successfully mixed business with politics, and when offered the invitation to speak before the historical society was serving as clerk of the circuit court. He was, by his activities and attitudes, the quintessential Bourbon, and as his address would prove, James Oscar Prude was just the man to explain to others why the political order that was taking form, and that would soon be confirmed by the Constitution of 1901, was what Alabama needed and deserved.

Titling his remarks "The Importance and Growth of Genealogical Work in the South," Prude began by explaining how southerners should take pride in the "intermixture of ancestral blood"—Anglo-Saxon with a tincture of Huguenots—from which were derived "the high and noble traits of character which have elevated and pre-eminently distinguished the Southern people in the field and on the forum." These southerners, he boasted, founded institutions based on "personal purity, personal independence, and political liberty," fought the Revolution to preserve them, then framed the Constitution, "the corner stone upon which was built the grandest monument to a liberty-loving people." Future southerners should learn from their example.

Then he got down to it. Those ancestors accomplished what they did because they owned slaves. He minced no words here. Slavery was "the most potent factor in producing and developing those true, honorable, and chivalrous traits of character which have marked with distinction Southern manhood and womanhood as the noblest work of God." This distinction was no accident. It was providence. And everyone benefited. "The savage Negro [was] Christianized and the Southern people [were the] benefactors by having this mission placed in their hands." "When the books are opened in which

are recorded all the benevolent works of all the Christian mission-
aries of modern times," he was certain that "it will be seen that the
greatest of these was wrought under the Constitution of the United
States by the slaveholders of the Southern States."

These advancements were accomplished, as he described them, in
an idyllic era—a time when the "inferior race" labored for kindly
masters who guided and protected them. True, these masters "speculated on that situation financially and accumulated wealth" in the
process, but this prosperity "was not confined to favored social
classes" but was spread among "almost the entire white population."
Everyone benefited; therefore everyone supported the system. The
challenges and rewards of this situation produced a class, one might
even say a race, of leaders who "were active, resolute, hardy, and
adventurous and of helpmates, wives and daughters," (Prude was effusive about southern women) who were "strong, courageous, refined, and elevated in their tastes and manners." These were the
people whom God charged "with the lifting up of barbaric slaves
into the 'full stature' of men and bringing them into the light of a
true Christianity and of a civilization."

But before the process was complete, the charge carried out, there
was the war. Then there was emancipation, and with it "new problems . . . which call into requisition the governing power, the self-
control, the courage, the wisdom, and the benevolence which made
the period of slavery, and the men who controlled it, so conspicuous
in American history." Though "their mission of civilizing the negro,
through slavery" had been taken from them, white southerners now
faced "the more difficult task of protecting society and the State
against the most dangerous enemy that was ever fastened by the
power of organic law upon the body politic." Then he got to the
point. "That enemy," we can imagine his shouting now, "is the voting and lawmaking power, given over to the control of an ignorant
mass of ex-slaves, who belong to a race that is socially and politically
irreconcilable to their former owners."

It's all the Yankees' fault, of course. They freed the slaves before the
slaveholders' noble work was done, then left former masters with the

problem, a problem that could be solved, he made clear without actually saying it, only by putting the masters back in charge. "Men of the South [who] still hold a relation to the emancipated slaves that no other people are prepared to deal with," must go into "communities where the negroes reside in great numbers, under conditions of extreme delicacy and embarrassment [and] exercise [their] . . . powers to govern." And who were these masters, these "men of the south"? The Bourbon Democrats. No doubt about it.

Then Prude returned to genealogy, reminded his audience that "the Southrons of to-day are worthy sons of noble sires, with minds and hearts broadened and liberalized by the results of the terrible conflict of arms which deluged the Southland with the blood of her best citizens." In conclusion he challenged them to make "the war for Southern Independence . . . a starting point for the heralding of 'the New South,'" a South founded on the beliefs, values, and habits of action of those who earlier led the way. And if this was done, he assured his audience that "descendants of the heroes of 'the Lost Cause' will need no heraldic crest to emblazon their escutcheon other than their lineage from ancestors who wore the gray."

It was, no one can deny, a stirring call to arms. Reading it today, more than a hundred years after it was delivered, one can feel the passion. Prude was a true believer, and he was preaching to the choir. In less than an hour he laid out the historical framework that would be taught in Alabama schools well into the next century and believed by many to this day—a glorious old South of benevolent planters, happy slaves, and prosperous yeomen (unhappy blacks and poor whites get lost in the telling); a war nobly fought by a united people (no hint of dissent, no mention of desertion); a black race freed before its time; and brave redeemers (Bourbons if you will) rescuing the South from—how did Prude put it?—"the most dangerous enemy that was ever fastened by the power of the organic law upon the body politic."

Prude was doing more than interpreting history. He was laying down the justification for what was to occur six years later, when Bourbon Democrats stripped the "ignorant Negro" of the precious rights of citizens and relegated them to a condition as near to slavery as the law would allow. Believing as Prude did, and believing what Prude did, it was the only thing decent men could do. It all made perfect sense. Except to poor whites. But they didn't hear Prude.

By the end of his speech non-slaveholders had all but disappeared from the story, save for those who wore the gray (voluntarily or not) and with that wearing became part of the pantheon of southern heroes (voluntarily or not). Although Prude claimed that most whites shared in the prewar prosperity, and did not deny that the yeoman fought as bravely as the planter when it came time to defend the southern way of life, once the battle was lost it fell the lot of the former slaveholder to endure Reconstruction and redeem the state. Only they, because they had been masters, possessed the "innate desire to govern" that qualified them for the task.

And that task would include governing poor whites as well. Prude didn't say that, but he really didn't need to. Still smarting from the populist challenge to their authority, it had become a matter of faith in Bourbon circles that another "revolt of the rustics" should be prevented at all costs. Taking the vote away from blacks took away from poor whites their natural ally and thus removed one of the greatest threats to Bourbon authority. To explain it as Prude did, to make disfranchisement a historical necessity, put a noble face on what later generations would consider both unconstitutional and unconscionable. But black disfranchisement, of course, was not enough. So it followed that the right, or at least the ability, to vote was slowly taken from poor whites—first by legislation, then by the constitution. And the Bourbon Democrats became the Bourbon Oligarchy, the few who ruled for the many.

Thus history, James Oscar Prude's history, told and would tell of a New South that was really the Old South reborn. Prude and others like him would weave the story of noble men and women who assumed the responsibility of governing an inferior race that could not govern itself and leading an inferior class that needed to be led almost as badly. So the Bourbons used history to justify what they did and would do, and because they rewrote history as they rewrote the Constitution, and taught both to the children who were fortunate enough to be taught at all, the status quo they created appeared an ancestral arrangement, hoary with age and confirmed with the wisdom of the ancients. It was a system so beautifully laid out and so logically explained that one could argue that it was accomplished through "the providence of God," which was what the Bourbons did argue.

But those being governed, poor blacks and their white counterparts, knew better. Trapped in a system over which they had little control, denied political solutions to their problems, and finding little sympathy among the "worthy sons of noble sires" who governed them, they struggled to feed their families and maintain some shred of independence and dignity. Yet they knew there were limits to what they could do. In the cabins and on the branchhead farms, in the mill villages and the mines, they told tales of those who rebelled, of outlaws like Rube Burrows and "Railroad Bill" who became folk heroes because they challenged the system, and of politicians like Reuben Kolb, who did the same. Even in the telling they preserved the status quo, for the heroes were martyrs, and the victory went to the Bourbons. Given these examples, rebellion was futile.

They understood the futility in places like Mitcham Beat, where just a few years before Prude spoke, local Bourbons had crushed what they believed was a Populist-inspired uprising, had killed or exiled suspected leaders, and had terrorized those who remained. Then the county's Democratic establishment built itself a new courthouse, a visible symbol of their victory. It opened its doors in 1899, and two years later the men who governed from it sent delegates to Montgomery to write the constitution to confirm their authority once and for all.

But the farmers of Mitcham Beat did not need a new courthouse to tell them who had won. They knew, and their bitterness did not die easily. For years to come they would brood over the way townsmen, courthouse politicians, planter landlords, and furnishing merchants controlled their lives, and they dreamed of the day they could do something about it. Excluded from the establishment by laws that discouraged them from voting and alienated by memories of what those in power had done to family and friends, citizens of Mitcham Beat, like marginal folks all over the state, withdrew unto themselves. As they did, they warned their children that if they heard "the whinney of a horse and the squeak of good leather to run and hide." Most farmers in the Beat rode mules with croker-sack saddles and rope bridles. The sound of anything else might be the Bourbons, the county's "first and best citizens," back again.

9
White Man's Alabama

So the Bourbons settled in.

James Oscar Prude opened a "bond and brokerage business" in Tuscaloosa, which he operated until 1909 when he retired to his plantation, "Owenwood." Now a planter like his admired ancestors, he made a reputation for himself as a farsighted agriculturalist who applied "modern methods" to raising cotton and livestock. By then a widower, he delighted in his children, one of whom graduated from West Point and remained a staunch Democrat and devout Methodist the rest of his life.

John S. Graham continued as editor of the *South Alabamian* and was recognized as an innovator in the use of illustrations to attract subscribers and advertisers. A man of many interests and activities, he studied law and served as a justice of the peace. Like Prude, Graham was "unbending in his advocacy of the principles of the Democratic Party," and until his retirement in 1910 his paper was known for being "fearless and aggressive in its efforts to expose the fallacies of the populists." Elected to the Alabama House of Representatives in 1918, Graham battled "valiantly for public measures, which he deemed right and sound, and [was] equally valiant in opposition to all measures which he deemed unwise or contrary to the public good." Always the local booster, John S. Graham used his paper to promote his town, his county, and his state, and when he died in 1928, he was eulogized as a man devoted to the "affairs of his community."

John Graham and Oscar Prude reveal both the diversity and the consistency of Bourbonism. A Bourbon could be found anywhere, in small towns, on plantations, in the state's larger cities, in the legislature, and in local offices. What bound Bourbons together was an unwavering belief in white supremacy, a devotion to low taxes and fiscal restraint, a commitment to keeping government out of the affairs of citizens like themselves, and a determination to maintain this status quo by every means the law allowed—and they were the law. White supremacy meant, of course, that black Alabamians were no longer part of the body politic. Some 140,000 blacks had voted in 1890. Over 100,000 cast ballots in 1900. In 1903, two years after the constitution was ratified, fewer than 3,000 African Americans went to the polls. The new restrictions also worked their magic on poor whites. In 1900 there were more than 230,000 whites registered to vote in the state. By 1903, despite a growing population, some 40,000 whites had disappeared from the rolls, the victims of poll taxes, literacy tests, and property qualifications. The Bourbons had done their work well.

But other whites, qualified whites, also were staying home because, it seems, voting just wasn't worth the trouble. Regardless of what they did or how they cast their ballots, the same folks filled the courthouses, sat in the legislature, and executed the laws, so why bother? In 1902 the Democrats held a primary. It was one of the "reforms" demanded by the Populists and instituted by Bourbons once the Populists were beaten and could no longer use it against them. Nearly 50 percent of the qualified voters did not show up at the polls. This would be the way of Alabama politics. Republicans became a toothless enemy. The Democratic primary, soon a "white-only" affair, became the real election. And except for the occasional "hotly contested" race, low turnout was the rule. So who voted? Who ran the state? Who governed Alabama? The answer: a relative handful of propertied white males, the people that the Constitution of 1901 was written to secure in power. The authors of that document did their work well.

Still a low turnout can reflect satisfaction. One must not discount the fact that many qualified voters were comfortable with the system and had no desire to change it. Unless their vote was needed to keep things as they were, they'd just as soon stay home. Yeoman farmers who owned their own land were as committed to low taxes as any planter was, and though they might want better schools, roads, or law enforcement, they had little faith in the ability of government to deliver those things for their kind. And given Alabama's record, that lack of faith was justified. Besides, their Bourbon betters had put the black man in his place and guaranteed that he would stay there. For many, that was reason enough to support the system, no matter who led it.

SMALL-TOWN BOURBONISM

Because the majority of Alabamians still earned their living on the land, and because so many others were clumped together as a definable unit in mill towns and mining camps, it is understandable that most studies of local life and culture at the turn of the century have focused on these two groups—size and convenience count. However, when we want to see the values of Bourbon Alabama at work, the best places to look are Alabama's towns and villages, where a rising middle class of merchants and professional people created a culture comfortable with Bourbon rule and dedicated to its principles. It was a world of tightly knit social groups, classes if you will, based on and sustained by church affiliations, family ties, and interconnecting occupations. And it was a world from which many of the state's leaders were drawn. Alabama's cities—Mobile, Birmingham, Montgomery—were small towns writ large and would be well past mid century. In short, if you wanted to find Alabama's essence, as well as its future, head for a county seat or market center. Hang around for a while. You couldn't miss it.

At the top of the social order were the "in-town" elites—businessmen, lawyers, doctors, and such—who dominated and directed the economy. As mayors, councilmen, judges, and officers of the court, they governed as thoroughly and at least as effectively as their state-level counterparts—maybe more so, for they were on the ground with those they governed. Sharing interests and attitudes, they boosted their communities, built schools, beautified business districts, lived in attractive homes, and conducted themselves as the solid middle-class burghers they were. They met in lodges—Masons, Goodfellows, Elks, the Order of Redmen—which admitted only themselves, bourgeois versions of Hell-at-the-Breech, dedicated to maintaining the order that allowed them to meet in the first place.

Their wives, solid middle-class ladies of unimpeachable piety, gathered in clubs ("women's study clubs" were a particular favorite) and Sunday School classes that met outside the Sabbath. Interested in local affairs, self-improvement, charitable works, new recipes, and the latest gossip, they were the arbiters of good taste and the foundation of family life.

They were also, in many cases, the visible, progressive conscience of the community. In 1895 many of the scattered societies united to form the Alabama Federation of Women's Clubs, and in the years to come they worked tirelessly for the good of their towns, their cities, and their state. Individually and collectively they were concerned with such things as education, convict leasing, and child labor. Some of them believed that if women had the right to vote, Alabama's ills might be addressed and maybe even alleviated, so they worked with that goal in mind. These women gave inspiration and support to the likes of Julia Tutwiler, who became both the "mother of co-education in Alabama" when she "forced" the state university to admit women in 1893 and the "Angel of the Prisons" for her efforts to reform one of the worst penal systems in the nation. Tutwiler was not alone. During this era more and more Alabama women began "stepping out of the shadows" to accomplish things that, left to the men, might never have been done. Through their efforts the "male only" club that governed the state was slowly, often grudgingly, forced to acknowledge that it could not, should not, govern alone. That change in attitude may have been this generation's most valuable legacy.

Still, for most middle-class Alabama women of the era, duties domestic were the main concern. So while their husbands bought and sold, calculated and considered, and recorded the ebb and flow of commerce in ledgers and journals, these women kept the home and raised their children to be, they hoped, carbon copies of themselves.

They also directed the servants, black servants. Though not every middle-class family had a maid or cook or yardman (or yard "boy" as they were apt to call them, regardless of age), it seemed they did, an appearance that was not so much a testament to the relative affluence of these whites as to the limited options open to blacks. Demeaning as it might have been, a job as a "kitchen mechanic in the rich folks' house" put food on the table and clothes on the children. So they took it, the job, and became the "drawers of water and the hewers of wood" that Bourbons wanted them to be.

RACE AND CLASS AT
THE TURN OF THE CENTURY

It followed that during those first decades of the twentieth century, race relations in Alabama coalesced around customs and ceremonies that defined superior and inferior, master and servant, and drew clearly the line that marked separate but equal, with everyone knowing that equality was a sham. Anyone who grew up, white or black, in this culture—a culture that would continue, seldom challenged, for more than half a century—remembers how it operated and can pick out examples that defined the differences as much as or more than the color of skin.

There was the practice of white children's calling black adults by their first names. Or if the black person was really old, calling them "Uncle" or "Aunt," which whites told themselves was out of respect, but blacks knew better, knew it was only another way of denying that they were individuals, people, worthy and deserving. And the custom, the courtesy, accepted by whites as their due, of blacks stepping aside, tipping the hats so often that the brim was worn smooth, calling whites, even white children, by titles, Mr., Miz, Missy, Cap'n, boss, little boss. And seldom speaking unless spoken to. These were the slights, humiliations, insults, that whites directed toward blacks to draw the line, draw it so often and so vividly that it could not be erased.

This subservience was acted out every day, done so frequently that whites did not have to convince themselves that it was the way things should be, because it was the way things were, so they never thought it should be otherwise. A politician in a neighboring state put it into words when he told his constituents that the only place for a black man was "at the back door with his hat in his hand." That was a little harsher than the kindly racists of small-town Alabama might have said it, for most of them seemed to believe that segregation, indeed inequality, was all right, correct, justified, so long as both sides were courteous about it. So they, the whites, convinced themselves that blacks were as happy with the system as they, the whites, were, and blacks, having little choice in the matter, played the game—at least when they were around the whites. But down in the "quarters" things were different. How different? Well-to-do whites didn't have a clue.

Poorer whites had a better sense of things. Although they were often overlooked, every small town had its lower orders, separated from their "betters" not by race but by condition, class if you like, and held there suspended—superior because they were white, inferior because they were poor, as if somehow poverty mitigated their whiteness, made it less significant. They were, of course, a varied lot, ranging from skilled laborers who could lay brick or tune an engine (when cars replaced horses) down to those who competed with blacks for menial jobs and as a result lived as bad, and badly, as the other race. Those at the top of the group were, in their place, admired members of the community. Those at the bottom? The kids, children of the bourgeois, rhymed it up, as children often do:

Had a little dog, his name was Dash,
Rather be a nigger, than po' white trash.

But they were only saying in public, to hurt, what their parents said privately, to confirm. And in the scheme of things they, the bourgeois children, were expected to learn racial and class courtesies and become their parents. The "trash" was expected to learn as well, only they were excused for not being as good at it, and become parents too.

Yet we must not make too fine a point of class. While the distance between the middle of the middle class and the bottom of the lower was great, as the classes closed together the line blurred, just as lines between planter and yeoman blurred back in slavery days. The small-town mechanic with grease under his nails might own his own shop (or at least his own shade tree with a limb for a hoist), and the brick mason might work his own crew, have more men taking orders from him than the merchant had clerks. They were businessmen, and regarded as such. Their children went to school with the children of the burghers. They played together, at least until the sons of the proletariat began spending afternoons and Saturdays working with Daddy, learning the trade. Then the working class children disappeared from the schools, and playmates separated. But because the line was not clean and clear, some crossed it, married above or beneath themselves, and drifted up or down, or both.

Thinking back, it seems it was the sweat that defined them. Or what you did to make you sweat, since in the heat of an Alabama summer, sweat was a common denominator. Still, sweating gently sitting in a store or office set you above sweating hot and heavy in the heat of the day, at a machine, in a kitchen, on a scaffold, or in a ditch.

God also separated them. Or at least worshiping God did. Middle-class folks went to middle-class churches. Methodists had an edge at the turn of the century, though in-town Baptists had taken on a patina of civility, had moderated their method if not their message, had taken to shouting less, and were attracting more and more converts from that class. Some towns had enough Presbyterians to make up a congregation. In a few there were enough Episcopalians to form a parish. The biggest bunches of Catholics were in Mobile and the Birmingham District, where southern European immigrants dug the coal, but most larger towns contained a few. And there were Jews, solid citizens who, in those days before the "reborn" Klan, stood out only incidentally. So on Sunday small-town Bourbons went to church together, nice churches, with stained glass, a piano or organ (or both), and, eventually, electric lights and fans. There, together, they were admonished for their sins (few of them serious), charged to obey God's laws, and told that they should be kind to those less fortunate. Then they went home for Sunday dinner and rested just as the Lord commanded.

The other classes, and races, went to their churches. Smaller, out on the edge of the village, built with more enthusiasm than skill, uncluttered by adornments, uncomplicated by theology, they were visible testimonies to rejected materialism since it was easy to reject what you couldn't afford. Preachings there got closer to the marrow. Real sins were admonished, real sinners read out, real confessions heard, real tears shed—and salvation? It seemed real as well. Change the color of the congregation, and the message was strikingly similar—though blacks seemed to sing better, or so said the middle-class whites who would ride out during revival and sit in the grove and listen. The message was not of a logical God but a loving one, a God who cared for the least of these, and a God who would smite the sinner and raise up the sinned-against come judgment day. A God of sanctification and justification, and if you could just hold on, keep your faith, you would see his face one day. And when the preacher finished, sometimes late into the afternoon, the flock went home to get ready to return to a world that was not their own.

The farther out you got from the town, the further you were from town culture. During the first decades of the 1900s, life for farm folks was in many ways an extension of the old century rather than an entry into the new. Had their fathers, and in some cases their grandfathers, appeared in the fields, they would have recognized the work and the sort of people working. And those ancestors would know, probably, that their descendants' sweat wasn't falling on their own land—especially if they were black. Sharecropping and tenant farming, the exploitive expedients that settled in the region after the war, never left. Instead they got stronger, and as they did the influence and the image of the independent yeoman declined. White supremacy counted for little here, for both races suffered under the system. But on the whole, only one race benefited from it.

AN EXCEPTION: DAVID CRUTCHER

At the turn of the century over 70 percent of Alabama's black farmers were tenants and 'croppers, so those who did own their land, and were able to keep it, were as unusual and important in their contexts as any planter was in his. In Madison County just over 7 percent of African Americans worked their own fields, and David Crutcher was one of them. In 1906 Crutcher and two friends borrowed money from the Federal Land Bank, an agency set up to assist people like him, and purchased 154 acres north of Huntsville. Born a slave on a nearby plantation in 1851, Crutcher had farmed as a tenant after the war, dreaming always of working for himself instead of "the man." When he got the chance, David Crutcher took it.

Five years later the three friends divided the land among themselves, and Crutcher and his wife, Lucy, settled down to raise their crops and eleven children. Deeply religious, Crutcher gathered a congregation about him and held services in his living room until he could build a church to house them. In 1919 Union Hill Primitive Baptist Church opened its doors, with the Reverend Crutcher in the pulpit.

Holding the land was not easy, and in at least one instance Crutcher took out a second mortgage with a local lender to pay the note due the first. But playing one side against the other was the way farmers, black and white, survived. And the Crutchers made it.

Not everyone was so skilled, or so lucky. Though much has been made, and should be made, about the way white landlords, merchants, and bankers took advantage of small farmers, landed and landless, those farmers understood, as one of their number, Ned Cobb of Tallapoosa County, put it, that "all God's dangers aint a

white man." There was the weather, which could dry fields to blowing dust or turn them too wet to plow; there were the insects,
worms, and, in time, the boll weevil; and there were the countless
setbacks that could befall—sickness or injury hits, a plow breaks, a
barn burns, or a mule dies. "God's dangers" were more than just men.

BOURBONS BECOME PROGRESSIVES

Then a funny thing happened to the Bourbons. Right at the moment of their greatest triumph, right at the time when they were so
firmly in control that they might have kept things as they wanted
and no one could have done anything about it, a few of them began talking about changing, reforming, the very system they had
worked so hard, risked so much, to establish. Maybe, because the
Constitution of 1901 had done away with race and class as political
issues, they thought it was safe to raise other questions, safe to suggest that the best could be made better. But what is important is that
they did more than just talk. This bunch went out and tried to turn
talk into action and from action get results. So it didn't seem right
to call them Bourbons. They were too forward looking, efficiency
obsessed, business oriented, and image conscious. So newspapermen,
familiar with similar attitudes in politicians outside the South, took
to calling these Alabamians what counterparts in other states were
called—Progressives. Meanwhile, those Democrats who could not
generate much enthusiasm for reform were labeled "conservatives."
Truth was, scratch the surface of both and you found a Bourbon. It
was just that with the Progressives, you had to scratch a little deeper.

The new century had hardly begun before these reformers made
their presence known. Often allied with former Populists, they
amended the constitution to let the state spend money to improve
roads. They set up a railroad commission to put a lid on rates, got
the legislature to mandate that a high school be built in each county
(white first, black later), and funneled more money into higher education. Because conservative forces opposed any significant change

in the tax code, reformers continued to rely heavily on income from convict leasing to fund their programs. In good Progressive fashion, they decided that if they could not abolish the system, they'd make it more humane and more efficient. How humane they made leasing is questionable, but they certainly made the system function better and more profitably. In 1906 Alabama earned $400,000 from convict labor, more than four times what it collected a few years before. Reformers might decry how the system profited from human misery, but no one could deny that in Alabama crime paid.

Significantly, this urge to reform seems to have been shared by a majority of Alabamians, or at least a majority of those who were Democrats and voted. This may say as much about the persistence of populism in party ranks as it does about the popularity of progressivism among party leaders, but either way, people were talking change. As a result, in 1906 textile baron Braxton Bragg Comer, an outspoken Progressive, was elected governor with 61 percent of the ballots cast. Despite opposition from conservatives who claimed Comer's call for railroad regulation was just a way to get cheaper rates for his Avondale Mills, and who hinted that he would not support child labor legislation because it would reduce his workforce, Comer carried the day. Then the governor went out and did most of what he said he would do. It was, on the whole, a good way to start the century.

But before we get too excited, let's remember that these progressive governors would only go so far in their efforts to improve the lot of run-of-the-mill Alabamians, a stance that often put them at odds with populist elements in the party. Their attitude toward unions is a good case in point. As Bourbons the Democrats had opposed labor's efforts to organize, passed laws to prevent strikes, and willingly called out state troops to keep workers in line. The Bourbons did this, so they said, to protect the public, although once they also claimed, with as much guile as hypocrisy, that the military went in "to protect the lives and liberties of the much despised negro miners." The Bourbons knew and understood that the "despised" were "despised," not because they were black, but because they had been hauled in to break the strike. On this issue the transformation of Bourbon to Progressive made no difference.

For example, in 1908 Tennessee Coal, Iron and Railroad Company (TCI), the state's largest mining firm, laid off some workers and cut the pay of others. Already upset by low wages, dangerous working conditions, and competition from convict labor, the miners turned to their union, the United Mine Workers (UMW), and the union called the strike. Some eighteen thousand workers left their jobs, and as tempers flared, TCI officials asked the state to intervene. Governor Comer sent in the National Guard. The strikers lost.

While Comer and his ilk were hardly "progressive" on labor matters, there was at least one issue on which they lined up solidly with the national movement—prohibition. For years there had been efforts, mainly by church groups and the Women's Christian Temperance Union, to prohibit the sale of alcoholic beverages in the state, and during Comer's administration those efforts gained momentum. Nationally, reformers saw prohibition as a way to improve health, mend broken families, and provide industries with a sober, dependable workforce—all noble goals with which Alabama progressives agreed. Yet progressive Alabamians, like most southern Progressives, also saw prohibition as a means of racial control. Calling on the legislature to safeguard "the white man and white woman from the violence of the liquor-crazed black," many of the state's "better citizens" pressed first for a "bone dry" law and then for an amendment to the state constitution outlawing intoxicants.

But there was opposition. Some in the state believed prohibition should be decided county by county, others were concerned with the loss of tax revenue that would follow, and there were those in the Birmingham District who feared workers would leave if prohibition passed. Many, true to their tradition of hardheaded individualism, simply did not want any government telling them that they could not take a drink. Although Comer stumped the state for the amendment, it lost—and lost big.

In the end Comer lost more than the prohibition battle. Constitutionally prohibited from succeeding himself, the governor sat on the sidelines for the next four years, then offered himself in 1914. The offer was rejected. Railroad interests, organized labor, and local-option advocates united to defeat him. It was a strange alliance, but there would be stranger ones.

But let's give credit where credit is due. Comer and others like him did some things that needed to be done. Educational appropriations increased, though the state remained near the bottom in most categories—except maybe illiteracy. Moreover, to Comer's credit, he refused to give in to those who thought black education was a waste of money. Roads got some necessary funding, though a heavy rain could still bring most counties to a halt. Railroad rates were lowered a bit, property was assessed a little (just a little) closer to its real value, and parents were told that their children *had* to attend school until they were sixteen, a regulation that was the back door through which reformers were able to limit child labor. Like so much of the legislation passed in Alabama, before and since, the measures were halfhearted, and the results were halfway. But they were better than nothing.

NOT SO PROGRESSIVE ALABAMA

The next few years were interesting ones for Alabamians who happened to be paying attention, who had the time to pay attention. Statewide prohibition eventually was passed; the constitution was amended to let counties levy a small "special" school tax, which some in the Black Belt never got around to doing; and the United States entered World War I. On top of that, a Democrat was in the White House—Woodrow Wilson—and a Democratic majority in Congress, so Alabama's congressional delegation, full of vigor and seniority, got ready to slice the patronage pie. There was even talk of an Alabama senator, Oscar W. Underwood, as a possible presidential candidate, the first from the South since the Civil War. Maybe, some suggested, all was finally forgiven.

Forgiven, maybe, but not forgotten, at least not in Alabama. Here white citizens celebrated Confederate Memorial Day with songs and speeches and created civic deities from veterans living and dead. As for black Alabamians, they watched and wondered, surely, just who had won after all. Yet Alabamians of both races were also determined to show that they were loyal Americans, so when their country called they answered. In 1898 they rallied to defeat Spain and to free Cuba, and in 1917 they went off to Europe to make the world safe for democracy. Most who went came home to tell of wonders, like Paris, and horrors, like trench warfare. But some did not return. So when it was over, citizens wanted to raise monuments to the fallen. Except that some of the fallen were black. So what to do? One town solved the problem by ignoring the African American dead and listing only whites. Another, seeing the hypocrisy in that, devised a solution more in keeping with the spirit of age. A local committee, which included at least one black member, decided to put up a granite slab with the names of one race on one side and the other race on the other—white facing east, black facing west, separate but equal.

AN ALABAMA BOY GOES OFF TO WAR

Emmett Kilpatrick was one of those Kilpatricks from Camden. Scion of a wealthy and politically powerful family, like southern gentlemen of old, he received a classical education, one that revealed in him a particular facility for languages. Knowing that a southern gentleman was not a very profitable occupation, Kilpatrick turned to the law, was admitted to the bar, and settled in his hometown to practice and be bored. Then war broke out in Europe, and when America got involved Kilpatrick enlisted. It was to be his grand adventure. He had no idea how much of an adventure and how grand.

In France his knowledge of "six or seven" languages—and fluency in French—landed him a translator's assignment and, eventually, a place on the team that negotiated the Treaty of Versailles. That done, Kilpatrick decided Camden could wait, so he stayed, worked for a while at the U.S. embassy in Paris, and, finding no excitement in that, headed east to Russia, where various groups were fighting against the Bolsheviks. After a brief stint as a mercenary in the Lithuanian army, he landed with the Red Cross and was sent to distribute food in the Crimea, where the Bolsheviks (the Reds) and the anti-Bolsheviks (the Whites) were slugging it out. Kilpatrick had been there only a short time when, on 29 October 1920, he and his party were captured by the Reds. Not sure what to do with an American, his captors sent him to Moscow.

While young Kilpatrick (he was only twenty-six) languished in what he described as a "loathsome cell," the news got back to Alabama, and things started happening. Bibb Graves, adjutant general of the Alabama National Guard and a man of no little political ambitions, called on the United States to declare war on Russia to get its citizen back and vowed that if Washington would not act, he would take the guard and conduct the invasion himself. Newspaper headlines screamed the challenge. The *Mobile Register* editorialized its support. But before Alabama's finest could be mustered out and sent abroad, a negotiated settlement brought the captive's release.

Emmett Kilpatrick came home to a hero's welcome. Comfortable in his celebrity status, he toured the state speaking out against, as John Graham put it, "bolshevism, socialism, and every other 'ism'" but Americanism. Camden could no longer hold him, so he moved to Uniontown, set up a law practice, got into politics, and was elected to the state legislature. Later, when asked to describe his constituency, he summed up the situation as neatly as any Bourbon could have: "There were only two Republicans in Uniontown and all the rest were Democrats and my adherents." Who could ask for anything more? Emmett Kilpatrick was home.

THE MORE THINGS CHANGE,
THE MORE THEY STAY THE SAME, MOSTLY

For those who stayed in Alabama, the war brought good times. Cotton prices rose, industries boomed, military camps pumped money into the local economy, and folks were able to buy things they had only dreamed of earlier. Jobs opened up, and in a tight labor market women took many of them. Alabama Power Company, which had completed its first hydroelectric dam just before the war, is a good example of what took place, for although men still handled things in the field and still held top positions in the company, the "girls of the office" ran the office. Many were young women who had moved from the small towns where they had been raised to the big towns and the cities where there were jobs. There they lived as independently as their incomes and social restraints allowed, and in doing so they pushed against the boundaries that once confined them.

Now, of course, most Alabama women did not take jobs in the city, did not stray far from the Victorian standards imposed on them by parents, husbands, religion, and society in general. They did not bob their hair, roll their hose, rouge their knees, or sport about in "knickers" (as some Alabama Power girls on holiday at Lake Mitchell did to the shocked amazement of the good citizens of Clanton). But even those who did not, even those who stayed close to home, could feel the winds of change and were exhilarated by it.

Of all the changes promised, the most exciting of all was the possibility that finally, at last, women might get the right to vote. Women's suffrage was not a new issue, nor was it the cause of "a few cranks strolling over the state" as future U.S. senator Tom Heflin claimed during the Constitutional Convention of 1901. Heflin's remark came at a time when it appeared that the gathering might allow married women who owned property to vote on certain matters and had even invited Frances Griffin, president of the Alabama Equal Suffrage Association, to address the meeting. It was one of those interesting little moments that speak volumes about turn-of-the-century Alabama.

With the gallery "packed" with her supporters, Miss Griffin systematically demolished the arguments that had been raised against giving women the vote. And to calm the fears of men who were as interested in excluding "unqualified" whites as in excluding blacks, she stressed that she and her allies were seeking the franchise for "good women . . . not the naughty, fast damsels, adventuresses and the like." Then, no doubt to the surprise of many, Miss Griffin revealed that she and others like her already voted, and the state had not suffered for it. Whenever there was an election she sent her black gardener to the polls with instructions on how to cast the ballot. That she was disfranchising him to enfranchise herself apparently caused her no concern. What did bother her was that if the convention took the vote from blacks as intended, it would also take the vote from responsible citizens like herself. Her solution, give the vote to white women, "good women," so they could help white men "purify politics" in the state. In other words, let women like her help men like those running the convention maintain white, upper-class supremacy.

When she finished there was "prolonged applause" from the gallery, but not from the delegates. Frances Griffin's argument notwithstanding, members of the convention apparently agreed with former governor Emmet O'Neal that woman's suffrage was contrary to "the theory of southern civilization," which held "that woman was the queen of the household and domestic circles" and should stay as such. The proposal was defeated. But women's groups continued to push the issue, continued to organize and reorganize, and during the Great War momentum began to swing in their favor. Slowly but surely social, political, and religious conservatives accepted the fact that southern civilization would not become unhinged if women voted, and finally only a few of the most traditional remained to oppose the issue.

John Simpson Graham was one of them. As far as he was concerned all the talk about women's voting, getting into politics, changing things for the better was just a lot of "tommyrot." Writing in 1919 Graham argued that men had already reduced a woman's workweek to fifty-six hours—a little over nine hours a day, Sunday off. Men had prohibited night work, secured women's property rights, and limited child labor. "Women," he concluded, "have gotten everything they have coming to them . . . and they should be satisfied." As for Alabama's suffragettes and the national leaders who inspired them, "If I had my way," Graham growled, I'd "wipe [them] out . . . as God did the people of Sodom and Gorromah."

A year later women got the vote.

Men like Graham pouted.

ALABAMA IN THE '20S:
WHAT ROARED AND WHAT DIDN'T

It is difficult, and perhaps fruitless, to say just how the "Roaring '20s" played out in Alabama. Certainly in larger cities and on college campuses there were young men and women who adopted the culture of the Jazz Age as enthusiastically as anyone in the nation. In small towns a filtered version, influenced by movies (theaters were popping up everywhere) and magazines, took hold of kids, and soon teachers were trying to figure out how to deal with "flappers" and their beaus. For these youngsters and their solid middle-class parents, life was good. A slowing economy hardly affected them. An automobile was in the garage, electricity in the house, a radio in the living room, and a refrigerator in the kitchen. Women had the vote. Evangelical Protestants had prohibition. Birmingham industrialists had labor under control. Although many blacks were leaving the state, planters had sharecroppers and tenants in the fields. The Democrats had statehouse and courthouse. To these folks, Alabama looked just fine.

But there was another side. Back before the Great War, Gov. Charles Henderson had asked the Russell Sage Foundation of New York to study conditions in the state. The governor received the report in 1918, just before he went out of office, and, considering what it contained, he was probably happy to leave the matter to his successor. Describing what historian Wayne Flynt has called "a grim landscape of neglect and inequity," the report chided the state for refusing to finance necessary reforms though it had the resources to do so. Or to put it another way, the Sage Foundation found well-to-do Alabamians too cheap to do what needed to be done for the least among them. Some of the conclusions in the report were probably expected, among them the revelation that the legislature preferred profitable convict leasing to a humane penitentiary system, or that child labor laws let factories continue to employ more than a hundred thousand children between the ages of ten and seventeen. Nor could anyone who ventured out into the countryside, or went into the mill towns and mining camps, have been unaware of how hookworm, pellagra, malaria, and a host of other diseases of poverty handicapped the people. They might have been surprised to learn how little the state's leaders seemed to care. The year the report was issued only one southern state allocated less money to its board of health. To put those priorities in perspective, that same year the state spent $26,000 on treating sick people and $83,000 treating sick animals. There was no way to deny what the legislators believed was most important.

Meanwhile, if those reading the report thought it might at least say something nice about the improvements recently made in education, they were disappointed there as well. "Progressive" reforms notwithstanding, Alabama still spent just over half the national average on its pupils, teacher pay was over 20 percent lower than the average, and on higher education Alabama spent less per capita than any state but Arkansas. That was on the white side of the ledger. On the other side separate but equal was an illusion—at least the equal part. Fewer than half the black elementary school-age children had a school to attend, and there were only three public high schools for blacks in the state. William Oates's conviction that most children should not be educated beyond the primary grades seems to have been shared by Alabama legislators—at least where black children were concerned.

Truth was, poor white students didn't have it much better. Anyone who lived through that era, or in the decade that followed, can remember children's appearing when the school opened, how they sat in class for a few weeks, then disappeared to pick the cotton. Picking done, they appeared again, usually late in the fall, and wandered in and out until spring, when the weather warmed. Then they were gone again, into the fields, to plow, plant, and chop. By the time the crop was laid by and they could return, school was out. Compulsory attendance laws were weak, but even if they had been stronger it hardly would have mattered. Alabama's cotton economy dictated how often rural children attended school. That same economy also determined how much they learned when they got there. The story was told of how a group of youngsters from a tenant farm arrived at the schoolhouse, lunch pails in hand. One of the pails rattled as the owner walked along, and at recess a curious classmate slipped back into the cloakroom where the lunches were stored to sneak a peek. In the pail were a handful of hickory nuts and two rocks for cracking them. Not much to sustain a growing child. Not much.

PROGRESSIVISM AT LAST: SORT OF

While it is difficult to gauge the impact the Sage report had on Alabamians in general, some citizens took it to heart, and in the decade that followed they elected two of the most reform-minded governors in the state's history—Thomas E. Kilby and Bibb Graves.

Kilby, a wealthy Anniston businessman with a deep concern for society's less fortunate, set a never-to-be repeated example (at least in a race for governor) when he refused any campaign contributions, spent only his own money, and got elected without any debts to "special interests." Then, with help from businessmen who thought of him as one of their own, he got property assessments raised to the legal limit and set about building new prisons and mental health facilities. He also got a state dock authorized down in Mobile, pushed through a worker compensation law, and increased funding for public health by 50 percent. At his urging the legislature finally set up a child welfare department, and Loraine Bedsole Tunstall, a veteran child labor inspector, was chosen its director—the first woman to head an executive agency in the state. Black Belt planters complained bitterly about higher taxes, but to little avail. In his last year in office, every bill Governor Kilby submitted to the legislature was passed, another record that remains unbroken. Moreover, Kilby left the state treasury in its best condition since before the Civil War.

In its follow-up report an impressed Russell Sage Foundation noted that Alabama had gone "from the rear ranks to the front ranks of states of the union in her social progress."

But convicts were still being leased, and reformers swore not to rest until that blot on the state's character was removed. Kilby had wanted to do it but found that he needed the money for the prisons being built, so the practice continued. Besides, some of his business supporters liked the system, so the best Governor Kilby could do was get the legislature to pull convicts out of the timber and turpentine industries. They stayed in the mines, and it was in the mines that the scandal broke. Under Kilby's successor, William "Plain Bill" Brandon, word got out of a convict who died after he was beaten and dunked in scalding water. The murder made the national news, and soon it seemed that everyone not only knew of the incident but also knew that Alabama was the last state to lease its convicts. It was not the image that progressive Alabamians wanted to project to the rest of America. So Bibb Graves decided to make ending it the main plank of his platform when he ran for governor.

PROGRESSIVISM, ALABAMA STYLE

If credentials and experience count for anything, Bibb Graves may have been the most qualified candidate yet to run for the state's highest office. A civil engineering degree from the University of Alabama gave him that sense of order and efficiency characteristic of Progressives, and his Yale law degree certified his energy and intellect. Service in the legislature, a failed congressional race, chairmanship of the state Democratic Party, and wartime service in France that made him a real "colonel" added exposure and experience. By the early 1920s he was recognized gubernatorial timber. But Black Belt planters found his views on taxes and spending suspect, industrialists were troubled by his sympathy with labor, and social conservatives wondered just how much influence his intelligent and attractive wife had over him. Dixie Bibb Graves had been a suffragette, a leader in the fight for prohibition, and was now an active member of the newly formed League of Women Voters. She was also a staunch advocate of child labor legislation and an eloquent speaker on behalf of human welfare causes. In short, she was not the sort of person supporters of the status quo wanted advising the governor.

Dixie Graves was only one of a number of progressive women who were letting it be known that getting the right to vote did not limit them just to that. In 1922 three women ran for the state legislature. One of them was Hattie Hooker Wilkins from Selma. Early and active in the suffrage movement, Wilkins enjoyed the support of the League of Women Voters and other reform-minded groups in her district. However, lest her reformist tendencies appear too radical for Dallas County voters, she was careful to emphasize in her campaign that she considered "her most significant accomplishment that of wife and mother, and maker of a beautiful home." That apparently calmed enough fears, and Hattie Wilkins was elected. She served only one term and declined to run again, but while she was in Montgomery she chaired the committee on public health and supported legislation to improve education, children's services, and (naturally) local issues for the folks back home.

Representative Wilkins would have been a good ally for Bibb Graves if he had been as successful in his 1922 run for the governorship as she was in her legislative campaign. But with conservatives skeptical and most of the state's newspapers endorsing his opponent, Graves was badly beaten. In 1926, however, he was able to overcome opposition from the old Bourbon coalition of planters and Birmingham industrialists (whom Graves branded the "big mules") and narrowly carried the day. It was not a ringing endorsement, but Bibb Graves did not care. He was ready to reform.

Graves won by putting together a coalition that was unique, even for Alabama, a collection of interlocking interests that represented the best and the worst the state had to offer. With a strong core of support among fellow veterans on which to build, Graves ran as someone dedicated to enforcing prohibition, as an advocate of women's rights, and as an opponent of the convict lease system. Claiming to be a friend of both the working man and the business-man, Graves promised to convince the legislature to better fund so-cial services and internal improvements, and he vowed to improve education. This platform gave him the support of newly enfran-chised women, labor, educators, and evangelical Protestants, groups that could, and often did, overlap.

The support of evangelical Protestants was especially critical, for a significant portion of the electorate was either Methodist or one of the various shades of Baptist. Whether rural, small town, or ur-ban, these denominations shared a common opposition to alcohol and a common (though not equally intense) commitment to moral reformation and social justice—so long as it did not involve ra-cial equality. Locally focused, evangelical Protestant preachers pre-ferred to encourage individuals in their congregations to reject sins such as "gambling, low-neck dresses, hugging and kissing, [and] Sab-bath desecration . . . [which included] playing baseball on Sunday," rather than rely on the state to legislate social reform. Prohibition, however, was another matter. Alcohol—whether you were for it or against it, drank it or didn't—had become a litmus test used to de-termine the worthiness of an individual to be part of "good" so-ciety. Those who opposed prohibition (or were believed to oppose it) were just the sort of people that evangelical Protestants, espe-cially small town and rural evangelical Protestants, believed the state needed to regulate. This group included Catholics, foreigners, and big-city businessmen, not to mention the poor whites and blacks who turned to drink to help them escape their misery. Bibb Graves promised to deny these folks whiskey, that "passion inflamer," and the profits from it.

Helping Graves in this crusade was the Ku Klux Klan, to which he belonged and of which he served as Grand Cyclop of the Mont-gomery Klavern. Revived just before the War, in Alabama this new Klan differed significantly from the Reconstruction version. Since blacks and Republicans no longer were threats, this Klan declared itself the champion of 100 percent Americanism, Christian values, and moral living. Drawing its strength from many of the same groups that energized evangelical Protestants, the Alabama Klan spoke out for what it considered the common man, for prohibition, and against the planters and urban businessmen who dominated the state. Indeed, if the Klan had not also denounced Catholics, Jews, and other "foreigners," and if it had not taken to enforcing its own moral code with the lash and the noose, it might have gone down in Alabama history as one more manifestation of the old populist struggle against privilege. But that didn't happen.

So this unlikely combination of evangelicals, Klansmen, educators, women, and organized labor put Bibb Graves in office in 1927, and once there he set out to do what he said he would do. Convict leasing finally was abolished, and revenue bonds were issued to build roads and bridges (financed by drivers' license fees and gasoline taxes). Graves also convinced the legislature to give education the largest appropriation it had ever received, and over the next four years schools got more than twice the money allocated to them under his predecessor. Funding these increases with taxes on tobacco and corporations, Graves also was able to raise teacher salaries and put more resources into teacher training institutions. Allocations also went to social services, and public health received nearly three times the money under Graves as under the previous administration. Child welfare services also were expanded, and the Division of Negro Education was established. Although in most cases the state still funded its agencies below the national average, most observers agreed that under Bibb Graves, Alabama had taken a giant step forward.

Most observers, but not all. The big mules didn't like the taxes levied on them and were quick to criticize using state bonds to pay for roads and such. But it wasn't just the wealthy who were unsettled by Graves's reforms. Many small-town politicians and professional folk felt too much was being spent on people who did not deserve it; some did not like child labor legislation's being enforced; and others worried how long such spending could be maintained before the state would have to tax them. But so long as Graves was able to hold his coalition together, there was not much they could do about it.

THE ELECTION OF 1928: ALABAMA'S DEMOCRATIC PARTY IN CRISIS

Then it happened. In 1928 the national Democratic Party nominated Al Smith for president, and the Graves coalition began to come apart. So did Alabama's one-party system. Smith was a Yankee, a Catholic, pro-labor, and he favored repealing Prohibition. Long associated with New York's Tammany Hall, which southerners saw as a seat of patronage and corruption, Smith was just the candidate to outrage evangelicals, the Klan, industrialists, and many reformers. On top of that, he was a city man and knew little or nothing about the problems of the agricultural South. Hearing the news of his nomination, some Alabama Democrats cringed. Others went on the attack. One of the attackers was J. Thomas "Cotton Tom" Heflin.

It has been suggested that Tom Heflin is the closest thing to a pure demagogue Alabama has ever elected. That may be going a bit far, for the field is pretty crowded, but, sufficient to say, few if any were able to play on populist racial and religious fears better than "Cotton Tom." Resplendent in a white cotton suit, complemented in later years by flowing white hair, he struck the pose of the quintessential southern Democrat. During his eight terms in the U.S. House of Representatives and his two terms in the Senate, no one could recall one piece of meaningful legislation he authored—unless you count the act creating Mother's Day, as he did, and as almost everyone else did not. Yet it could not be denied that he was a stirring orator, a clever debater, and an entertaining attraction who could excite almost every popular prejudice and use it to his advantage. Put simply, his constituents loved him.

In a sense Heflin was a throwback to the age of Israel Pickens, when politicians listened to the people, catered to their whims, and rode to victory as their champions. And as it was then, with Heflin it was difficult to tell whether he was promoting the people's cause or convincing the people to promote the cause of Tom Heflin. Either way, in the 1920s Heflin matched or bettered them all with his Negrophobic, anti-foreign, anti-Yankee, anti-Catholic rhetoric. So when Al Smith was nominated, Heflin rose in protest and denounced Smith as a Papal-controlled, race-mixing threat to the southern way of life and Christian civilization—which Heflin suggested were one and the same. Evangelical Protestants joined the fray, denouncing Smith not only for his religion, but also for his opposition to prohibition, which the Methodist *Alabama Christian Advocate* claimed would unleash drunken Negroes, "this child race not far removed from their savage haunts in the jungles of Africa," on defenseless whites.

With Heflin and others like him threatening to do the unthinkable and vote Republican, loyal Democrats once again played the race card. Claiming that Republican nominee Herbert Hoover had forced white girls to "sit along side buck Negroes" when he was secretary of commerce, Democrats reminded voters that their party was the party of white men, the party of the Lost Cause, the party of redemption. They took special delight in telling how Oscar Stanton De Priest, an Alabama-born African American, was up in Chicago running for Congress as a *Republican*—proof enough that the party of Lincoln had not changed. It was as if the campaign would be decided on the basis of which side was the most racist, most bigoted, and most obnoxious about it. Things got so rough that one writer suggested that the newspapers should report the campaign on the sports page. It was the best and the worst show in town.

Hoover won the presidency, but Al Smith carried Alabama, just barely. As a good Democrat should, Smith ran strongest in those places where race mattered more than evangelical religion or prohibitionist morality. The Black Belt in particular proved its loyalty to the party. The Graves coalition, however, was shattered. Almost every group, with the possible exception of labor, saw some of its members defect to the G.O.P. To some observers, it appeared that an Alabama Republican Party, a party made up of conservative business interests, middle- and upper-class elites, and evangelical Protestants might just emerge from the chaos of 1928.

But it didn't. Not just yet anyway. Less than a year after Hoover took office, the stock market crashed, and America was plunged into the Great Depression. And Alabamians knew where to lay the blame. In their own inimitable way citizens of this state assessed the causes and reached their conclusion. As an unknown Alabama poet explained it:

Heflin blew the whistle,
De Priest rang the bell,
Hoover hollered "all aboard"!
And business went to hell.

10

Depression and War

It was an old, worn saying that the Great Depression came to Alabama at a bad time, because things were already awful so nobody noticed. But for many, that was true.

It was true for cotton farmers, nearly 70 percent of whom were tenants. Prices for their product had been sliding since the war, and hopes for paying out, catching up, getting ahead had faded back into the old cycle of borrowing, debt, and carrying over. That was for those who could make a crop. During World War I cotton country was invaded by the boll weevil, an insidious insect that bored into the cotton boll, laid its eggs, and disappeared while its larva ate away the farmer's future. When the boll opened, there was nothing there, nothing for the tenant, nothing for the landlord, nothing for the merchant. Nothing.

So tenants started leaving, those who could, joining a migration that had begun back before the war, only then it was mostly black, and now it was integrated, as poverty and despair always seemed to be in Alabama. During the first decades of the century, black Alabamians had left by the thousands, pushed by Jim Crow and pulled by the promise (or at least the hope) of a better future in the North. Whites who left the farms in the '20s usually did not go that far, but they left. There was a labor shortage, especially in the Black Belt. But planters were, if nothing else, resourceful, so many of them turned crop land to pasture. Cattle, of course, needed less labor than cotton. Now tenants left behind were turned off the place, "broken up" they called it, action that gave the lie to the old saw about landlords loving their "people" like one of the family. So they really did become "hands," wage-workers hired from the towns and settlements where they clustered to plant, chop, and pick in those seasons and left to get by as best they could the rest of the year. Some observers, romantics mostly, bemoaned the end of the landlord-tenant relationship that in rose-tinted theory promised security for both, peace to grow old in. But landlords were realists. So were tenants.

Still, you might have thought that with less cotton being grown, scarcity would have driven up the price. But the world market was glutted, so the price stayed low, and farmers stayed poor. They weren't alone. During the '20s a glance at newspaper ads, at popular magazines, at downtown city stores, and at small-town businesses would lead you to believe that times were good, and for many they were. But there were wrinkles in that economy. As went cotton, so went cotton mills, and as workers struggled to get by on cut wages, short runs, and stand-downs, merchants sold less and ordered less, which passed the problem on up the line.

And it wasn't just cotton. Through the '20s Birmingham, the state's industrial giant, rode the economic roller coaster, not because of its product, but because of who owned it. When orders lagged U.S. Steel cut pay, reduced hours, and even closed plants in the Magic City so it could keep its Pittsburgh operations running at full capacity. To add insult to the injury, northern owners destroyed Birmingham's competitive advantage by charging customers according to the so-called "Pittsburgh Plus" formula that based freight rates on an imaginary route from Birmingham to Pittsburgh and then to market. That scheme, in practice, meant that a Birmingham businessman from one side of the city who bought steel from a mill across town would be charged as if the load had been shipped from Pennsylvania, some eight hundred miles away. So even before the crash, times were hard in the city. Banks failed, businesses went under, people were evicted, children went hungry. Birmingham did not have to wait for the depression to suffer. If you wanted to get mad at Yankees exploiting the South, Birmingham would have been a good place to begin.

So why didn't someone raise some hell? Why didn't the newspapers editorialize the injustice? Why didn't Birmingham businessmen raise a voice? Why didn't labor take to the streets? Why didn't some politician pull an Israel Pickens or a William Lowndes Yancey, expose the villain, and champion the people against it? Why? It was because they, the newspapers, the businessmen, politicians, even the workers were, themselves, the enemy.

In hot pursuit of the Yankee dollar, the press praised, businessmen courted, politicians promoted, and labor (or at least labor leaders) accepted conditions that seem today tantamount to servitude and convinced themselves that it was good for all concerned. And for a while it was. Yankee money built Birmingham, made many if not rich then at least prosperous enough to move across the mountain ("out of the smoke and into the ozone" was how one real estate ad put it), to upscale suburbs like Homewood and Mountain Brook. Outside investments and mill payrolls fed the state's only true urban economy, and the native middle and upper classes saw themselves not as agents or overseers but as beneficiaries.

Workers, as one might imagine, were less enthusiastic, for it was their wages that got cut, their hours reduced, their plants shut when Pittsburgh balanced the books. But with no more options than their counterparts in the cotton mills or on the tenant farms, they suffered through it. And besides, during the '20s, things always turned around.

So citizens rarely protested, and when they did, it made little difference. U.S. Steel and its allies controlled city hall, managed the local economy, and sent their endorsed and approved legislative delegation to Montgomery, where they sat with endorsed and approved legislators from the Black Belt and voted to keep taxes low, services minimal, races segregated, and white folks supreme. Nobody called them Bourbons anymore, but that's what they were.

COME THE CRASH, NOT WITH A BANG

It should be no surprise that when the national depression hit, Pittsburgh sacrificed Birmingham first. A labor force of a hundred thousand, in two years' time, was reduced by 25 percent. More layoffs and closings followed, and eventually fewer than twenty thousand held full-time jobs in the mills and mines. The shock waves were felt all the way up and over Red Mountain and into the ozone. And everywhere else.

Downstate, in Mobile, uneasy bankers watched the market drop and turned conservative, rejected loan applications from such institutions as the *Mobile Press* and the Battle House Hotel. Meanwhile deposits dropped as equally concerned depositors withdrew their money and put the cash in safe deposit boxes, or in their mattresses. And they kept it there, didn't spend it.

Middle-class, white-collar folks, the ones with bank accounts, began to economize, get rid of the frills, and that meant black folks. On the eve of the depression, more than half of Mobile's households had at least one black servant. The largest employment category in the city was "female domestic"—4,570 in 1930, and few if any were white. They weren't fired, just "let go," as if the softer term made a difference. And they went, along with the gardeners, butlers, and cooks. Other towns and cities may not have had as many domestics as Mobile, but working for white folks was the way many black men and women were able to keep their families fed, clothed, and hoping. Losing the job meant losing all that.

So those who had money hung on to it. As for those whose wages were cut, whose jobs disappeared, whose farms were broken up, they just hung on. Slowly the economy ground to a halt. By the time Herbert Hoover got ready to run for reelection in 1932, statewide retail sales were down by nearly 50 percent, and the sale of durable goods was only a tenth of what it had been four years earlier. As the doggerel said, "business went to hell." Along with everything else.

THE POLITICS OF DEPRESSION

The Democrats blamed the Republicans, and the Republicans took it. Any suggestion that the fault lay elsewhere was laughed off, and

GOP hopes raised in 1928 faded. But those forces that opposed Al Smith and the direction he seemed to be taking the party of redemption still were there. Though conservative businessmen and landlords, evangelical Protestants, white supremacists, and their sort again swore loyalty to the Democrats, there was a feeling that some of them were simply biding their time until something better came along.

It was also a good time to blame Tom Heflin and the "bolters" who left the Democrats in '28. And a good time to blame Bibb Graves, whose willingness to borrow and spend was denounced by conservatives as cause for the state's unsteady financial condition. So in 1930 conservatives turned to one of their own, Benjamin Meek Miller, "The Sturdy Oak of Wilcox," who ran for governor on a platform that included as much attention to roads, child welfare, and public health as a commitment to no new taxes would allow, which of course was little or none. He also promised to fire any state employee who belonged to the Klan, but everyone knew that was a slap at Graves, not a commitment to racial or religious toleration. No, "Meek" Miller, who once boasted that "a man could walk six miles in a straight line and never leave [his family's] land," was running to put the planter-industrialist coalition, the big mules, back in power. When he defeated five opponents to win the Democratic primary, then took the regular election, he appeared on his way to doing just that.

Conservatives figured Miller was the sort of leader the state needed in that time of deepening economic despair. Reserved, dignified, and known for his parsimony, the new governor prided himself in the fact that he still used kerosene lamps on the Miller plantation, because electricity was expensive. The cost of gasoline being what it was, Governor Miller allowed only two automobiles in his inaugural parade, and, not about to pay Montgomery prices for milk and butter, he arrived at the governor's mansion with his favorite milk cow in tow. If nothing else seemed certain, everyone knew that B. M. Miller would return Alabama to the fiscal conservatism of Bourbon days.

Everyone was wrong. Taking office in 1931, Miller found a state with thousands out of work, hungry, and afraid and a government without the resources to do much about it. So to the dismay of his conservative colleagues, he quickly borrowed $500,000 just to keep state agencies functioning. Then he set to work.

Although the case can be made that Miller was a conservative because conservatism benefited him and his class, one must remember that there were those who truly believed that low taxes, limited government, and a balanced budget were best for the state as a whole. B. M. Miller was one. But the crisis forced Miller to reconsider, forced him to do things he normally would not have done. To many, the governor did not do enough. But considering his own beliefs, some of the action he took was downright revolutionary.

Like a good conservative, Miller started by cutting the state expenses and laying off "unnecessary" workers, which hardly helped the chronic unemployment situation. People who didn't work didn't pay taxes, so as revenue declined the governor was forced to throw the "no new taxes" pledge out the window and push through a gasoline levy. Then, to the surprise of his neo-Bourbon allies, Miller rejected a sales tax because its burden fell on those who were "battling for bread, hunting for food, seeking clothes . . . and begging for the necessities of life." Instead the governor announced that he intended to balance the budget by taxing those whose "profits and incomes have never been taxed," those Alabamians "who have money, [and] who have the ability to pay." This would be done through a graduated income tax. It was heresy.

The debate over the income tax laid bare the class divisions that racial politics had covered up for years. The crash caused poorer whites to realize that their vaunted "supremacy" counted for little when their families, like black families, were ill-fed, ill-clothed, ill-housed, and just plain ill. State revenues had fallen to the point that social service agencies opened during the Graves years could do little to ease the suffering. Meanwhile teachers and other employees were being paid in IOUs, scrip, that some merchants accepted for goods and services, some accepted at a discount, and others did not accept at all. Yet there were those out there who were doing well, or so it seemed, and the gap between those who were and those who were not was growing.

So Miller took to the stump to push the income tax, went out to argue that only the selfish, the unconcerned about the plight of their neighbor, would oppose this solution. But the selfish rose against him. They called the plan un-American, "socialist," "communist," even "Republican." Such a scheme, they charged, took money from hard-working Alabamians and gave it to the idle, lazy, and "sorry as gully dirt." Though Miller claimed that the tax would fall on only seven thousand, the seven thousand warned that they were just the beginning. A few may be taxed at first, they said, but soon the burden will fall on all. Stop it now.

And they did. In 1931 and again in 1932, attempts to amend the constitution to allow an income tax went down in defeat. But Miller kept fighting, and as he did, events came to his rescue.

IT CAN'T GET NO WORSE THAN THIS

With new sources of revenue denied and old sources rapidly drying up, Alabama's state government simply collapsed. Conservatives had sown the wind; now they harvested the whirlwind. Moreover, most realized it. What happened in education dramatizes the point.

By the time the second income-tax vote was counted, only 16 of Alabama's 116 school districts were able to pay their teachers a full salary. As 1932 drew to a close officials in Montgomery were warning that as many as half the schools in the state would not open in January. And the Alabama Education Association, acting more and more like the union it would become, vowed that teachers would no longer work without pay. Faced with this vow, cracks began to appear in the opposition.

Although agricultural interests, organized under the Farm Bureau Federation, continued to oppose Miller's plan, some businessmen saw disaster in the making and told representatives to compromise. But legislators did not need to be told. Folks back home demanded action, hinted of a revolt at the ballot box, or maybe a real revolt, a revolution; things were that bad. So the people's representatives hurried to Montgomery when Miller called a January special session, and there they quickly increased corporate taxes and proposed an amendment that would tax incomes over $4,000 a year. Then, once again, Miller went to the people.

The campaign was a throwback to the pre-Bourbon era, when politicians identified enemies and promised to bring them to task. Today, we can recreate it from memories and believe it went something like this:

Standing before farm folk in little country schools that might not open again, or before mill folk without jobs, or on courthouse steps before town folk fading from middle class, the governor would ask, "Who among you paid federal income tax last year? Raise your hands."

There were never many. Miller knew there would not be. In 1930 only fifteen thousand Alabamians paid the federal levy. By 1932 nearly half of those failed to qualify.

"If you don't pay Washington," Miller told them. "You won't pay Montgomery."

The point was made. The tax would fall on those who could pay. It passed.

Yet as with so much in Alabama history, symbolism took precedent over substance, and the symbolism itself may be more important in retrospect than in reality. Governor Miller was acting in a crisis, and it is doubtful he would have done so otherwise. In most areas his administration was consistently conservative. On record believing that "a dollar a day [was] enough for any working man," he opposed organized labor's efforts to raise wages and continued the tradition of using state troops to put down strikes. His record on race was mixed at best. Though he intervened to prevent two lynchings, he failed to stop a particularly brutal one that he had the time and resources to halt. Moreover, Miller refused to help protect lawyers defending the "Scottsboro Boys"—young black men accused of raping two white women—because the attorneys were communists. In other words, with a few notable exceptions, Benjamin Meek Miller acted like most of his predecessors. And, except for the exceptions, Alabama's oligarchy liked it that way.

IF THIS BE REVOLUTION, THEN MAKE
THE MOST OF IT, 'CAUSE IT AIN'T MUCH

Still, Alabamians had done something many thought could not be done. They had forced the legislature to violate one of Bourbonism's most sacred principles and tax the wealthy. True, this action came too late to prevent most of the schools from closing in the winter of 1933, but doing it was something. Yet keep in mind that, like Miller, legislators were responding to a crisis both economic and political. The once-docile electorate created by the Constitution of 1901 was restive, uneasy, and ready for something new. Though the Democrat Franklin Delano Roosevelt carried the state in 1932, the fact that the Socialist candidate got more votes than Hoover in some counties was not lost on conservatives. In Mobile an "army" of unemployed marched on city hall demanding action, and one local newspaper warned that there were "sparks of revolution in the air that may burst into flame any moment." Conservative legislators feared for the future, and if they could get by with limited corporate and income taxes, those were a small price to pay.

There were other reasons for conservative concern. Rumors were reaching them that the "New Deal" Roosevelt promised included federal intervention on a scale unseen since the days of Reconstruction. Conditioned to believe that nothing good could come from Washington, they got ready to fight the invaders. So it followed that during the next decade, pro– and anti–New Deal forces went at each other, argued over the constitutionality and social (read that racial) consequence of federal programs, claimed history was on their side, and warned of impending disaster if the other carried the day. But for most Alabamians it was not history or constitutionality or even social upheaval that mattered. They wanted to know: "Will the programs give me a job? Will they help me feed my family? Will they allow me a measure of dignity?" For the out of work, out of options, out of hope, those were the only questions that counted.

From this debate would emerge a cadre of politicians who were called, and called themselves, liberals. Today, more than half a century later, the term has become muddled and in many cases pejorative. What it meant back then, however, was fairly clear. In Alabama a "liberal" was someone who, having given up on the state's doing anything to make life better for its poorer citizens, turned to the federal government for help. This inclination made Alabama liberals natural allies of the New Deal and suspect among conservatives. Moreover, liberals' willingness to work with Washington associated them with ideas and attitudes, especially on race, that stood in marked contrast to the way things traditionally were done in the heart of Dixie. And while most Alabama liberals were staunch segregationists, conservatives were able to overlook that fact and use race against them—eventually.

In 1933, however, race was not the issue on most minds. Recovery was. And considering how little the state would and could do to revive the economy, it was no wonder that so many Alabamians ignored warnings that money from Washington would come with strings attached. With state relief checks averaging about $8 a month, some mothers fed their children only twice a day—and some not that. A Mobile man told of how he was awakened by wild knocking, went to the door, and found a hysterical woman with a sack of scraps, begging for anything, willing to do any work to buy milk for her baby. Banks were closing, and the once-prosperous middle class was beginning to panic. Their only hope, it seemed, lay in Washington and with Franklin D. Roosevelt.

THE NEW DEAL: HOW NEW? WHO CARED?

Historians continue to disagree over how successful New Deal programs were in ending the depression in the nation and in the state. By the end of the twentieth century, that debate had become political as rising Republican politicians played down the New Deal's accomplishments and claimed instead that what FDR really did was lip-lock Americans to the federal teat. But the older generation, those who came of age during the depression, have been hard to convince. Alabamians who found jobs in one of the "alphabet agencies" set up to put people to work, and who lived to draw Social Security, do not believe that these programs undermined fundamental American values by making people dependent on the government instead of themselves. No, to that generation the New Deal set government to working for the people instead of propertied interests, and in the process saved America. To those people Franklin D. Roosevelt is a hero.

There were, of course, other heroes, little ones who did little things to help people get through: merchants who let profits disappear rather than lay off clerks, store owners who accepted teachers' scrip at face value not knowing if the state would ever redeem it, churches that set up soup kitchens, landlords who let tenants stay on the place while other owners turned to cattle, housewives who set out plates of cold food (biscuits and sweet potatoes seemed the fare of choice) so transients could eat without begging, railroad "bulls" who turned the other way when hoboes slipped on and off the trains, affluent families that carefully wrapped leftover food because they knew that residents of "Hooverville" down by the dump would be scavenging their garbage for their next meal, and more, and more. But they were not enough, could not have been enough, so when the government stepped in to help, those needing help were thankful.

In January of 1933 Franklin D. Roosevelt took office and went at it. In the famous "hundred days" that followed, he inspired Congress to enact legislation that reshaped the relationship between states and the federal government. The banking industry was rescued and restructured, millions of dollars were put into existing work relief programs, farmers (and in some cases even tenants) were helped, workers' right to unionize was protected (much to the displeasure of industrialists), and new agencies were created to put people to work. For the first time in the memory of many Alabamians, government seemed to care about the little guy.

Examples of New Deal successes, or what at the time many perceived as successes, abound, but few if any can match what was done up in the valley of the Tennessee River. At the end of World War I, the valley seemed ready for prosperity. The Wilson Dam and adjacent nitrate plants stood nearly complete at Muscle Shoals, and rumor was that Henry Ford had offered to buy the property, finish the project, and around it build a new metropolis—"Seventy-Five Mile City." But Ford and the Republican-controlled government could not agree, so the plan was abandoned, and the dam sat idle.

Then came Roosevelt. To rest up before the inauguration, the president-elect went to his retreat in Warm Springs, Georgia, where he often delighted local audiences by calling himself a "simple Georgia farmer." From there he traveled into North Alabama, into the valley, to see first-hand the conditions he had heard about. More sensitive to the South's situation than any president since Woodrow Wilson, Roosevelt returned to Washington and from the White House supported the passage of the bill that created the Tennessee Valley Authority (TVA). This agency would oversee the construction of dams to control floods and generate the electricity that would light the valley and attract a host of new industries. For the people of that region, it was a dream come true.

But not for everyone. Private power producers, the Alabama Power Company in particular, saw something fundamentally unfair, un-American, in a government agency supported by taxpayer money competing against a private company with only its profits to keep it going. The government's advantage was obvious, and Alabama Power sued to stop it. The suit failed, but in the aftermath the federal government chose to limit its efforts to Tennessee River development, while Alabama Power focused on the Coosa-Tallapoosa Valley. If it wasn't a compromise, it sure looked like one, and a lot of folks believed that's what it was.

While TVA's impact would last long after the New Deal was history, other, shorter-lived programs would be remembered fondly by those who were helped. The Works Progress Administration (WPA) put people to work in every county of the state in jobs that ranged from construction to records reorganization to theatrical productions to murals on post office walls. Critics charged that most of it was "make-work" and unnecessary. Some even raised the race issue, claiming that the programs favored Roosevelt's "African jungle friends," and rumors spread that northerners were being sent down to promote communism and interracial marriage—a linkage that seemed to delight conservatives. But the people who got the jobs didn't pay much attention to the rumors. During the first year of operation the WPA and other federally funded relief agencies put nearly 130,000 Alabamians, white and black, to work, paid them a living wage, and gave them the dignity of a job instead of the dole. In the process, Alabama got new bridges, public buildings, works of art, and other physical benefits, not to mention money to be spent in local stores. At the time, that was what mattered.

Still, if you seek out survivors of the depression living at the end of the century and ask them to tell about the era, the agency that so many of them recall, fondly recall, is the Civilian Conservation Corp (CCC). And why shouldn't they? The CCC was created to help unemployed young men, which is what so many of them were in the 1930s. It took them from worn-out farms and sent them back to reclaim the land with terraces and cover crops—including the kudzu that did its job and more. It took them from towns and cities, put them in camps with country kids, housed them in barracks, fed them in mess halls, and put them to work. Before the CCC had run its course, it had given employment to nearly seventy thousand Alabamians, black and white (but mostly white). For many it was their first real job, their first real paycheck, and the money, part of which was sent home, represented their first real relationship with institutional authority. They came to the camps a ragged, dejected, fearful bunch. There they were clothed (some recall the first decent shoes they ever owned), given a physical exam (another first for many), and organized. They learned to work together; some also learned to read and write, and others recall learning the fine art of poker. And today they take their great-grandchildren back to the state parks they helped build and show them their handiwork.

THE RETURN OF BIBB GRAVES

Although B. M. Miller went further than most Alabamians would have expected someone of his philosophy to have gone, most knew that he would not have done what he did had it not been for the emergency he faced. But Miller's limited efforts produced limited results. So with the school system still in chaos, the treasury depleted, and state services dribbling away into nothing, many concluded that Miller's successor should be a governor in the mold of FDR. They wanted a governor who could work with Washington, bring in federal funds and programs, a governor not tied to the old tradition of low taxes and limited services, a governor like Bibb Graves had been.

Graves was waiting in the wings. Constitutionally prohibited from succeeding himself, he sat out the probationary four years, built alliances, mended fences, and got ready. Then in 1934, with the backing of organized labor, small farmers, and New Dealers, he threw his hat into the ring. Declaring himself the champion of the "small mules," the ones who pulled the load while the big mules feasted on the fruits of their labors, he promised to put the burden where it belonged.

The big mules—industry, business, and planters—didn't like that one bit, so they rallied around Birmingham lawyer Frank M. Dixon, who attacked Graves's ties to the Klan and broadly hinted that the former governor had socialist leanings that would lead the state to ruin. But Graves's supporters were more concerned with economic recovery than with the Klan, more concerned with government aid than with socialistic suggestions, so in an election that revealed deep class divisions, Graves carried fifty-six of the state's sixty-seven counties and won by over twenty thousand votes. Taking his victory as an endorsement, Bibb Graves set out to serve the people who elected him.

Under Graves the state experienced its own little New Deal, or so it seemed to many citizens—critics and supporters alike. He pushed an often-reluctant state legislature to pass the laws required to get federal money, then set up the programs Washington offered. Through his newly created state department of labor, the governor carried out policies that increased the power of unions and outraged industrialists. In racial matters, however, Graves's Klan sympathies showed. Despite pleas from as high as President Roosevelt, Graves refused to pardon the Scottsboro boys. Though they were obviously convicted on flimsy evidence, and despite a worldwide outcry, Graves held his ground. It ultimately took action by the U.S. Supreme Court to get most of them released.

Graves did not cross Roosevelt very often, however, so the state was able to make the most of federal programs, and in time (and much to conservatives' distress) the ancient admonition that nothing good ever comes from Washington lost much of its sting.

BRINGING IT ALL BACK HOME

This was when Alabama liberals moved to center stage. Looking to Washington for help that the state could not provide, they found allies in the senators John H. Bankhead Jr., Hugo Black, and Lister Hill, who supported Roosevelt and in return brought home the federal bacon. No less significant were congressmen, especially William Bankhead, Henry B. Steagall, Bob Jones, George Huddleston Sr., and Luther Partick, who were as effective for their constituents as any representatives sent to the capital. And there was Loula Friend Dunn, who grew up in southwest Alabama, attended Alabama schools, and rose from a caseworker in the state's child welfare department to become the director of federal social and employment programs for six southern states, including her own. Eventually serving as commissioner of public welfare in Alabama, her subtle grasp of local conditions and needs and her ties to the Washington establishment made her an important ingredient in relief efforts. Governor Graves made the most of these connections. With New Deal public works money he rebuilt the state capitol complex. Funds from Washington helped underwrite a variety of social programs. And when it came to getting federal money to pave roads, only two states were able to blacktop more miles than Alabama.

But even the federal treasury had its limits, so when it came to educational reforms, Governor Graves had to turn to state taxpayers, and when he did, the limitations of Alabama liberalism became apparent. Most Alabamians agreed with the governor when he said Alabama needed to equalize educational opportunity for rural and urban students (though not necessarily for black and white), that free textbooks should be provided for the first three grades, and that there should be a fully funded seven-month school year. But when he proposed to fund all these promises with a gross receipts tax that would be paid by business, the big mules rose in anger. With the help of their Black Belt planter allies who were looking for a way to stop the Graves steamroller, these conservatives pushed through a sales tax instead. Fearing his whole program would fail, Graves signed the act into law. It was a fateful moment, for it set Alabama on a course that would in time give it one of the most regressive and unstable tax systems in the nation.

It was not as if the big mules and the planters suffered under the New Deal. Money from federal programs paid wages, and wages bought merchandise. More than that, New Deal construction projects bought steel, and though industrialists chided and complained about labor's growing power, the alternative would have been, could have been, closed mills and boarded-up mines. Planters also complained that hands would rather draw relief checks than work, a complaint that probably said less about laziness than about the work and what planters paid for it. Besides, planters sat on most of the committees that dispensed federal funds and directed agricultural programs, and they had no reservations about using their position to their advantage. So when cotton needed chopping or picking, it was not uncommon for federal money to dry up and workers, with no alternative, to be forced into the fields. Though landlords complained that government planning was socialistic, there is no record of any of them refusing the crop subsidies, and when attempts were made to force them to share the money with tenants, they fought them and generally won.

The big mules and the planters did well enough.

THE NEW DEAL FADES AWAY

Unable to succeed himself, in 1939 Governor Graves stepped aside and made way for the man he defeated four years before, Frank Murray Dixon. Now Dixon was not the stuff from which Alabama governors were normally made. First of all, he wasn't even a native Alabamian. Born in California and brought up in tidewater Virginia, prep school and Ivy League educated, with a University of Virginia law degree in the bargain, he wasn't what one expected to find running for office down here.

But here he was. And his being here says a lot about what connections and common concerns can do for a political career in Alabama. In Birmingham's "New South" economy, few professions grew more rapidly and richly than the law, and as law firms increased and expanded they began to attract graduates from top schools, which was why Frank Dixon landed a job in the Magic City. This was followed by marriage into Greene County, Black Belt landed gentry; service in World War I, in which he lost a leg; a prominent role in the American Legion; and finally a legal partnership that made him one of the city's most successful corporate attorneys. Add to these his active and loyal support for the Democratic Party through the Tom Heflin–Al Smith debacle, and you have the sort of fellow the big mules (many of whom weren't Alabamians either) couldn't help but love.

In Dixon we see many of the contradictory patterns that make up the Alabama quilt. He was a dedicated white supremacist, which would seem normal for the nephew of Rev. Thomas Dixon, author of the 1905 novel *The Clansman,* from which came the movie *Birth of a Nation* and, it is said, the revival of the Ku Klux Klan. Yet Frank Dixon opposed the Klan, not because of its racial prejudices but because it represented a popular political challenge to the big mule–planter alliance. So the Alabama oligarchy tapped him as their choice to challenge Graves in 1935, and, as we have seen, he lost. Four years later he was back. Putting together a coalition of progressive businessmen, courthouse conservatives, new voters, and, yes, even some union leaders, Frank Dixon defeated a weak opponent and was elected governor.

If nothing else, Frank M. Dixon was efficient, and he came into office determined to make Alabama efficient as well—no small challenge in a state where efficiency has never been a particularly high priority. But to the surprise of many, maybe all, he did make things better. Working with legislators, he cut duplication (which was not easy because it also cut jobs); instituted a civil service, merit-based system (no snap either, since it ate into patronage); established a teachers' retirement fund (which put that voting bloc in his corner); and made department heads responsible directly to him. He also went after taxes, or at least the way they were assessed, which led to modest increases in state property taxes, but when he tried to get counties to increase their assessments as well, landed interests in the legislature would have none of it. Still, his efforts to streamline government stand as the most successful in the state's history, a statement that may say more about Alabama than it does about Frank Dixon.

Through all of this achievement Dixon was adamantly opposed to Roosevelt and the New Deal. Part of this attitude rises from his obsession with inefficiency and waste, which to his way of thinking characterized Washington's efforts to revive the economy. His racial views also contributed to his feeling that money was being spent on the wrong people and for the wrong reasons. He also made clear that efforts to make lynching a federal crime amounted to a sinister attempt to interfere with the way a state enforced its laws and controlled its population.

At the core of his opposition, however, was a growing conviction that FDR and his advisors were falling under the influence of labor and its supporters, and for corporate lawyer Frank M. Dixon, nothing could be worse. So he was not long in office before the few union leaders who had supported him discovered that they had made a big mistake. Of Dixon it has been said that the legislature could never "pass enough anti-labor bills to please him," and a union newspaper denounced him as a "peg-legged bigot whose creaking cork leg is moved to take each step at the command of Birmingham's industrial barons." But what else did they expect?

The point to be made about Dixon, indeed the point he made himself, was that he had come to believe that the national Democratic Party was deserting Alabama, his Alabama, corporate conservative, antiunion, white supremacist Alabama. And before his term in office ended he was saying so, was warning that if the national party did not mend its ways, Alabamians might just have to find another home. Those were the same sentiments whispered by Democrats who voted for Hoover in '28, Democrats whom Dixon had vocally opposed. But things had changed, and Frank M. Dixon was beginning to believe Heflin and his "bolters" might have been right. He was not alone.

TWILIGHT OF THE NEW DEAL

A core of Alabamians was skeptical of the New Deal from the outset. And as the programs multiplied and the changes came, their skepticism, to them at least, was confirmed. There were others, of course, who were New Deal supporters at the start, supporters to the end, and whose ideological descendants today look back in wonder and envy at what was accomplished. But by the time Roosevelt's second term ended, most Alabamians, one suspects, were just a little tired of it all. On the programs that worked, like TVA, they heaped pride and praise. Those that fell short—like the government-sponsored cooperative communities of Skyline Farms up in the Jackson County mountains and Gee's Bend down on the Alabama

River—they wrote off as noble efforts. As for the rest—the CCC, AAA, WPA, PWA, and all their alphabetized ilk—interest in them waned as government funds were cut and shifted. By the end of the 1930s there were war clouds on the horizon, and American priorities were changing.

As for Alabama, as 1940 approached the state seemed to be settling back into patterns that defined it and its people before the crash. Most citizens still lived in the countryside and made their living from the land. Sharecropping and tenant farming were common, as were poverty, privilege, and the gap between. Federal money notwithstanding, many (maybe a majority) of the state's residents were poorly educated, poorly housed, poorly fed, and poorly doctored. But one senses that nevertheless things were better. Birmingham, though not yet booming, had turned the corner, while at the other end of the state, reforms instituted during the Graves and Dixon administrations had increased activity at Mobile's state docks, and when the docks were busy, Mobile was busy.

In small towns and hamlets, in mill towns and mining villages, in mountain valleys and at branchheads, things were looking up. Always more interested in recovery than in reform, Alabamians had taken the New Deal as a means of getting through the depression and, if possible, getting some things they could not get otherwise. So they took government money and did as much of what they were told as they could reconcile with existing beliefs and values. In some cases these programs and agencies changed lives. In most cases they didn't.

Surely change was felt the most in northern Alabama. TVA and a host of subsidiary programs transformed the landscape, the economy and the political outlook of the people. Long the home of independent, populist-minded, mostly white farmers whose opposition to concentrated power and wealth set them at odds with Birmingham industrialists, Black Belt planters, and Montgomery politicians, North Alabamians emerged from the depression as the most pro-Washington, pro-union, pro–national Democratic Party section of the state. From this region and with its peoples' votes would come some of Alabama's most liberal legislators—state and federal. Corporate interests looked on with horror, and Black Belt planters decried the dangers inherent in getting too dependent on federal money, but they really had little to fear. North Alabamians were still Alabamians, and, when put to the test, they acted like Alabamians.

In other parts of the state the New Deal left less of a mark, but even so, at times the alterations were significant. By 1939, and largely with Washington money, every county in the state but Choctaw had at least one paved road. A federal highway system linked most of the major cities and some minor ones along the way, changing lives and living the way railroads had once done. Public buildings, parks, reclaimed land, and the like made differences where they were, but where they weren't things remained pretty much the same. And, for the most part, they weren't in the Black Belt. There planter hostility to anything that interfered with the right to exploit a largely black labor force led local officials—all white and landed—to reject what few programs were offered—except, of course, crop subsidies, which went, mostly, to them. The rest—CCC camps, WPA projects, and the like—were nothing but creeping socialism, especially if they offered alternative employment during picking season.

And yet by 1940 most Alabamians, even black Alabamians, could say, honestly, that things had improved, that the New Deal had made a difference, and that the federal government was not the enemy conservative Alabamians claimed it to be. Franklin Roosevelt was still a hero, and they had no qualms voting him into office for the third time.

Besides, he was a Democrat.

WAR

Let us understand this. The New Deal was important; it altered things. But World War II transformed Alabama and Alabamians. The New Deal made *a* difference. World War II made *the* difference.

On the surface the story is simple enough. Blessed with a good climate, cheap, plentiful, and in some cases already government-owned land, electricity from TVA and Alabama Power, a network of WPA-built and -improved roads, an excellent river system with a port for ocean commerce, Alabama was a perfect place for training bases, war industries, and distribution. And Alabama played the role well. Airfields in Montgomery, Selma, and Tuskegee trained thousands of cadets and crews, including black pilots who fought discrimination to fight the Germans. Forts were built, or reopened and expanded, to prepare infantry for the conflict. Huntsville got a chemical facility. Birmingham's steel mills glared red night and day, and textile mills ran round the clock. Muscle Shoals welcomed Union Carbide and Reynolds Metals. In Mobile some thirty-five thousand workers launched a new freighter or tanker almost weekly. Near Childersburg, in north-central Alabama, Du Pont Chemical built the largest smokeless powder and explosive plant in the South, and what had been a town of some five hundred souls had to find a way to accommodate some fourteen thousand construction workers. Many of them were local. Most were from Alabama.

It all did not happen overnight, of course, but it happened. Alabama congressmen who had helped Roosevelt called in their chips and made sure the state got its fair share, and more. All of which, of course, meant jobs, payrolls, money earned, and money spent. The New Deal did not end the depression in Alabama. World War II did.

But at what cost? In all, over three hundred thousand Alabamians served in the armed forces. More than forty-five hundred lost their lives. Thousands more came home with physical and mental wounds that would be long to heal. It seemed that every community, every town, hamlet, neighborhood, sent someone away who did not come back. And for years afterward those who remembered would visit the cemetery, visit the stone that said "in memory of," lost over Germany, missing near Guam, buried in France. They went a long way from home to die.

Those who stayed behind learned that war transformed more than the warriors. There was work now, and the migration to the cities that had abated during the dark days of the depression, when on the farm at least you could eat, began again, and what was once a trickle became a flood. If Birmingham had been the nation's most depressed city a decade earlier, Mobile must have become the most congested. In 1940 Mobile's population stood at just under seventy-nine thousand. In the next three years that figure more than doubled. Public services were overwhelmed. Police and fire protection was stretched to the limit, schools went on double sessions, medical services were inadequate, housing shortages were epidemic, and some workers rented rooms in eight-hour shifts.

As the city became more crowded the story was told of two shipyard employees meeting each other as one arrived on the job and the other left.

"You look familiar," one said.
"So do you," replied the other.
"Where do you live?" said the first.
"Out on Government Street. Where do you live?"
"I live on Government Street too. What address?"
"1422, apartment 4–B."
"That's where I live. What's your wife's name?"
"Sally."
"My wife's named Sally too."
"Why," they exclaimed in unison, "we must be husbands-in-law."

It probably never happened, but it might have, if Sally had been able to schedule the two of them around her third shift at the shipyard. When men went off to war, women moved into the workplace, did men's jobs, and did them well. Although the women's rights movement of the 1960s and 1970s is credited with bringing women into the workforce in a meaningful way, truth is, for Alabama at least, it began during the war. Though the trend waned slightly with peace, the door had been opened, and Alabama women would not let it be shut again.

Women were not the only "minority" that benefited from worker shortages. Black Alabamians left towns and farms, headed for the cities, and joined the labor force. The Black Belt, close to Mobile and Montgomery, was especially hard hit, as planters who had been hiring former tenants for seasonal work discovered their labor supply depleted. Even though defense contractors initially hired them as unskilled workers, pay and conditions were better than what they left, so they made the journey. Besides, they were still in the South, in Alabama, close to home, and that counted for a lot.

But things were changing for the African American worker. In 1943, after months of pressure from the National Association for the Advancement of Colored People (NAACP), the federal Fair Employment Practices Commission barred defense contractors from discriminating in hiring. Conservatives like Governor Dixon denounced the rule; in Mobile white workers rioted for two days when blacks were promoted to comply with the order, and finally the promoted workers were put in segregated units, but it was a beginning. Before the war was over, African American Alabamians got the opportunity to learn new skills, earn more money, and prove themselves. A new day was dawning.

JOHNNY COMES MARCHING HOME

Alabama servicemen and women were seldom philosophical about the war. When asked why they were fighting, the most frequent reply was "to win and get home." The folks they left behind sensed this longing and did what they could to let them know that home wanted them back. Countless letters were sent overseas assuring loved ones that what they were fighting for would be there when they returned. Preachers and politicians spoke eloquently and romantically of the way of life the war was fought to preserve. So did merchants.

In December 1944, with Germany all but defeated and Japan's days numbered, a South Alabama newspaper decided to publish a special edition with pictures of the hundreds of county citizens then in uniform. When the newspaper approached local merchant Will Dunn, owner of the Big General Store, he quickly agreed to take out a full-page ad. But Dunn did not use the space to tout his merchandise. His advertisement sold something else.

"IT'S JUST THE SAME, JOHNNY, JUST THE SAME" was the headline imposed on a drawing of a village. It was not Will Dunn's village, but every village and town and city in the state and the nation. It was a generic advertisement, reprinted in countless papers, but that didn't matter. It said what Mr. Dunn and others like him wanted to say, and what they believed servicemen who got the paper in the mail, maybe a month or more later, wanted to hear.

The old town is just as you left it, Johnny. All the things you've been fighting for are just the same . . . and we're counting the days till you can take your place among them.

The lights still shine in the drug store of an evening. The cars still park along the main stem. You can still wake up at night and hear the echoing whistle of the through freight. And though the floodlights turn off a little earlier in the filling station than they used to, there's still someone there to wipe your windshield off while the gas pump rings up the fare.

Baseball and double-features, chicken on Sunday, and the church where you worshipped . . . all these are just the same, too, Johnny—and all the sights and sounds and, most of all, the friendliness that go to makeup this American town— your home-town!

Of course, Johnny, it won't be the same until you get back, until you step off the train in your uniform with its campaign ribbons, tanner, stronger, leaner, perhaps a bit taller than when you went away—but otherwise the same young fellow we used to know.

So here we are, looking forward now to your homecoming. Looking forward to the day we can shake your hand, to the day when you will hang up those Khakis or blues in the closet, resume your place among us and take up the good American life just where you left it.

We've kept things for you just the way you knew them, Johnny. We know you want it that way.

Problem was, it wasn't true.

11

Alabama after the War: "Big Jim" and Beyond

JOHNNY AT HOME

It wasn't the same. Johnny (and Jane) knew it right off. The buildings had not changed much. Though people were a little older, their faces were comfortably familiar. But these folks were prosperous, had jobs, money in the bank. When the inductees left for war the effects of the depression still hung around like an unwelcome guest. Not any more. Things were different, and returning servicemen and women wanted to enjoy the difference. No one had kept things "just the way you left it," and that suited Johnny (and Jane) just fine.

But they weren't surprised. During the war, home on leave, they noticed changes. They had listened to parents and friends talk about work and wages, heard them complain not about layoffs and standdowns but about rationing, shortages, and nothing to spend their money on except movies. Then someone would wink and say that if you knew the right people, greased the right palm, there was gasoline to be had, and tires, and nylons, and steaks. Then someone would recall the depression and how important it was to save and how war bonds were a safe investment and everyone would nod in agreement because they had some squirreled away. More than $1.5 billion in bonds were bought by Alabamians, the highest per capita sales in the nation, and when the war ended that money was sitting there, waiting to buy cars, waiting to buy appliances, waiting to buy houses, waiting to buy into the middle class. Johnny and Jane heard the talk, the plans, and liked what they heard. They didn't want to go back to the way things were before the war. They wanted to be part of the way things were when they returned.

Of course, not everyone who stayed behind planned for the future. Some just enjoyed things that came their way and hoped the good times would last. The Hurts, a Northeast Alabama clan, were of that breed. According to hill country chronicler H. C. Nixon, they were a "household of two double-up families, former share-croppers," who had struggled through the depression. Then the war came, and they struggled no more. Three of them worked as farm laborers, positions that gave the family a house and a garden. One was a pipe fitter at the Du Pont plant, while the rest went "near and far to industrial work." But despite a middle-class income, the Hurts rejected middle-class values. "Neither saints nor money savers," in four months they bought, sold, traded, or wrecked some thirteen automobiles. At one point four of them were in jail at the same time, where they stayed until the others pulled together enough to bail them out. Two of them reported for the draft but were rejected. How the others avoided service is a mystery. They were, and intended to remain, an Alabama social type, the "good ol' boy." They worked hard, paid their bills, and except for those times when they got drunk and started fighting, they usually left folks alone. Some found them "dynamic and cooperative." Others claimed they were shift-less and undependable. Both were probably right.

In one sense, the Hurts do represent the majority of Alabamians, for by the end of the war many of them—Hurts and other Alabamians—worked in towns and factories instead of on farms. Not that agriculture suffered. After the ups and downs of the New Deal era, wartime demands turned everything upward. Every year between 1941 and 1945, the value of state agricultural products increased. At the same time, however, farm acreage declined. The path was an easy one to follow. Fewer acres meant fewer hands, fewer tenants, fewer sharecroppers, and with their departure went the ancient system of lord and vassal, master and retainer. What led to what, which to which, is difficult to divide out. Did farm laborers leave for "defense work?" Or were they pushed off when landlords found that with fertilizer and a tractor they could grow as much and earn more on less land? It depends, I suppose, on where you were. And who you were.

Down in the Black Belt, what was left of the tenant farming system after the depression crumbled during the war, as most of the workers who had remained on the plantations finally took off for the war industries and the sawmills. Landlords who tried to preserve old relationships complained but adjusted quickly to the new situation. "I miss their labor," one planter reflected, "but at the same time I am putting more land into pasture" and buying tractors, for "the more machines I use, the less labor I'll need." Wages for the few hands who stayed to drive the tractors had risen to $1.50 a day, three times what they were before the war, but as the landlord noted, "the price of cotton is higher too. We will manage all right." Still, he knew the war would end and confessed, "I dread the time when those tenants who left come knocking at my door after their city jobs close down." He knew that by then their cabins would be gone and the land they farmed would have disappeared into larger fields. There would be no place to live and only seasonal work to do. They had not left much behind when they went to the city. They would find even less if they came back.

Of those whose lives were changed by the war, place black Alabamians near the top of the list. Supported by the federal Fair Employment Practices Commission, African Americans held jobs and got promotions unheard of before the war, and at one point nearly half of the Du Pont workforce was black. Though still relegated to common labor more often than their white counterparts, black Alabamians nevertheless seized opportunities when they could, learned new skills, and earned more in four years than some had hoped to earn in a lifetime. They did not intend to give up these gains, just because the war was over.

Actually, they wanted more. Returning black servicemen brought with them an acute sense of the irony of a nation fighting against Nazi racism and tolerating American racism at home. Some white

Americans (though not many white Alabamians) also saw the dilemma, and by the time all the soldiers returned, perceptive politicians could see that segregation and discrimination would no longer go unchallenged. Black Alabamians, encouraged by changing attitudes elsewhere, began to look for ways to alter the old system. White Alabamians, unsettled by what they saw and heard, prepared to defend what they had.

SO HOW NEW WAS POSTWAR ALABAMA?

That's a good question. The answer, of course, is the unsatisfactory "it depends." But it does. It depends on where you were.

Some cities changed, some didn't. To longtime residents, Mobile seemed to have been made anew by the conflict. Before the war it was an easygoing, tolerant, loose-around-the-edges, moss-draped, Catholicked and Epistocratic place where establishment families and establishment values kept a lid on class conflicts and racial tensions, such as there were. Then the war came and with it immigrants, hard folks from worn-out farms, for whom the move to the city was a financial windfall and a cultural shock. Remembering how sermons preached in the country had told them that Sodom and Gomorrah were cities, they came on their guard against sin and, to help them hold evil at bay, built among them churches like the ones they had left. But with more money than they had dreamed they would ever have, what they once denounced seemed less a threat to their salvation than it had been before. If, as they had been taught, God would reward the faithful, then God was settling up just fine.

Then the conflict was over and, to the distress of longtime residents, the immigrants stayed. Cold War tensions kept military bases busy. Mobile got its fair share of federal largesse, and civilian workers reaped the benefits. Well, not all of them. Women, whose contribution to the war effort was widely praised, found themselves required to step aside and give their jobs to returning servicemen. Some refused and were forced out. Others, those with skills and dedication that could not be duplicated, were able to stay. But most went home quietly, just as they were supposed to. Their resignation, however, was deceptive, for though they accepted their fate, they went away different from what they were when they came. Alabama women had proved themselves, to themselves and to others. Traditional barriers had been broken, and though it would be their daughters and granddaughters who would benefit most from the example wartime women set, their contribution to postwar Alabama was no less significant than their contribution to winning the war.

So you could have gone to Mobile, visited the old homes and, if you knew the right people, mingled with the old families in the sort of garden party, seersucker and spring-frock gentility that was pictured, on society pages at least, as the province of the poised, the patrician. Or you could have moved out a bit, to the faster-paced, narrowly focused, uptight, scrub pine, and paved Protestant enclaves full of working-class parents and tow-headed children. Yet in some cases the two cultures would merge, or at least coexist close enough to see each other and wave, as they did during Mardi Gras.

Mobile's Mardi Gras was, at its core, an exhibition of social status and economic power. Old families with both ran the show, sponsored the floats, paid for the costumes, underwrote the balls, and announced their accomplishments with a place on the court of the king and queen of carnival. As wartime immigrants prospered in the postwar years and began looking for ways to move into a society that had never really accepted them, they naturally sought a place in the carnival culture. Most, however, found the door closed. The older, snobbish mystic societies that put on the parades for everyone and then held parties for themselves were not about to accept the unpedigreed, no matter how financially successful they might have become. So the new Mobilians founded their own societies. Then they paraded just as enthusiastically as their betters. But looking at the old pictures, it seems, the first few years at least, that their masks were a little larger, covered a bit more, as if they were not sure they wanted to be recognized and branded "social climbers." Or maybe they were afraid their preacher might be in the crowd and they would find themselves the subject of next Sunday's sermon. It was not something to worry old-line Catholics or Episcopalians, but Methodists or Baptists of a shorter Mobile lineage could not forget their raising, even if they tried.

Birmingham, on the other hand, seemed less changed by the war. A steel and coal company town before the conflict, it was a steel and coal company town afterward. Working and living patterns set earlier stayed in place, and though like most cities it experienced housing shortages, neighborhoods grew along familiar lines. The well-to-do resided on the south side, or inched over the mountain and into the suburbs, leaving the city overwhelmingly working class, white, and segregated. Still, as a transportation hub, an industrial giant, a business and banking center, Birmingham was considered by many to be the "most unsouthern of southern cities."

It was also the most southern; at least it was if the way blacks were treated is the measure by which you go. As in Mobile, where African American life was centered along Davis Avenue, many Birmingham blacks lived and worked in the city proper, around Ingram Park, an ill-kept block where black children played and around which the black business community took root. But in Birmingham, African Americans also were squeezed into poor pockets of land between white residential sections, where they rented white-owned, poorly constructed "shotgun" houses, and where they stayed because city ordinances prevented them from buying or living in areas set aside for whites. Though most Alabama towns had a "Negro section," the "quarters" as it was frequently called, few if any segregated so rigidly as Birmingham, and few made it as difficult for blacks to alter "approved" housing patterns. In the years after the war, blacks protested many things in Birmingham, but few of the restrictions placed on them were as resented as those that kept a majority of them in substandard houses with little hope of improvement.

Small towns also felt the changes. Huntsville, a rural market center in the '30s, took the influx, and from it came the core of trained engineers and technicians that, as the space program grew, would turn the town into Alabama's best-educated, most progressive city. Childersburg, on the other hand, watched its immigrants leave almost as quickly as they arrived, and then it settled back to being the quiet little village it had been before Du Pont came to town.

Rural counties and county seats had changed, and were changing still, when the veterans came home. The New Deal and the war had altered the landscape, redrawn and reordered it to meet the needs of the automobile. Better roads carried people and commerce to places where the trains did not run, redirected trade, and set in motion the decline of railroads and railroad towns. It would be decades before the transition from train to car and truck was complete, but in the lifetime of most veterans it would happen.

Rural veterans who paused to look around saw the change at a deeper, more fundamental level. They noticed it most on Saturdays, market days, when country folk came to town. When the veterans first returned they found Saturday friendly and familiar. Many farm families arrived as they always had, in wagons. They hitched their animals under a tree, fed and watered them, then went about their business. Closer to the stores, parked not hitched, were cars and a few trucks, precursors of the popular pickup, prewar vintage, worn, and weary from four years with little relief. Sometimes there were as many automobiles as wagons, sometimes more. Then, as factories re-tooled for civilian consumption, war bonds were cashed in; and cars and trucks were bought, driven in, and parked, spilling out into the groves. Year by year the balance shifted until finally the wagons and the steady ones that pulled them were gone.

They would soon be gone from the farms as well. Though the mechanization of agriculture had begun decades before, wartime demands and mechanical innovations combined to put more tractors in the fields. So farmers sold their animals, took the money, made a down payment on something that ran on gasoline, which they parked in the stall that was empty now. And they grew less hay and bought more fuel. Some held on though, kept the beast that had served faithfully, claimed it made a good pet for the kids and grand-kids. Only they knew better.

By the mid 1950s the agricultural allotment system set up under the New Deal had been reworked to further favor large interests over the family farm. Planters, the cotton barons, were allowed to plant substantial fields, and the man with a few acres was limited to the leavings. It fell the responsibility of the local agriculture department to send out workers—"field-men" they called them—to measure the plots, just to make sure no one planted more than their allotted acreage. One day a field-man arrived at a small house and was greeted by the farmer, an elderly fellow—lean, loose jointed, overalled, and booted—who willingly took the visitor around back to measure his cotton patch. He was proud of it, and he should have been. The middles were plowed clean, the rows were chopped and thinned, no grass competed with the stalks that were about bloomed-out and ready to make bolls. If there was ever a planting capable of bringing in the cotton farmer's prayed-for bale-an-acre, this was it. But there was no acre. Two-tenths was what the government allotted him—two-tenths of an acre. And he planted it all.

The measuring did not take long, because the field-man brought his son to help. And when they finished he complimented the farmer on his crop, then wondered aloud why so much trouble was taken on so little. The question came from the perspective of efficiency, and economy, and use of time—things that mattered to the field-man. And the answer:

"But I gotta have something for my mule to do."

That came from the perspective of a man whose life was spent around cotton and animals, and he would stay with them as long as he could. And the field-man, who had grown up on a farm himself, and had gone off to war, and had come back to work in town and be part of the middle class, understood. And he would be happy to know that the boy, whom he had made help him measure the field when his friends were playing summer baseball, understood too.

US VERSUS THEM

It has never taken much to convince Alabamians that sinister forces were out to get them. For Israel Pickens that force was the Royal Party and its bank. William Lowndes Yancey warned the state of the antislavery conspiracy, laid and incubated by abolitionists, hatched by Republicans, and forced on the South by federal authority. After the war, Bourbon Democrats rallied white citizens with warnings of carpetbagger government, black rule, and federal occupation. Then the populists placed the blame for agriculture's problems at the feet of Bourbon merchants, industrialists, bankers, planters, and various combinations thereof. The Bourbons countered, shifted the blame to those they claimed "corrupted" the system—blacks, poor whites, and residual Republicans—and constitutionally cut them out. The depression briefly brought back populist urges, as Roosevelt denounced Republican "economic royalists" and set up agencies designed to make things better for the "little man." Meanwhile Alabama's own "economic royalists," Democrats of Bourbon ancestry, continued to control city halls and courthouses, congregated in banks and boardrooms, and waited for their chance to strike back.

About this same time, up in Washington Alabama's congressional delegation became masters at bringing popular programs to the state while comforting conservative constituents with the knowledge that the money for these efforts did not come directly from their pockets. Politically astute and socially sensitive for the most part, these senators and representatives first parlayed New Deal loyalty into generous federal grants to help people recover from the depression. After the war, with seniority on their side, the delegation continued this tradition. In time, Alabama was receiving so much aid from Washington, and sending so few tax dollars in return, that northerners began to complain that they were subsidizing the state. But as far as Alabama was concerned, it was just sour grapes. Yankees were jealous, that was all.

Well, not all Yankees were jealous. Because the programs created and championed by Alabama congressmen during the 1940s and into the 1950s—social services, housing, health care, highway projects, farm subsidies, and such—had an impact beyond Alabama, some folks liked what they were doing and said so. Or at least that was what it sounded like when, in 1955, the managing editor of the left-leaning *New Republic* wrote a friend asking "Why is it that Alabama in the last generation has produced so many more liberally minded public men than any of her neighboring states?"

We don't know what the friend answered, though "beats hell outta me" surely would not have been inappropriate and might even have been the truth. Or the friend could have pointed out that a stalk of corn stands tall in a field of peas, pointed out that it was not hard to appear "liberally minded" around congressfolk from Georgia, Mississippi, Tennessee, and Florida. Or he could have told the truth, that Alabama's public men looked "liberally minded" because they supported the Washington-based initiatives that "liberally minded" New Republic readers supported. And maybe he should have added that if the New Republic would send a reporter to Montgomery to meet the "public men" Alabamians sent there, instead of hanging out with the "public men" Alabamians sent to Washington, they'd see something else altogether.

Because that's what, by 1955, Alabama's liberally minded folks had become—something else all together. But we are getting ahead of the story.

JUST HOW LIBERAL WAS LIBERAL ALABAMA?

We must keep reminding ourselves that Alabama liberalism was linked, hip and thigh, to the federal government. Most liberal programs and reforms, those undertakings that improved the lives of poor-to-average citizens, would not, could not, have been undertaken, much less succeeded, without federal money and federal enforcement. Native, in-house attempts to use the resources of the state (including the wealth of its wealthiest) to improve the health, education, and welfare of the general population passed the legislature watered down and bland, if they passed at all.

And we must also remember that though some conservatives warned that federal money brought federal regulations, and that federal regulations meant federal enforcement, most conservatives did not get past the "federal money" part of the equation. They saw instead programs that relieved the pressure on them to do much for the common good. Washington would give liberals what they wanted, populist inclinations would be satisfied, voters would be happy, and no one in Montgomery would tell planters and industrialists what to do with their land, their labor, and their income.

It was a neat arrangement. Democrats sent to Washington could take a broad view of things, could author and sponsor legislation for the general welfare just like the constitution told them to do, and stand as a shining example for "liberally minded public men" everywhere—except, of course, at home. Back in Alabama they had to downplay their liberalism. So when visiting in the Black Belt they pointed out how the agricultural policies they supported were good for the planter and good for what economists were beginning to call agribusiness. When in Birmingham among steel barons and bankers, they reminded those folks of lukewarm labor stands and fiscal conservatism. What they did not say, but what conservatives surely noted, was that year by year Alabama's congressional delegation voted more and more like Republicans and less and less like Democrats.

But they were still part of the party of Roosevelt, as they told their labor supporters when they spoke to them. And labor, without many alternatives, took them at their word. Besides, when congressmen brought home the bacon, labor feasted with the rest.

Still, there were the grumblers. Back during the war, outgoing governor Frank Dixon, whose opposition to the New Deal seemed to grow with each year he was in office, warned fellow Democrats that "their own party [was] dynamiting their social structure, . . . arousing bitterness and recrimination, . . . [by] attempting to force crackpot reforms on them in a time of national crisis." Was he talking about fair labor policies? Was he upset over antidiscrimination efforts? Yes, both. And probably more. Concerned that the Democratic Party was becoming the party of organized labor, of urban interests, of expanded government, and of equal protection for all citizens regardless of race, Dixon and die-hard conservatives were beginning to feel their options narrowing. Pretty soon their choices would be down to two: They could either change the national party or get out. Then they would be down to one.

As disturbing to conservatives as the national party's drift was the direction state politics seemed to be taking. When Dixon went out of office in 1942, his supporters feared his cause would go with him. But then liberal champion Bibb Graves, who seemed certain of a third term, died before the election. With pro–New Deal forces in disarray, the big mule–planter coalition rallied around Chauncey Sparks, "the Bourbon from Barbour" County, and pushed him into office. It wasn't that hard, really. The only opposition left in the field was James E. Folsom, whose hulking six-foot, eight-inch frame gave him the nickname "Big Jim," and whose recognized sympathy for the common man got him some labor support. Sparks beat him without a runoff. But Folsom wasn't through, and four years later he made his second run for the state's top office. This time he won.

TAKING A RIDE WITH BIG JIM FOLSOM

Big Jim was the stuff from which legends are made, and though the legends are usually more colorful than the life, in Folsom, man comes about as close to myth as anyone could. Born on a small farm in the state's southeastern Wiregrass region, Folsom grew up in a politically active family, pulled together a high-school education, got a little college to go with it, held a variety of jobs, married well, played with politics, ran for Congress and lost, moved to Cullman, and was selling insurance when he got the news that Bibb Graves was sick and might not live to run for governor in 1942. A man of sincere populist sentiments, Folsom decided he would enter the race as a spokesman for the little man, and, if Graves faltered, he would pick up the liberal standard and run with it. But Big Jim was too new, too untried, and when Graves died, Folsom could not rally the fallen candidate's supporters to his side. Chauncey Sparks won, and Folsom went home.

He didn't stay on the sidelines long. During the next four years

Folsom shook up the Democratic establishment with his growing popularity among voters and with political positions that came down well to the left of Alabama's center. At the same time some of his personal foibles began to surface. Never shy about his love for liquor, Big Jim turned "bad to drink" when his wife died in 1944, and from then on alcohol plagued his career. Single now, he began the "woman chasing" that in time would have middle-class moralists shaking their heads and clicking their tongues in disapproval. So Folsom was carrying a lot of political baggage with him when he ran again for governor in 1946. He also had a lot going for him, for Big Jim Folsom was able to touch something in Alabama that had not been touched for some time—the popular mood.

That popular mood had more clout at the ballot box than it had since the days of Pickens and Yancey. Since the 1920s modest education reforms had increased the number of whites literate enough to pass the voter exam, and prosperity had given them the money to pay the poll tax, so scores of citizens who had once been disfranchised were qualified and ready. Many of these new voters were veterans, who saw Folsom as one of their own (he had served for a time in the Merchant Marine). These servicemen and women came home wanting and expecting more than the status quo. The federal government, with GI Bill educational and housing opportunities, was offering them something that was denied many before—entry into the middle class. Folsom promised that the state would help, that it would better educate the children they intended to have, remove the sales tax from the food they would feed their families, build farm-to-market roads to get them to town, improve worker compensation if they got hurt on the job, and have an old-age pension waiting for them as a reward at the end. And Folsom told them that the only folks who opposed the state's treating its people as they should be treated were landed interests in the Black Belt, big mules in the cities, and entrenched "courthouse gangs" in various county seats. Given the opportunity, Big Jim promised to revise the constitution that gave those few dominion over Alabama's many and to restore government to the people.

And he connected. Connected because Folsom seemed to understand, intuitively, that the culture from which he sought votes was essentially a folk culture, rural even in the towns and cities, personal, caring, suspicious, combative, rough around the edges, and proud of it. It was a culture in which feelings, impressions, meant more than rational conclusions, so the same intuition that told Big Jim how to approach them told them that he was "the little man's big friend," just as he said he was. And besides that, Folsom's Alabamians loved a show, and he gave them one.

With little support from courthouse gangs and big-city newspapers, Folsom fine-tuned the folksy style of his earlier campaigns and set out to meet people where they were. A county band called the Strawberry Pickers provided some of the entertainment, but the best performer was the candidate. Brandishing a "corn shuck mop" with which he promised to scrub Montgomery and a "suds bucket" which was passed around for contributions, "Big Jim" stumped the state. Speaking from the courthouse steps, from the back of a flatbed truck, outside in a grove of trees or in a union hall, he was willing to go to "the brush arbors and the forks of the creeks," anywhere he could draw a crowd, anywhere anyone would listen. And the people came, and they heard, and they believed.

Folsom's chief opponent was the lieutenant governor, Handy Ellis, former legislative floor leader for Bibb Graves, who would have been the liberal choice if Big Jim had not been a candidate. About all the conservative hopeful, Agriculture Commissioner Joe Poole, could do was throw the race into a runoff, which he did. And what a runoff it was. With most of the Graves gang supporting him, Ellis went to courting conservatives, driving the rest of labor into the Folsom camp. Then Ellis, desperate to break Big Jim's hold on the farmer vote, agreed to have his picture taken behind a plow mule—remember there were mules back then—just to show rural folks that he was more than city and sophistication. But whoever hitched the animal got the harness wrong. Folsom saw it right away. And soon Big Jim operatives were circulating copies of the picture around the state. Farmers were delighted. Conservatives cringed.

Meanwhile Jim Folsom did what successful politicians in Alabama have always done. He identified the people's enemies and called on the people to defeat them by electing him. The big mules and Black Belt planters, the courthouse rings and the big city newspapers, he told his audiences, "were satisfied with things the way they are. They are satisfied for Alabama to be way down at the bottom among the 48 states. They are satisfied for Alabama people to make less." But he wasn't satisfied, not Big Jim, and he swore that if they gave him the chance, things would change.

And he won. Smashed the coalition that had controlled the state for most of the century, dashed the predictions, upset the odds, then stood before an inaugural-day crowd of maybe a hundred thousand to celebrate his victory, their victory. All around rumors were flying that Folsom would see the poll tax repealed, would have the legislature reapportioned, would reform the tax structure, and would get the state a new constitution. It looked like a revolution. The old order was defeated on every level. Nearly three-quarters of the legislators elected that year were freshmen. Everyone expected, or in some cases feared, that a new day was dawning.

Then reality set in. Although the legislature was new, the system wasn't. The Constitution of 1901, written to preserve the status quo, was still in place, doing what it was designed to do. Barred from a second term, Folsom was a "lame duck" from the minute he took office. Opponents knew that if they could delay him, block him, wait him out, in four years he would be gone. So they went to work on the legislators, who would be running again and would need their support.

In Montgomery agents of the status quo seemed to come out of the woodwork. Friendly folks from the Alabama Power Company, the Farm Bureau, the League of Municipalities, and the Association of County Commissioners passed around estimates of how much Folsom's "People's Program" would cost and reminded newly elected legislators that raising taxes had ended many a promising political career. Leaning close, they warned that changes in election laws might open the door for blacks to vote. They whispered to rural representatives that a reapportioned legislature would let urban interests run the state. And they pointed out to anyone who would listen that a constitution rewritten by Folsom supporters would undermine the social structure on which Alabama's political system was based. United, perhaps, as never before, conservative forces lobbied, cajoled, coerced, and compromised in an effort to convince freshmen legislators that they should vote as the folks they replaced had voted.

All this effort notwithstanding, the conservatives' task was not all that difficult. Though many new delegates were elected on an "it's time for a change" platform, the changes they sought were seldom as sweeping as what Big Jim proposed. Firmly grounded in their counties and communities, freshmen saw service in Montgomery from a local rather than a state perspective. Their political base was back home, and back home most of them were friends with the very folks—courthouse gangs, landlords, merchants, mill bosses, and steel barons—that Big Jim ran against or ignored. They did not have to go very far to come around. Although a core of old populist, pro-labor, and antiestablishment legislators from the industrial towns and hardscrabble hills of North Alabama resisted conservative entreaties (if any were made) and hung in with Big Jim all the way to the end, they soon were reduced to little more than a reminder of what New Deal liberalism once was and a commentary on what it had become. As for the rest, once lobbyists "'splained" things to them, the "People's Program" didn't have a chance. The revolution ended, not with a bang, but with a whimper.

But Big Jim's biggest enemy may have been Big Jim. Distrustful of a press that did not support him, he seldom gave reporters from what he called the "lying newspapers" much of substance to write about. So they were left with the showman, which they dutifully reported with caustic enthusiasm. And since newspaper readers were, for the most part, establishment folk who were less than enamored with "Big Jim" in the first place, the stories reinforced their belief that he was a loose cannon who needed to be tied down, a potential embarrassment to Alabama and Alabamians.

This gnawing conviction seemed confirmed on 3 June 1946, the day before the runoff, when an article about the Alabama campaign appeared in *Life* magazine. In reality, it was an article about Big Jim, whom the writer described as "an indifferently successful insurance salesman," whose "burly backwoods friendliness" made him a colorful candidate but who did not have much of a chance of beating his "politically entrenched" opponent. By the time most *Life*-reading Alabamians got their copy in the mail, they knew that once again the national media had gotten it wrong. Big Jim had won. He was the Democratic nominee—which in Alabama meant he was the governor-elect.

And what a governor-elect *Life* introduced to the nation. Though most of the pictures were what one would expect—Folsom with his mop, Folsom with the bucket, Folsom shaking hands with voters— at the end were three obviously posed "candid" shots that showed what has been charitably called "the more undignified side of Big Jim." One caught the candidate for governor kissing a tiptoed candidate for Strawberry Queen full on the mouth, while two other beauties crowded close for their turn. A second, a family dinner setting, showed Folsom, barefoot and in his undershirt, shoveling food in with his hands (okay, it was probably fried chicken, but still . . .). And the third, an end-of-a-hard-day-on-the-campaign-trail shot, had the grinning candidate, all six feet, eight inches of him, folded into a suds-filled bathtub, his knees almost as high as his chin. For anyone concerned about Alabama's "image," it was a public relations nightmare.

And it wasn't over. A few weeks later in Daytona Beach, Florida, an Associated Press photographer snapped the city's mayor, dignified in his businessman's suit, extending an official greeting to Alabama's next governor, attired in a flowered shirt, swimming trunks, and, of course, barefoot. The picture went out to all AP affiliates, and the "good people of Alabama" cringed. Meanwhile up in Montgomery some of the very folks Folsom was counting on as allies were having second thoughts. "Big Jim can't help it if he's a fool," one of the newly elected representatives reportedly said, "but he could stay home." The tide was turning.

Once in office Folsom was again his own worst enemy. Proving no sounder in his ability to judge people than he was in his ability to order his personal life, the new governor consistently picked the wrong folks to guide his initiatives, so legislation languished in committees, where it was often amended beyond recognition. Efforts to undermine the coalition of interests united against him only made Folsom's position worse. Bill after bill went down in defeat. The poll tax was not repealed, the legislature was not reapportioned, and the constitution was not rewritten. There may have been a liberal in the governor's office, but in the house and in the senate, conservatives held sway.

Those who supported Big Jim in hopes that he would clean up corruption in Montgomery saw those hopes dashed when reports of rigged bids and bribery began to appear in the press. Critics, of course, had a field day, and their "I told you so" carping became a chorus when early in the governor's second year in office, a Cullman County woman claimed in court that he was the father of her twenty-two-month-old son. Now a man with Folsom's record for drinking and carousing had been the subject of all sorts of rumors, and sexual impropriety was one of the many. But Big Jim was usually able to deflect such suggestions with candor and humor. Once when he was accused of sleeping with a woman in a Phenix City motel, the governor shot back, "That's a lie, nobody slept." This latest charge, however, proved to be true, and though Folsom's friends paid off the woman and the case was dropped, the story made the national news and, once again, Alabama's governor stood accused of making Alabama look bad. In the midst of the scandal, Big Jim remarried, which quieted some of the gossip, but critics were not content to let the matter rest. One of them even memorialized it in a song:

She was poor, but she was honest,
Victim of a rich man's whim.
Took a ride with Big Jim Folsom,
And she had a child by him.

Now he sits in the governor's office,
Making laws for all mankind.
While she walks the streets of Cullman, Alabama,
Selling grapes from her grape vine.

Now the moral of this story,
Is don't ever take a ride,
With that southern, Christian gentleman, Big Jim Folsom,
And you'll be a virgin bride.

What it may have come down to was this: Though Big Jim might have intuitively sensed the popular mood in 1946, that mood rapidly changed, and Big Jim did not change with it. Or maybe what he missed was that the mood was many layered, and those layers were unstable, shifting. Part of Folsom's populist appeal was his "good ol' boy" disregard for the rules that governed middle-class society—folks like the Hurts, you remember the Hurts, voted for him as one of their own. But Folsom seemed to forget populism's pious side, a near puritanical faith nurtured in little country churches, where whiskey and sex were condemned as regularly, and with as much enthusiasm, as they were by middle-class moralists. Big Jim's personal conduct put these folks in a bind, for though they found a lot to like in his political and economic reforms, they found it increasingly difficult to support the man behind them.

Folsom also seemed to have missed, or at least ignored, the fact that a new struggle with new enemies was becoming more important to Alabamians than the class struggle against consolidated wealth and corporate power. No sooner was he in office than America was mired in the Cold War, and concern over Communism was being felt in every level of society. Playing on these fears, conservatives spread the word that leftist labor leaders had bought Big Jim with union endorsements. And when the governor vetoed a bill requiring an anticommunist loyalty oath for state employees, those charges seemed confirmed. The veto might have been an act of principle and courage, as liberals claimed, but to folks who feared that "Godless Communism" was abroad on the land, the man who swore to protect them was not doing his job.

Maybe the thing that really got him, and would get future reformers, was that many Alabamians were turning conservative because for the first times in their lives they thought they had something to conserve. Veterans came home ready to shake things up, but once educated on the GI Bill and comfortable in homes bought with VA loans, they began to take a different view of the matter. Becoming, and joining, rising merchants and first-generation professional folk in the cities, towns, and villages, or going back to the farm, selling the mule, and buying a tractor, they discovered that the status quo wasn't so bad when you were part of it. In short, they became the core of Alabama's new middle class, and as they settled into their status, they quickly adopted its values and its prejudices.

Finally making enough to pay income taxes, they resented sending their money to Montgomery where, conservatives told them, Big Jim and his buddies would spend some of it on women and whiskey and waste the rest. And they nodded knowingly when told of how Washington was squandering resources on useless programs and sorry people, while hardworking taxpayers like themselves footed the bill. The fact that Alabama was still getting back more federal money than it paid in taxes didn't matter. Where the money went was the issue. And they were sure it wasn't going to them.

Meanwhile all those rules and regulations that counted for something during the New Deal were becoming a burden, an intrusion into places where government didn't belong. Small farmers in particular complained about the Department of Agriculture's telling them how much to plant and penalizing them if they did not comply. But their complaints were mysteriously myopic. They realized that federal policy was designed to drive them off the land, calculated to force small, inefficient farms to fail. However, they did not seem to consider how this policy actually helped the planters and processors who were courting their support, asking for their votes to preserve the state status quo. So small farmers rallied to larger agricultural interests they believed were their allies, never seeming to understand why things got better for the big man and not for them. They resented the agencies that ran the programs but not the local landlords who benefited. And as their resentment of Washington grew, it would be easy to convince them that the federal government was a threat to their well-being in many other ways.

So it was that Alabama's new middle class, and those still striving to be part of it, began to look, think, and act more and more like the middle class of old. They began to complain about taxes and bureaucracy, about burdens without benefits. They were coming to see their interests tied more closely to those above them in the economic hierarchy than to those below. Class solidarity, on which Folsom's populism heavily depended, was crumbling. Big mules and planters weren't the problem—"gubment" was.

Or at least that is what these folks thought—these white folks.

RACISM REARS ITS UGLY HEAD

That's what they were, mostly, white folks.

Which is not to suggest that there was not a black middle class, for there was, or that there were not black Alabamians who were fed up with government rules and regulations, for there were, but just to point out what is probably obvious, that in Alabama at mid century, political trends were white trends. But don't go thinking that African Americans did not matter, for they did. And they would matter a lot more before the century was over.

It was just that they did not matter much in politics, not back then. Once again, the authors of the Constitution of 1901 had done what they set out to do. For all intents and purposes there was no black electorate in Alabama. Progressive Alabamians could brag that while there had been "incompetent governors, greedy governors, good, bad, and indifferent governors," Alabama had "been spared the shame of having a vicious governor or one willing to exploit the Negro issue," but it was a hollow boast. There was little reason for candidates to use race as an issue, because it wasn't one. Relegated to second class in every capacity of civic life, black folks simply did not mean much to white folks, unless there was work to be done.

Even Big Jim, whose liberal credentials were about as good as anyone's back then, did not have much to say on the matter. When he spoke of ending the poll tax, he spoke of how it discriminated against the poor in general, and it was in that context that he usually supported black rights. Though Folsom seemed to believe that African Americans were due what any citizen was due under the U.S. Constitution, he nonetheless supported segregation and may have been about as close to a true "separate but equal" governor as the state ever had. But Big Jim's admitting that "there are sections of Alabama where a Negro doesn't stand a Chinaman's chance of getting fair and impartial justice on an equal footing with white men" was one thing. Big Jim's doing something about it was another. In Alabama's conservative-dominated legislature, any bill that might improve the lot of black citizens was doomed from the start. Still, Folsom left no doubt that his sympathies lay with the poor of both races.

He also left no doubt that he believed that the Democratic Party, the national Democratic Party, had the interests of his supporters at heart. In 1948 when states' rights, white supremacy zealots from the lower South bolted to form a third party, dubbed the Dixiecrats by the press, Folsom welcomed their convention to Birmingham. Then he went back to Montgomery and from there fought Dixiecrat efforts to get control of the state party machinery. But the Dixiecrat platform struck the right note with Alabama's big mules, planters, and middle-class conservatives, and that proved enough to keep the Democratic nominee, Harry Truman, off the ballot. Though Big Jim did have the satisfaction of seeing the Dixiecrats defeated and Truman elected, he surely knew that they would return. He just didn't know when or how.

When measured against his other troubles, the Dixiecrats seemed a minor problem, or at least Big Jim dismissed them as such. Trying to get his bills through the legislature and bring order to his personal life was enough. If the big mules and the planters wanted to play with national politics, fine with him. He expected them to fail and was delighted when they did.

So it was that by the end of Big Jim's first term in office, Alabama seemed a state of two political minds. At home conservatives held sway, still preaching on the ancient text of low taxes, limited government, and white supremacy. And yet the same voters who supported the status quo in Montgomery sent a team of liberal senators and congressmen to Washington, charged with the responsibility of taking up the slack when the state failed to provide. Alabama was, in a sense, having it both ways. And if anyone saw the irony in this, they mostly kept it to themselves.

BIG JIM GONE AND BACK AGAIN

Folsom's failure became apparent in the election of 1950, when his handpicked successor was badly defeated by Gordon Persons, the quiet, easy-going, dignified president of the Public Service Commission, whose promise of "four years of no fussin', no fightin', and no feudin'" was welcomed by Alabamians rich and poor, urban and rural. Though clearly the choice of conservatives, Persons was a loyal Democrat, and in that sense he represented a victory over the states' rights wing of the party. Though his election was hardly evidence of Alabama liberalism getting "a new lease on life," as Birmingham's black press heralded it, it did represent a shift back to the center, or at least what passed for the center in Alabama. Prison reform, more money for education and highways were his priorities, and he succeeded because he did not aim too high. He also oversaw the hiring of a new football coach for Auburn, put a public cussing on a reporter from the *Montgomery Advertiser,* signed legislation to keep communists from holding public office (which must have worked, for none ever did), supported efforts to find new ways to keep blacks from voting (just in case federal courts struck down the ones they had), and was antiunion enough to keep the big mules off his back. In other words, he made a lot of folks happy, without making too many mad—a balance that can pass for success in Alabama.

The Persons interlude gave Big Jim a moment to recharge his batteries, and when it came time to run, he was ready. So were a host of other candidates, and once again the campaign for governor in Alabama became a national news event. Folsom, of course, was at the center. Playing the populist theme for all it was worth, he blunted criticism of corruption with the admission that "shore I stole, but I stole for you." Accused of nepotism, he responded, "you wouldn't want me to hire a stranger, would you?" And when anyone brought up his weakness for women, the now happily married candidate would grin, and admit that "if my political enemies troll a pretty gal by ol' Jim, they'll catch him every time."

The people loved it.

But Folsom had learned in his last term that the populist appeal could go only so far. Though farmers and union workers were still his core constituency, his slogan—"Y'all Come"—hinted at his openness to a more diverse coalition of supporters. Working for the election of friendly legislators while he sought votes for himself, Folsom made sure that he would have allies when he needed them. So when the votes came in and Big Jim Folsom had won the 1954 Democratic primary without a runoff, there was a general feeling that the failures of his first administration would not be repeated in the second.

Then, one week after his victory, the United States Supreme Court handed down its decision in the case of *Brown v. Board of Education of Topeka, Kansas.* That changed everything.

12

Old Times There Should Not Be Forgotten

A LITTLE SOMETHING ABOUT THE WAY THINGS WERE, AT LEAST TO WHITE FOLKS

It is hard to explain, even now, after thinking about it so many years, just why segregation worked. Not how it worked—rules, regulations, customs, conventions, laws, and legalisms can accomplish all sorts of injustices—but why? Why so many good white people, church-going decent people, moral middle-class people who would give to the poor, visit the sick and shut-ins, comfort the afflicted, and bring hope to the hopeless, would allow it. But they did.

Acknowledging this is difficult, for I grew up in the mid-century white middle-class of small-town Alabama. These people were my people, so a lot of what follows is memoir as well as history. I knew them well. They were the first to respond with money, clothes, and such when a black family (or even a poor white family) lost everything in one of those winter house fires that flared up when cold weather came and people in drafty shacks tried to keep warm. No hearts were ever moved more frequently or more sincerely, yet no eyes were ever averted more easily. And no people were ever hurt more deeply when outsiders pointed to the inconsistency, the irony, the hypocrisy of the system. It was bad enough to be told that you were wrong. It was worse still when you suspected, feared, that the other side was right. And understand this. I am convinced that deep down in some silent recess, we knew it.

Why else would we go to such lengths to justify—"They can't take care of themselves, so we gotta look after them." (Notice how often black folks were reduced to pronouns.) Rationalize—"They would rather keep to theirs, just like we would rather keep to ours." Biologize—"Their skulls are thicker than the white man's, so there is less room for brains," a high school science teacher told his class. Sanctify—"God made the races different because he didn't want them to mix." Even glorify—tell of how an always-unidentified black man was heard to say "if you ever a nigger on Saturday night, you'll never want to be white again."

We white folks knew, suspected, but we did not speak it out. Why? In part, I am convinced, because we came to believe our own excuses. Or, at the least, to prefer them to any alternative. White southerners had done that before. We did it with slavery. And we also did it with poor whites, who were accepted as a breed apart. And we, in this case the white male "we," did it with women, convinced ourselves that they should not serve on juries and should stay out of politics—except to vote. Put simply, white Alabamians came to accept the system as being what it was because that was what it was meant to be. Outsiders, Yankees usually, may call it hypocrisy, but it really wasn't. It was conviction.

More than that, white folks assumed it would never end. Big Jim might warn one of his Black Belt opponents to watch out because when the courts extended the franchise to African Americans "you'll be seeing more niggers in the legislature than you have ever seen on your farm." But it was said in jest and heard the same way. A third-grade teacher might tell her class that if you take the skin off a black person and a white person and lay them side by side "you can't tell the difference," but she would never suggest that the same thing might be true with the skin on. And come Sunday whites could sing:

Jesus loves the little children,
All the children of the world.
Red and yellow, black and white,

They are precious in his sight.

Jesus loves the little children of the world.

because nobody seemed to think the song was about the ones down in the quarters, swinging on rusted swings in a tumbled-down park that showed "separate but equal" for what it was. To most white middle-class Alabamians, segregation was just there. It had been there before they were born, and despite what they heard the Supreme Court had ruled, they were sure it would be there long after they were gone.

But there were some whites, those down a little lower on the economic scale, those whose whiteness was about all that separated them from blacks, who did think about it. And when the word came that some court had said they had to integrate, these whites asked what "integrate" meant, and recoiled in horror when they were told. One of them sent his son to school to ask his teacher, "What you gonna do when the niggers come?" as if black kids had already packed their books and were waiting for the bell to ring so they could walk out and over and in. And when she told him, "I will teach any child that wants to learn" he went and told his daddy who told his friends, and that night the teacher's phone rang and a sinister voice at the other end explained to her that it wasn't the right answer and she better think again. There was fear, then, on both ends of the line, only the caller wouldn't have admitted it.

So the "good white folks" got scared, scared by threats from white folks they hardly knew and with whom they had little association, and who they believed—and said to each other—were "as sorry as the sorriest nigger." These others knew how "good white folks" felt about them and suspected, believed, that if blacks kept pushing, the middle class would compromise, would give blacks a little so they would not take a lot. And they figured, the whites at the bottom did, that what blacks would be given would come from them. So when whites wavered, looked like they might give in, diehards called them "nigger lover," and the wavering ceased.

Words mattered back then, just as they do today. Children from "good" families were told to use "colored," since that was what "they preferred to be called," not thinking that "they" might have preferred not to be identified by race at all. And were told that only "trash" called them "niggers," and no one wanted to be "trash." So children learned what not to say, or what to say if they wanted to cut deep, and in time it was hard to tell which was the worst insult—to be called one, or someone who loved one.

What did the black folks call whites? Whites didn't know. Blacks didn't say it where whites could hear. Not yet.

But understand this: It wasn't just a class thing. When it came to simple humanity, many of the "best" white people were poor, and their poverty taught them that race didn't matter as much. And many of our most hardened racists drove nice cars, lived in nice homes, and sent their kids to nice schools—schools that were among the last to integrate, just as working-class whites had figured.

Still, putting it simply, this can be said: Whites of all classes liked for blacks of all classes to be at the bottom. Whites liked blacks courteous, deferential, subservient, cheerful, and available when there was work to be done. The rest of the time they liked them out of the way. Which is where most African American Alabamians stayed—for a while.

"IT AIN'T NECESSARILY SO"

You will never lose money betting on how little segregated white folks like me knew about segregated black folks. And, from talking to black Alabamians who today finally feel comfortable discussing race relations under segregation, it is safe to say that they didn't know much about whites either. But, let me add, both sides thought they knew more than they did. Further, the two sides seemed to act more often on what they believed was true, but wasn't, than on what they believed wasn't true, but was.

Confused? So were things back then.

Like most other whites, my contact with the black side of segregation was incidental and episodic. Most of what I know came later, from reading memories written down or told in an effort to explain how it was to be "colored" in a world run by whites. Or one that whites thought they ran. So it was that I became familiar with the way black Alabamians created a culture that was vibrant and strong, colorful, sophisticated, spiritual, and a little sassy. And so it was that I came to regret that I never knew this culture except from a distance, an observer, one of those whites who would drive out to a black Baptist church on Sunday night and sit outside in cars to hear the singing—but never go in.

Had I entered I would have found myself among people who, denied access to white establishments, had created their own. In Mobile, along the street named, with a sweet irony, for the president of the Confederacy, black Alabamians built "a city within a city." There they operated and in many cases owned department stores, specialty shops, motion picture houses, lodges, a social center, drugstores, and offices. The same was true in Birmingham, Selma, Montgomery, Huntsville, and most other cities and towns where there were enough African Americans to constitute a community. There were also the churches, descendants in name (sometimes) and spirit (always) of those churches that were created during Reconstruction, that comforted members during the dark days when the state turned lynchers into heroes and continued to sustain and encourage despite all the indignities heaped on by Jim Crow.

And the schools. In spite of the obvious disparities between the physical settings in which black and white children were educated, black schools were at the center of the black community. They offered hope, instilled values, taught self-respect, and pointed the way for a better life. Say what you will about the people who marched and sacrificed and struggled for the rights others took for granted, among the things they had in common, the most significant may have been that they were educated in Alabama schools.

So then, there were two worlds, apart, and yet both of them came together from time to time to let the populations of each get a glimpse of what life was like in the other. But it was only a glimpse, and imperfectly seen. So it was easy to assume that things were the way you wanted them to be.

THE MOVEMENT BEGINS

In 1941 an anonymous employee of the Federal Writers' Project revealed just how little white folks of what might be called the "liberal persuasion" knew about the feelings and frustrations that dogged Negroes. Commenting on black Birmingham, the writer admitted that "color prejudice" handicapped that race but assured readers that the situation was not as bad as it seemed. Blacks were at ease in their world. Whites were at ease in theirs. Even when the two appeared to intersect, as they did when the races used public transportation, they contentedly stayed apart. And why shouldn't they, the writer went on, since the black "end of the street car [was] as comfortable, if not as commodious, as the other"?

See what I mean? Today we know, have been told, that it wasn't a matter of comfort. Nor even where you sat. It was having to sit there, like having to use "colored" restrooms and drinking fountains and waiting rooms and such. It was those daily indignities piled high by white folks not so much to keep blacks out of their lives as to remind blacks who was in control. And it was that black folks were expected to abide by the rules and act as if they liked them, for by the liking they assured the rule-makers that segregation was, as whites would later argue, "preferred by both races."

It came down to this: Whites believed there was an understanding, an arrangement, unspoken but binding, under which blacks agreed to accept white authority in matters between them so that, in everything else, they would be left alone. That the agreement was not negotiated but imposed mattered little to whites, who liked to believe that blacks were as comfortable with it as they were. This defined race relations in Alabama. Those who accepted the arrangement, lived by its rules, were generally admired by and in both communities—at least that was the way it seemed to whites. As for those who didn't? Whites who violated the rules, who abused blacks "for no good reason" (a revealing phrase if ever there was one) became the object of disdain and, occasionally, legal redress, while blacks in violation usually "got what they deserved." One incident brings this into focus.

There was this sheriff—who and where doesn't matter. He was the law in his county. He never carried a gun. He didn't need one. He was the "High Sheriff." No one crossed him. Usually. But one night a young black man challenged the sheriff's authority, said something the sheriff thought was uppity, impertinent, so the sheriff took out a blackjack and knocked the man to the ground. As he lay there bruised, maybe bleeding, he looked up and accused:

"You hit me 'cause I'm a nigger."

"No," the sheriff replied, "I hit you 'cause you forgot you are a nigger."

And that should have been the end of it. Under the arrangement the violator, put "in his place," should have gone back to being what he was supposed to be—or at least should have given that appearance to whites—and the matter would have been closed.

Only it didn't end there, it couldn't. You see, that incident occurred outside a meeting where black folks were listening to a speaker telling them that it was time to abrogate the agreement, to end it. That, reduced to its essence, was what the Civil Rights movement was really about and why it unnerved so many whites. The movement freed black folks from pretending to like what they hated and told whites to quit pretending as well.

It seems only fitting that it all began in a bus.

"MY SOUL IS RESTED"

It seems also fitting that it began in Montgomery. At mid century Alabama's capital was about as segregated as any town in the state, but among its population was an African American community that had been pushing, sometimes not too gently, against the limits set by the white establishment. Black ministers, returning veterans, faculty from all-black Alabama State College, club women, and labor leaders had, at various times and in various ways, challenged the rules that defined their second-class status. And of these restrictions, few were more galling than the city's segregation ordinance that governed who sat where on city buses.

Here was the deal, the arrangement. Ten seats in the front of the bus were set aside for whites, while the remaining twenty-six were for blacks. Whites considered this ratio fair since a solid majority of the riders were African Americans. The line between the two sections was marked by an arrow attached to the last white seat. But the arrow could be moved, so if the white section filled, the bus driver had the authority to take seats from blacks. Some whites wouldn't let the driver do it, refused to displace black riders, and stood instead. And if the white rider was a woman, it was not uncommon for black men to move even before the bus driver ordered them to—common courtesy. But far too often whites took what they considered theirs by right of color. And each time they did, black anger grew.

Anger was one thing. Action was another. And when it came to action, Montgomery's black community was divided on what to do. For years many black leaders had lived within that unspoken agreement, had worked with white officials, and had tried to minimize points where confrontations might occur. Seeing little to gain from challenging white authority, they tried to keep restive blacks in check, control that, by 1955, was getting more and more difficult. In March of that year when a fifteen-year-old girl was arrested for refusing to give up her bus seat, the grumbling began. But black leaders, men mostly, discussed the issue among themselves and decided that the girl's "attitude" during the incident would keep her from being a sympathetic symbol and that her case was not one on which to make a stand. It should be noted, however, that not everyone agreed. The Women's Political Council, led by Alabama State English professor Jo Ann Robinson, let it be known then and again when a similar incident occurred in October that they were not sure how sympathetic black men were to the indignities suffered by black women.

Then it happened to Rosa Parks. That was another matter altogether. Mrs. Parks was, as Dr. Martin Luther King Jr. later described her, "one of the finest citizens in Montgomery—not one of the finest Negro citizens, but one of the finest citizens in Montgomery." Refined, gentle, soft-spoken, a skilled seamstress at a major department store as opposed to a domestic worker, she was considered by blacks (as well as the few whites who knew her) to be a "lady." She was, again to see her in white eyes, an example of "what a Negro can be if she puts her mind to it." But there was another side to Mrs. Parks. She was a long-time, active member of the NAACP, and she had attended meetings where ways to challenge racial restrictions had been discussed. In short, though Rosa Parks may not have planned to do what she did that December day in 1955, she was prepared to do it.

The bus was almost full when Mrs. Parks got on and sat just behind the arrow. Soon there were no empty seats in either section, so when the next white got on—a man by the way—the driver ordered the four blacks in the front row of their section to stand. They hesitated; the driver came back and insisted. ("You better make it light on yourselves and let me have those seats," he said.) Three obeyed. Rosa Parks did not.

Mrs. Parks calmly told the driver that she was not in the white section so there was no reason to move. The driver responded that the white section was where he said it was, and she was in it. Again she refused. So he told her that the ordinance that drew the line gave him the power to arrest her. She knew that, of course, but still refused. So he ordered her not to leave her seat, which was the whole point anyway, while he went for the police. He left and returned with an officer, and Rosa Parks was taken to jail.

A word about jail. While most white Alabamians never gave jail much thought, to black Alabamians jail, incarceration, was the ultimate symbol of their oppression. Among the questions movement leaders asked recruits, "Are you able to endure the ordeal of jail?" may have been the most frightening. Blacks of every age and class had heard the stories of how so-and-so was "picked up" and taken to that place beyond help or hope, and how he didn't come back—or if he did, he was much changed. And the horrors that awaited there were magnified if the crime was a violation of the racial code, for blacks instinctively knew that white supremacy could not be maintained by laws alone, that terror had to be used as well. So it should come as no surprise that once Mrs. Parks was finally allowed to use the jail telephone, she called her mother, whose first question was, "Did they beat you?"

But back then arrest and jail also divided the black community, separated the solid, upstanding, law-abiding Negroes from what even some of them called "niggers," in the same tone that solid, upstanding, law-abiding whites spoke of "trash." The arrest of Mrs. Parks required a reevaluation. She was not one of the incorrigibles, not one of the troublemakers whose names seemed always on the list of "usual suspects" when the law was broken. She was respected and deserved to be. Yet they arrested her. And the news spread round:

"They've put Mrs. Parks in jail."

Then someone would ask, "Why?"

"'Cause she wouldn't give up her bus seat to a white man."

And people started thinking, "That ain't no crime. That's just doing what's right." And maybe, at that moment, some people began to believe that there were worse things than jail, and that there were good reasons for going there.

So Mrs. Parks's mother called E. D. Nixon, head of the local NAACP, and Nixon called Clifford Durr, a white lawyer whose rare racial liberalism had cost him most of his clients, and together they bailed her out. Then they took Mrs. Parks home and put the question to her—"Are you willing to use your arrest to challenge segregation?" She understood what they were asking. So did her family. Her husband didn't want her to: "The white folks will kill you, Rosa." And she feared they might. So she thought it out, then she said "yes."

It was night by then, Thursday night, and in the darkness the decision by one brave black woman standing up to the system was transformed, remade, and sprung upon an unsuspecting and unready white Montgomery. There is still some disagreement about how it happened, whose idea it was, but the fact remains that before dawn Nixon and Jo Ann Robinson had decided that a one-day bus boycott on Monday would dramatize their determination. While Nixon called black ministers and other community leaders, Robinson and the Woman's Political Council circulated hundreds of leaflets telling what had happened to Mrs. Parks and challenging "every Negro to stay off the buses on Monday in protest."

Over the weekend black people talked, preachers preached, and white people worried because blacks were not acting black anymore. And they pulled it off. It was still dark and bitterly cold when the first buses rolled into the black neighborhoods, pulled up at their usual stops, then drove away, empty. It was like that all over town. White officials sent out word that black "goon squads" were keeping blacks from riding, but the police never found any. What they found instead was what whites had come to believe would never, could never happen. They found a revolt against segregation.

One demonstration was not enough, so the blacks kept it going, going for 381 days of carpooling, of hitched rides, of crowded taxies, and of walking—miles and miles of walking. They faced and withstood angry employers, lost jobs, taunts, and threats. But they succeeded, succeeded one suspects, because at the core of the protest were walkers like the seventy-two-year-old woman who, when someone (maybe a white rider passing by) asked her if she was tired, answered, "My feets is tired, but my soul is at rest."

MLK

The story of that woman was told a little over eight years later by the Rev. Martin Luther King Jr. in a letter he wrote while being held in jail in Birmingham for leading demonstrations there. A lot had happened between Montgomery and Birmingham, and King had been at the center of most of it. But the bus boycott was not his boycott. He came to the cause late and, by his own admission, reluctantly. The recently arrived minister of the small but influential black-establishment Dexter Avenue Baptist Church, King was not well known, especially by whites, which Negro leaders saw as an advantage. So when the Montgomery Improvement Association was created to carry the boycott to whatever its conclusion would be, King was picked as its president. He was twenty-six years old.

Almost overnight, or so it seems now, looking back, this young preacher became one of the most admired, and most hated, men in Alabama. Arrested with Nixon and others, for "conspiracy to boycott," he made the national news, and soon King was in demand as a speaker and was gone from the state. From then on, though Dexter Avenue would still be his church, Alabamians would hear more of him as the head of the Southern Christian Leadership Conference (SCLC) and of his attempts to do in other states what he and Nixon and Robinson had done in Montgomery. But King would often come back, back to preach the Gospel and inspire his people. And when he did, white Alabama took note.

It has been said that a people reveal their deepest anxieties when their reaction to a threat is far greater than the threat itself. Look at the boycott's initial demands. Fairer seating was certainly a priority, but above that, maybe above all else, African Americans wanted "to have more courtesy on the part of bus drivers, to eliminate them calling our women . . . cows and niggers and things like that," to be, in short, treated like human beings. But Montgomery officials would not give in, would not compromise, and some whites, reading into their intransigence permission to act, acted.

Once the boycott began, the dark, desperate, mean side of segregation, the side that hid behind jailhouse walls and under the cover of night, came out where it could be seen and reported throughout the land. It came as bombers, to Nixon's house, and to King's, and to the homes of other civil rights leaders in other cities. The bombs, the violence came courtesy of Klansmen, working-class whites who feared and resented at a deep, gut level and responded the same way.

No one was really surprised. That was the sort of people they were. But now there was something new in the mix. Now the Klan had allies from higher up the social, economic, and political ladder. And the nation was about to see just how far white Alabama would go to preserve white supremacy.

Not long after the *Brown* decision, a group of Mississippians, middle and upper class mostly, politicians and those with political connections, folks who, for the most part, would never have joined the Klan, got together and organized the White Citizens' Council. Its purpose was to use economic intimidation to force blacks to give up any efforts to integrate the schools, or anything else for that matter. The fact that they had the economic clout to make good on their plan separates them from most Klansmen, whose financial status was generally closer to that of the blacks whose ambitions they opposed. Violence was a Klansman's only resort, and he used it.

Brown wasn't enough to get Alabama's more affluent racists to follow Mississippi's lead, but when blacks started boycotting buses in Montgomery, that attitude changed. The first Alabama White Citizens' Council was formed in Dallas County shortly after the boycott began. Soon it moved its headquarters to Montgomery, closer to the action, and by the end of January 1956 membership in the capital was up to over nine thousand. So now the classes, at least the white classes, were united. And though the White Citizens' Council is often pictured as more moderate than the Klan in its response to black restiveness, the fact remains that the two groups complemented each other and the line between their attitudes and tactics was a fine one indeed.

But where was the governor? Where was Big Jim? Now of course Big Jim was not the mayor, so he really did not have much to say about how the city responded to black demands. However, with his office came a certain authority, clout, which he might have used to bring the two sides together, if he had a good rapport with each. But he didn't.

Though Folsom was generally trusted in the black community, segregationist whites had long wondered just how committed he was to their cause. Now as we have seen, Big Jim was no integrationist, but he did believe that blacks, like poor whites, had been treated unfairly. He also felt that both should have all the rights due them as citizens—including the right to vote. Such sentiments did not sit well with politicians from the Black Belt, where African Americans were in the majority, and Montgomery, of course, was in the Black Belt.

To make matters worse, the governor seemed to delight in pointing out that if Negroes "had been making a living for me like they have for the Black Belt, I'd be proud of them instead of kicking them and cussing them all of the time." No, local white supremacists did not figure they would get much sympathy from Big Jim.

This feeling was confirmed by an event that occurred just before the boycott began. In November 1955 Harlem congressman Adam Clayton Powell arrived in Montgomery for a rally to encourage blacks to make every effort to register and vote. Powell was, to put it mildly, white Alabama's nightmare—a Negro who did not act like a Negro because he did not have to. Articulate, sophisticated, self-assured (arrogant or uppity, according to whites), politically powerful, and economically independent, he was not the sort of role model Councilmen and Klansmen wanted at large in the state. But to Folsom Powell was a visiting congressman and deserved to be treated as such. So he sent a car with his personal chauffeur (who was black) to pick up the congressman, show him the city, and bring him to the governor's mansion, where the two of them discussed race relations over drinks. Then that evening when Powell addressed the gathering, he thanked Folsom for his hospitality, mentioned how pleased he was to find a southern governor who would invite a Negro into his home as a social equal and over "scotch and soda" would admit that integration in Alabama was "inevitable."

White folks went ballistic. If Big Jim and his advisors had actually wanted to alienate all but the most liberal segment of state society, they could not have come up with a better way to do it. Who Powell was, what office he held, made no difference to most white Alabamians. What he was—a black man, and one with an attitude—

was what mattered. Folsom should have known that sending a state employee with a state car to bring Powell to the governor's mansion would enrage many white Alabamians. Then to sit down with him and have a drink. Of the things whites and blacks did not do together, *sitting and drinking* were high on the list. Big Jim should have known that would make more whites mad and the already mad even madder. And he should have known that for the leader of the Democratic Party, the "white man's party," to confess that segregation, the cornerstone of white supremacy, was crumbling would be too much for just about everyone else.

So the governor should not have been surprised when his political enemies jumped on him. They had been looking for an opportunity since he came into office, and he handed it to them. Efforts to downplay the event fell flat, and in the weeks that followed Jim Folsom, who may have been the state's best hope for an easy end to segregation, found himself having to adopt a more conservative, less active stance than he and the black community might have wished. He did hold some private meetings with the leaders of the bus boycott and, according to those leaders' recollections, urge them to broaden their demands to include an end to segregation throughout the state. But publicly Big Jim kept his distance. He had to. "Adam Clayton Powell," the governor told his aides, "is one son of a bitch I wish I'd never seen!" Many black Alabamians probably agreed.

DOING ALABAMA POLITICS RIGHT

On the other hand, no one could say that race relations were high on the list of the governor's priorities. He had come to office promising farmers paved roads, promising old folks pensions, and promising everybody constitutional revision. Those were promises he planned to keep. Moving quickly, while his victorious allies were inspired and his defeated enemies in disarray, Folsom called the legislature into special session and handed them a farm-to-market road bill, complete with a tax increase to pay for it. Opponents warned that the legislation gave the governor patronage power unheard of in recent years, but since no representative wanted to have to explain to constituents why *their* roads didn't get paved, Big Jim was able to bring most of the reluctant over to his side. The way was greased by "personal courtesies" that ranged from seats on important committees to "mystery whiskey," which appeared in their hotel rooms when legislators arrived in town. And if these inducements did not work, the governor's operatives—the house speaker, Rankin Fite, the finance director, Fuller Kimbrell, and floor leaders George Hawkins and Joe Dawkins—knew how to trade for votes, reward supporters, and punish obstructionists. A little rhyme from the time explained it to those who did not understand:

> Hawkins, Dawkins, Kimbrell, and Fite;
> If you want a road, you'd better vote right.

Those were mighty men back then, and because of them the road bill cleared the house. It took a bit more maneuvering, along with some compromising, to get it through the senate, but it was done. Folsom got his bill. Alabamians got their roads. And a lot of the governor's friends, so it was said, went into the asphalt business.

On the last day of that special session, Governor Folsom called another, this one to deal with pensions for the elderly. So the legislature gathered again. Who could oppose helping old folks? One week later the bill was on the governor's desk, and later that year older Alabamians began receiving their pensions—$50 a month.

That was as far as Big Jim could push his exhausted legislators. Though he called a third special session to deal with constitutional reform, when the representatives gathered they simply appropriated the money to cover their expenses and adjourned. Enough was enough. Besides, constitutional reform included reapportionment, which Black Belt representatives believed would mean a loss of clout for them in Montgomery, so everyone knew that the third session would be long, bitter, and (probably) unproductive. All things considered, they'd rather be home, so that was where they went.

But in those sessions, and in the sessions that followed, Alabama legislators—conscientious in some cases, corrupt in others, and on occasions both—laid down a legacy that confirmed state representatives as a breed unto themselves. They may not have been efficient, though at times they were. They may have been self-serving, though at times they were not. But no one could call them dull. When the legislature met, it was the best show in the state. It was also serious business, for as Folsom finance director Kimbrell observed years later, when he and he alone was left to tell the tale, back then "politics in Alabama was a dirty business, if it was done right."

Once again one incident, one story, reduces the system to its essence. Speaker Rankin Fite was, in his time, one of the most powerful men in the state. But even he could have trouble getting a bill passed if what he was seeking was more than legislators could stomach (or explain to their constituents). There was once such a bill, and it was being blocked by two freshmen legislators. So the speaker called them into his office and put the matter plainly.

"Fellows, I need your help."

There was silence, then one of them spoke up. "But Mr. Speaker, this just ain't right."

"When I'm right," the speaker replied, "I don't need your help."

In the months that followed those special sessions, racial matters became the legislators' main concern. And on those issues, it was easier to get votes for things that weren't right—only back then, white folks, most of them, thought they were.

HISTORY, BIG JIM, AND "LIBERALLY MINDED PUBLIC MEN"

Alabama just can't seem to escape its history. Whenever the state appears about to break the chains that bind it to the past, something always happens—and usually that something involves race. Big Jim's second term is a case in point. It began under conditions that inspired the *New Republic* editor to ask why it was that Alabama had "produced so many more liberally minded public men" than her neighbors. Considering the state's progressive congressional delegation and its new governor, the question seemed logical. And looking at those first two special sessions, it seemed that liberally minded public men were indeed pointing Alabama to a new, more progressive future.

But it was not to be. The *Brown* case awakened Alabama segregationists from their complacent slumber and warned them of the struggle that might come. Then the bus boycott brought the struggle home, showed segregationists that the system was vulnerable, and inspired them to find ways to defend what was theirs. The solution, or what they hoped would be the solution, appeared a few months after the boycott began when an incident occurred that determined the direction the state and its leaders would take to thwart black hopes and preserve white supremacy. Tragically, it was a direction that could have been altered if liberally minded public men in general, and Big Jim Folsom in particular, had not done what they did.

In the fall of 1955 a federal court ordered the University of Alabama to allow a black student, Autherine Lucy, to enroll in the coming spring semester. When she arrived on campus and registered, protests broke out, spontaneously at first, then planned. Tensions mounted as a slogan-shouting mob, many of the protesters from off campus, congregated outside the building where the young woman was in class. Fearing for her safety, school officials took Miss Lucy out a back door and into a waiting car. The mob, alerted to the escape, tried to block her way, then pelted the vehicle with sticks and rocks as it drove off.

And where was the governor? Although he should have anticipated trouble (or maybe because he did) Folsom did not stay home to enforce the law. Instead he joined what has been described as a "drunken party" on a boat in the Gulf of Mexico and let university trustees expel Miss Lucy for inciting the mobs that rioted to prevent her enrollment—as if she were personally responsible for the incidents. It was a rationale not unlike the one Bourbons used back in 1901 to explain why taking away the black man's right to vote was the best way to prevent white men from stealing it. Autherine Lucy was punished, the mob was rewarded, and liberally minded public men let it happen.

More importantly, the incident convinced segregationists that if the state would hold the line, refuse to give in, Washington would have to recalculate the cost of forcing white Alabama to comply with those court orders. And finding the price too great to pay, the federal government would see the light and segregation would survive.

But did they really believe they would succeed? Some did, surely. They believed they would succeed because they still believed they were right, still believed that the races should be separate and that blacks were as happy with the status quo as whites were. Others weren't so sure. But unable to accept, much less comprehend, a state where blacks and whites enjoyed the same rights and privileges, and enjoyed them together, they hoped the zealots would succeed. As for those whites who may have believed that segregation would, and should, be overturned, that Alabama should break clean from its troubled past and treat all of its citizens the same, they fell silent.

Could Jim Folsom, or anyone for that matter, have energized the center, given hope to the moderates, offered white Alabamians an alternative to resistance? I doubt it. White Alabama's cultural racism was, in all probability, too strong. But we will never know, because no one tried. Lacking allies among the "liberally minded public men" that Alabama had supposedly produced, and among the good white folks who were out there, black Alabamians had to go it pretty much alone.

And those of us who remember the time remember how it no longer seemed quite right to still sing that song in Sunday school, that song that went:

Red and yellow, black and white
They are precious in his sight.
Jesus loves the little children of the world.

Not quite right unless we added another line at the end. Unless we added "in their place."

So Folsom and those liberally minded public men missed their chance. And so did Alabama.

But give Big Jim credit for this. He left us with some pretty progressive legislation and a wealth of stories. Unfortunately, tragically, most of the tales revolve around his drinking and his rapid descent into alcoholism, but they give him legendary quality that fixes him in our minds, and often in our hearts. Many still delight in telling of a governor who, with unabashed but slightly tipsy candor, could compliment a minister on "a damn good Baptist prayer," and many secretly wish (I suspect) that modern politicians were a little more colorful and a little less concentrated. And we remember moments like the time Folsom, again in his cups, joined a host of dignitaries at a Southern Governors' Conference in Norfolk, Virginia, to inspect a new aircraft carrier. As the planes buzzed about in a take-off and landing demonstration, something went wrong. There was an explosion. A plane burst into flames. The pilot ejected safely, and as he floated down his craft crashed with a roar, not far from the ship. While everyone sat in stunned silence, Big Jim slapped the knee of the naval officer sitting beside him and proclaimed, "Admiral, if that ain't a show, I'll kiss your ass."

Unfortunately, Jim Folsom's gubernatorial career is sort of like the events of that day. A lot of good things happened, but it is the show that folks remember. They also remember what came next.

WHO WILL LEAD THE CHILDREN
TO THE PROMISED LAND?

As Folsom prepared to leave office politicians hoping to succeed him did what politicians had done since the state was created. They set about to find an issue, define an enemy, and offer themselves as the champion who could protect and defend. As usual, there was a host of aspirants, but from the pack two emerged—George Wallace and John Patterson.

Wallace, who had been preparing for this moment since he was a student at the University of Alabama, was a Folsom operative who as a member of the house had organized and delivered South Alabama votes when Big Jim needed them. Already associated with progressive legislation in education and industrial development, he naturally took up his mentor's populist banner, played down racial issues, and ran on a platform which, within its Alabama context, was downright liberal.

John Patterson had taken another route to get where he was. In 1954 his father, Albert Patterson, had been chosen the Democratic nominee for attorney general on the promise that he would clean up Phenix City, Alabama, where every form of vice flourished to entice and exploit soldiers from nearby Fort Benning, Georgia. Underworld elements, fearing the future his victory promised, decided to act, and a few weeks after the election the senior Patterson was gunned down near his office.

The Democratic party quickly put Patterson's son on the ballot to replace their fallen hero, and with no Republican opposition, John Patterson was elected. Once in office the new attorney general went out after the Phenix City crowd and drove them from the state, an effort that brought national press attention and made him the subject of a B movie. Hoping to enhance this media-made image of the incorruptible lawman, Patterson then began investigating members of the Folsom administration who were accused of kickbacks, payoffs, and backroom deals that feathered their own nests. It was no surprise, consequently, that Patterson's name began to surface as a candidate for governor.

But by the time the campaign rolled around, Phenix City was clean, and efforts to link Folsom and his folks to corruption in Montgomery had generally fallen flat. Patterson needed something else, and, unfortunately for Alabama, he found it.

While attorney general, John Patterson had investigated the NAACP and, in effect, banned it from the state. That action, plus his

enthusiastic defense of the racial gerrymandering that kept Tuskegee's white government in office, made Patterson a hero to segregationists throughout the state. Although none of his opponents favored integration, John Patterson made his record defending the
racial status quo into the cornerstone of his campaign. Wallace, perceived as "soft" on segregation, fought back in kind, but it was no
use. Patterson and his advisors seemed to instinctively realize that
where a person stood on integration had become the standard by
which white Alabamians measured everyone else, including their
politicians. And in this campaign no one stood firmer on that issue than John Patterson. So Patterson won. In the bitterness of defeat George Wallace is said to have told an aide, "John Patterson out-
niggered me. No one will ever out-nigger me again."

Wallace always claimed he never said it. Others report that he did.
But that's not the point, really. What matters is that Patterson won
because he used race more effectively than Wallace, that Wallace
knew Patterson had won because he used race more effectively, and
that Wallace set out to make sure it would never happen again. It
never did.

While white Alabamians were looking for their champion, black
Alabamians had found theirs, and it wasn't just Martin Luther King
Jr. Throughout the state black folks were speaking out, marching,
protesting, petitioning, and demanding. Led by the likes of Birmingham's Fred Shuttlesworth, Selma's J. L. Chestnut, and Montgomery's E. D. Nixon and Jo Ann Robinson, they made the movement local even as men like King were making it national. And like
King, they made it nonviolent. Which may have unnerved their opponents more than anything else.

Whites could not comprehend what was happening, could not
believe that happy, content, loyal black folks could find fault with the
system. It must be, whites reasoned, the work of "outside agitators,"
as if it took someone from somewhere else to reveal to unsuspecting
Alabama African Americans that whites had better schools, better
jobs, more opportunities, more respect, and more advantages.

And yet there were whites who believed just that. So it followed that whites also believed that if those alien influences could be kept out, then everything would go back to the way it was, back to when blacks and whites abided by the "agreement" and lived happily "separate but equal." So whites applauded when Governor Patterson refused to protect the "freedom riders" who came into the state to desegregate bus stations, applauded when he announced that "the state of Alabama can't guarantee the safety of fools," and applauded when he vowed to uphold the state's segregation laws.

But did they applaud when racists burned a freedom rider bus outside Anniston? Did they applaud when a mob attacked freedom riders in Birmingham and Montgomery? Did they applaud the bombings? The assaults? The acts of violence the state seemed to sanction because it did little to stop them? We don't know. We only know that those who should have spoken out didn't. And knowing that may be enough.

SO IT CAME DOWN TO RABBITS

Once again it was a little thing, a bit of mindless lunacy that revealed white Alabama for what it was. A few weeks after Patterson was inaugurated, the local White Citizens' Council announced in its newsletter that subversive, integrationist, miscegenationist, maybe even communist literature was being promoted by a state agency— the Alabama Public Library Service. What the council had discovered was that in a library service–recommended children's book, *The Rabbits' Wedding,* one of the wedding rabbits was white and the other was black. Convinced that this was part of a sinister scheme to warp the minds of little children, segregationists raised the alarm, and when the legislature convened a few months later, Sen. Edward O. Eddins of Marengo County, down in the Black Belt, was primed and ready.

Announcing to the press that "this book and many others should be taken off the shelf and burned," Eddins went out after the library service director and threatened that the agency "won't get an extra cent if I can help it." Speaking for the White Citizens' Council as well as for himself, Eddins rejected the assertion that "a library must be a repository of all sides of a question," and announced that "the South has room for only one viewpoint. The integrationist doesn't have any right to express his opinion, not down here."

When the northern press got wind of all this, it had a field day, as it often does when southerners do something to confirm the belief, widely held up there, that Dixie is full of neo-Nazi bumpkins, the sort of people who would burn books and brutalize black folk. Eddins, of course, cared not one whit for what Yankee journalists wrote, and he expected other white Alabamians would feel the same way. So he must have been surprised, shocked even, to discover that not everyone was behind him.

Alabama editorial writers, among whom an integrationist was as rare as a violinist, roundly criticized the senator for the "silly spectacle" he had created and wondered if "the mature citizens of Alabama would be willing to take on Sen. Eddins as their literary tutor and censor." Not one Alabama newspaper, weekly or daily, rose to the senator's defense—at least on the matter of censorship. Firmly committed to the First Amendment, Alabama journalists did what journalists throughout the nation would have done under the circumstances—they took the senator to task.

But it was not just censorship that troubled the editors. Many among them feared that Eddins's tactics would undermine segregation rather than strengthen it. "We haul many a prop out from under a cause when we allow ourselves to appear ridiculous," wrote the *Birmingham News*. "This has made us just that." And the *Montgomery Advertiser* chimed in, "In addition to all the external idiocies by which Alabama is bedeviled, we also have to contend with internal idiocies."

So there you have it, the proof, if you need proof, of the unity among white Alabamians and the challenge faced by black Alabamians. Of all the institutions in the state, none more reflected the prevailing opinion held by good white people than their newspapers. That press and those people believed that segregation should be defended, could be defended. And they were sure that if people like themselves did the defending, it could be done with dignity in the courts of law and public opinion. Though they knew that there were those in the state to whom Eddins was a hero, a defender of a cause so dear that dignity in its defense was a trifling matter, these moderates did not believe, could not believe, that the zealots would take charge. How could they? Who would inspire them? Not the Eddinses of this world.

Then who? The answer was not long in coming.

13

The Age of Wallace

"AND THEY STOMPED THE FLOOR"

This is how George Wallace summed up his situation, his dilemma: "I started off talking about schools and highways and prisons and taxes, and I couldn't make them listen. Then I began talking about niggers—and they stomped the floor."

That's about the nub of it. That's what got 'em excited. The wonder is that after his candid assessment of John Patterson's victory in 1958, George Wallace continued to hope that something other than race would move white Alabamians. But race was the issue. Patterson did not originate it, lead Alabamians to it. Nor did Wallace in his turn. No, when it came to race, segregation, supremacy, white Alabamians did the leading. Patterson and Wallace, especially Wallace, did the following.

Actually if John Patterson had not let hooligans and Klansmen assault the Freedom Riders, he might have appeared in history as a fairly good governor. In areas like education, health care, and such, his administration deserves a strong "OK" by Alabama standards. But we don't remember that, mainly because it was not what got the juices flowing back then. It was when Patterson talked about how he wasn't going to let outsiders come in and stir up trouble, come in and tell Alabamians how to treat "our colored people" (note the possessive) that he became the popular hero—at least to white people. George Wallace watched this, watched and understood.

Now we get to that often-asked question: Was George Wallace out to champion the cause of the people, the white people? Or was he trying to find a way to get the people, white people, to champion the cause of George Wallace? The answer, in this case at least, to both is "yes."

Let's be honest. This is one of those instances where politicians did not have to find an issue, uncover an enemy, and promise voters protection. After the *Brown* decision, and especially after the bus boycott, white Alabamians knew who the enemy was, knew what was at stake. What they wanted was someone to lead them the way Dr. King was leading black folks.

So they elected John Patterson, who could say, by the end of his term in office, that in Alabama the barricades had not been breached, that segregation still stood. Where legal maneuvers and foot-dragging had worked well enough for Patterson, news of federal troops enforcing integration in Little Rock suggested that the next governor might have to do more. By the time the election of 1962 rolled around, white Alabamians were primed and ready to vote for a candidate who would not only "draw the line in the dust and toss the gauntlet before the feet of tyranny," as Wallace said he would, but would go to the wall for them, fight the battle for them, stand up for white Alabamians no matter what the enemy threw at them. Black folks were willing to go to jail for their rights. White Alabamians wanted a governor who would do the same for theirs. George Wallace convinced voters that he was that man. That was how he won.

ELECTING WALLACE

The enemy, of course, was the federal government, that ancient adversary against whom conservative Alabamians had been railing since Reconstruction. More to the point, it was the federal court system, "the sorriest . . . in the world" according to Wallace, and Federal District Court Judge Frank Johnson, whom Wallace called, with a fine feeling for history, "an integrating, scalawagging, carpet-bagging, race-mixing, bald-faced liar." Johnson, a North Alabama "mountain Republican" whose attachment to the GOP was rooted in that region's pre–Civil War anti-planter past, was an Eisenhower appointee who was already issuing orders to desegregate public fa-cilities, and white Alabamians feared he would issue more. He was also Wallace's law school classmate and friend, not that it mattered to the candidate who would later suggest that someone should give the judge "a barbed-wire enema." In Johnson Wallace found just what he needed, a visible symbol against whom he could rage but about whom most folks knew, deep down, he could do little.

Even as Wallace convinced conservatives that he could effectively fight for them, he also appealed to what still passed for liberalism in Alabama. Imbedded in his racial rhetoric were promises to improve education, help old folks, build roads, and promote industry—things he claimed would benefit the working man. He even promised to end the state's wasteful, profligate practice of entertaining "big shots" on the state yacht where they would be wined and dined and "taken for rides in the moonlight." Having learned his lesson in '58, Wallace in this campaign offered something for everyone—so long as they were white. Race, of course, was the whole point.

So Wallace won. And his victory raises the question that later will be critical to assessing his career. Was George Wallace a populist, a people's candidate who really wanted to do something for working folks but understood that before he could help, he had to get elected, and to get elected he had to campaign as the racist he really wasn't? Or was he really a racist, a hardcore segregationist who not only believed in white supremacy but willingly took the lead in its de-fense? These are fair questions, because earlier in his career Wallace appeared to advocate the racial liberalism associated with Big Jim Folsom. Later, an older, kinder, gentler Wallace would claim that he never hated blacks, claim that though his approach was flawed, he was just trying to find a way to help the little man. But of course, George Wallace's little man was always white.

EYES ON THE PRIZE

On that blustery January day in 1963, when an equally blustery George Wallace stood on the steps of the Alabama Capitol, "stood where once Jefferson Davis stood . . . [in the] very Heart of the Great Anglo-Saxon Southland" and pledged "segregation now . . . segregation tomorrow . . . segregation forever," it was a call to arms, and though no one came out and said it, both sides understood that blood would be shed in the battle. It already had been. The Freedom Riders were beaten just a few blocks from where he spoke, and folks were already calling the state's largest city what it was, "Bombing-ham." By not denouncing this violence, by announcing instead "that anything worthy of our defense is worthy of one hundred percent of our defense," Alabama's new governor gave lawlessness legitimacy. He may not have meant to do it, but he did.

Most white Alabamians rejected violence. Most preferred to resist integration in other ways. Cities closed parks, padlocked playgrounds, drained swimming pools, and in one case went out to public golf courses, out onto the greens, and ceremoniously removed the flags and poured concrete in the cups. But if you looked around you could see that already the defense was not 100 percent. Some white Alabamians, businessmen mostly, had begun to make adjustments, crack the door a bit so blacks could claim progress and would continue to spend money. In Birmingham, which Dr. King called "the most thoroughly segregated city in the United States," merchants fearing economic boycotts tried to integrate public facilities in their stores, and a few even went so far as to take down the "Colored Only" signs. But the city's leading segregationist, Public Safety Commissioner Eugene "Bull" Connor, had those stores cited for building code violations, so the signs went back up, and Birmingham went back to being what it was. Which is also why Birmingham became what it became—the city that had to be broken if the Civil Rights movement was to succeed.

BUT FOR BIRMINGHAM

Birmingham became a battleground because both sides wanted it that way. Although moderates in the city had united to defeat Connor when he ran for mayor, Dr. King refused to call off downtown demonstrations planned for the spring of 1963. Stinging from setbacks in Albany, Georgia, feeling his leadership of SCLC in jeopardy, King was determined to use the organization put together by local minister Fred Shuttlesworth to challenge segregation in Magic City department stores. Meanwhile Commissioner Connor, still in office while the courts sorted out the election results, and backed, indeed urged on, by some of the city's most powerful business leaders, was just as determined that the protests would not succeed.

The only person in the state who might have prevented what followed, who might have brought the sides together to hammer out a compromise, was the newly inaugurated governor, George Wallace. But of course Wallace wouldn't do that, couldn't do that. There was no way that the man who was elected rejecting moderation and compromise, who had told voters that "there is no middle of the road," that "you are either for [segregation] or against it," could turn mediator. So Birmingham was left to solve its own problems.

The story, by now, is old and well told. King's leading the nonviolent demonstrations. Connor, the fire hoses and the dogs out to stop him. Marches carefully scripted, held before noon so network cameramen could film them, fly the footage to New York, develop it on the way, and have it ready for the evening news, ready to show the rest of the nation how far Alabamians would go to keep its black citizens from enjoying the same rights and privileges enjoyed by whites. Hundreds were arrested, including, finally, Dr. King, who was hauled away in the city's windowless police van and put into solitary confinement. It was 12 April 1963. Good Friday.

That was when eight white ministers published a letter in the *Bir-*

mingham News calling the demonstrations "unwise and untimely," suggesting King was an unwelcome troublemaker, and urging negotiations instead of demonstrations. King, the story, the legend, goes, wrote his answer on scraps and margins, smuggled it out, and saw it published as a "Letter from Birmingham Jail," a title not unconsciously but perhaps ironically drawn from a classic ballad of loneliness and loss:

> "Send me a letter, send it by mail,
> Send it in care of the Birmingham jail."

And King's letter too was a classic, a document of commitment to nonviolent protest that explained, as the author would explain in a book a year later, "why we can't wait."

But blacks in Birmingham did not have to be told why waiting would not do, did not have to be told, as King told the clergymen, that " 'Wait' has almost always meant 'Never.' " So the demonstrations grew, and when whites threatened to fire demonstrators, the economically vulnerable went back to work and young people left school to march. Whites claimed it was all a lark, all an excuse to skip classes, but blacks knew better. They knew they were sending their most precious possessions, their children, into the fray. They were frightened. But they did it anyway. So there were more demonstrations, more dogs, more fire hoses and nightsticks, and more arrests, while the nation and eventually the world watched in horror.

Meanwhile, finally, Pres. John Kennedy shifted his attention from the Cold War to the domestic conflict in Alabama. Things had begun to get out of hand, even by King's estimation. What had begun as an effort to desegregate downtown stores had grown to the point that many blacks were demanding that all barriers come down. With the question of who actually governed the city still in the courts and the situation growing worse, Kennedy pressed for a settlement. But the mediator he sent reported that whites would not talk to blacks if Dr. King was involved, while some blacks would not sit at the negotiating table with upper- and middle-class black business leaders who had been trying to work with whites—"Uncle Toms" they called them. Then there was movement. Dr. King suggested that he and his allies would scale back demands, that desegregation of lunch counters, restrooms, and dressing rooms and a vague promise of employee promotions would be enough for now. White business leaders agreed, and on Monday, May 10, the compromise was announced—at two separate news conferences.

Bull Connor was livid, denounced the accord as "capitulation by certain weak-kneed white people under threat of violence by the rabble-rousing Negro, King," and called for a white boycott of integrating stores. Some blacks also saw the deal as a sellout and were critical of King and the negotiators. But it was the Klan that acted. Rallying outside the city the night after the agreement, Klan leaders sounded the call, and before dawn bombs had exploded at the home of Dr. King's brother and at the motel where King had stayed. Hearing the news, blacks quickly gathered at Kelly Ingram Park, the staging area for many of the marches. Connor's police along with state troopers sent by Wallace to "keep order" moved in, a riot erupted, and in the rock-throwing, nightstick-swinging melee thirty-five blacks and five whites were injured. But cooler heads carried the day. Black leaders worked frantically to return their followers to nonviolence. White businessmen stood by the deal they had made. And President Kennedy announced that he would send in troops rather than see the accord "sabotaged by a few extremists."

It worked, but those close to the scene knew that there were more than a few extremists out there, knew it wasn't over. Events came fast and furious now. In June Wallace made his carefully scripted "stand in the schoolhouse door" to keep two black students from enrolling at the University of Alabama. The whole thing was worked out with federal authorities so Wallace could appear as bold in opposing integration as King had been in supporting it, but without going to jail, as King had done. Still, even Wallace must have known who was winning. Events in Birmingham and elsewhere had so shifted and focused national opinion that only the most unrealistic racists would have remained confident of their cause. In August more than 250,000 demonstrators marched on Washington demanding meaningful Civil Rights legislation, demanding that Congress act so Dr. King's "dream" might come true.

Meanwhile, back in Birmingham, emotions continued to run high. Now there was an uproar over the court-ordered integration of selected city schools. But it was not just the integrating that upset segregationists. Many were quick to note that the students in the chosen white schools came mostly from working-class families, while schools attended by students from affluent homes were not on the list. Once again, it was said, poor whites were the sacrificial lambs. So boycotts were called. Emotional mass meetings were held. Cars loaded with noisy demonstrators waving the now common Confederate battle flag as their symbol of defiance drove from school to school, blowing horns, shouting slogans, and causing chaos. But amid the noise, the protests, the loud defiance, a few of the hardcore fell back on the old ways, the attack by stealth, anonymous terror, against which there was no defense, against people and places that should have been safe, against children and a house of worship.

On Sunday morning, 15 September 1963, a bomb exploded at the Sixteenth Street Baptist Church, next to Kelly Ingram Park. Four young girls were killed. They had just finished their Sunday school lesson—"The Love That Forgives." As their bodies were pulled from the rubble, one of the men on the scene, a member of the congregation, probably, said to himself and anyone else who was listening, "I don't know how much more the Negro people of this city can take."

CARRYING ON

There are moments when tides of history turn, moments we can look back on and believe that people paused and said to themselves, this is enough. The Sixteenth Street Church bombing was one of those moments. From that day on segregation no longer had the unqualified support of "good white folks." The explanations, the excuses, no longer rang true. Never again would murderers be heroes. The fanatical few who held to the old verities of white supremacy, who claimed absolution and exemption for the beatings and burnings and lynchings, still might speak unchallenged. Fear can do that to good people. But the fanatics could no longer count on the support they had earlier. The change was slight at first, hardly noticeable to the untrained eye, but those who were there, who heard the question "who could do such a thing?" knew things were different and would soon be more different still.

Except maybe in the Black Belt. Now I am not suggesting whites down there approved of killing children. Nor do I believe a Black Belt jury, all white of course, would have found proven bombers innocent, though the standard of proof might have been a bit higher. What I am saying is that there the tragedy did not change things. Segregation was not only a way of life, it was the way whites protected themselves and what they had from blacks, who, whites seemed convinced, would, if in power, treat whites as poorly as whites had treated them. They thought the church bombing and the girls' deaths were a tragic, unfortunate incident and the guilty should be punished. But it did not mean that segregation was wrong or that it should be reconsidered. It didn't mean that at all.

It followed that when the Civil Rights Act of 1964 was signed into law and public accommodations throughout the state slowly began to integrate, not much happened in the Black Belt.

Here's why.

There is a story told about Lyndon Johnson when he was in the Senate listening to South Carolina's segregationist Strom Thurmond speaking against an earlier civil rights bill. As Thurmond ranted on about states' rights, racial amalgamation, and communist conspiracies, Johnson leaned over to a colleague and whispered, "Ol' Strom really believes that shit."

So did white folks in the Black Belt. They believed that integration would destroy the white race, they believed communists were behind integration, and they believed that states had the right to protect white folks if the federal government would not. Today all this may sound like what Johnson called it, but not back then, not to whites down there.

And how would the communists accomplish their evil ends? By the most American of means—the vote. In January 1964, the Twenty-fourth Amendment to the Constitution outlawed the poll tax in federal elections, and whites in those counties where blacks were in the majority knew they had a problem. Those whites also knew that they controlled the courthouses and those little rooms at the end of the hall where potential voters went to register. As long as they could keep blacks from registering, as long as they could keep democracy in its place, there wouldn't be any black vote to contend with.

ENTER THE OUTSIDE AGITATORS

Ever since the Civil Rights movement began, southern whites had complained that "our Negroes" weren't interested in integration and such, that the races got along just fine before strangers, Yankees mostly, came in to stir things up. And almost any one of those whites could have said, would have said, what Dallas County Sheriff Jim Clark said to a group who had come to Selma to help local blacks register to vote:

"You are here to cause trouble, that's what you're doing," Clark told them. "You don't live here. You are an agitator, and that's the lowest form of humanity."

And everyone knew what sort of "trouble" these agitators could cause. Nearly 60 percent of Dallas County's population was African American, but only 2 percent of them were registered to vote. In neighboring Lowndes County where the black portion of the population was even greater, no African Americans had voted for more than half a century. In other Black Belt counties the situation was the same. If outsiders got these blacks registered and voting, whites would lose control of the courthouse, of the local legislative delegation, and of the coalition that had kept taxes low and social services minimal. Yes sir, those agitators could cause trouble, a lot of trouble.

But not every "agitator" was an outsider. Selma black attorney J. L. Chestnut had been agitating there for some time, and in 1963 Alabama native and future Georgia U.S. congressman John Lewis arrived to lead a Student Nonviolent Coordinating Committee (SNCC) voter registration drive. Yet galling as local black agitation was to segregationists, what really got under their white skin was the presence of northerners who came, so Black Belt whites believed, to overturn a system that did not need overturning. And when these northerners, the white ones, thumbed their noses at the customs and conventions of white supremacy, when they lived with blacks, ate with blacks, walked hand-in-hand with and even embraced blacks in public, segregationists saw the barbarians at the gate.

It is hard to explain today how all of this change unnerved whites and, at the same time, emboldened blacks. But it did. The barriers were coming down, and though voting would prove the critical issue, the horror whites felt as they watched what was happening, and the exhilaration felt by blacks, makes it clear that this was as much a social revolution as a political one.

Still both sides knew that there would be no social revolution, no economic revolution, if the political revolution did not succeed. So through 1963 and 1964 black Alabamians and their white allies worked to break down segregationist resistance. As they did Selma began to attract media attention, which in turn revealed to the nation that the Civil Rights Act of 1964 had not turned things around, that discrimination still existed, and that in the most democratic of nations people could still be denied the right to vote because of their race.

Once again incidents led to action. On 16 February 1965 the evening news showed footage of Sheriff Clark assaulting SCLC staff member C. T. Vivian in front of the courthouse. Two days later, in the nearby town of Marion, a white mob attacked a demonstration, and a black man, twenty-six-year-old Jimmie Lee Jackson, was shot and killed, apparently by a state trooper. Jackson was no outside agitator. He lived there, and he died there.

Jackson's death outraged members of the movement, and from it came the suggestion, the challenge, that marchers take their cause to the Alabama capitol, to Governor Wallace, and force him to deal with their demands. Wallace, hearing the news, announced that he would not let marchers tie up traffic along the fifty miles of highway between Selma and Montgomery and alerted the highway patrol. Even in the black community and among black leaders, there was disagreement over whether such a march would succeed or simply invite more violence. Meanwhile word drifted out of Washington that Congress was ready to pass an enforceable voting rights bill, news that doubled the determination of SNCC and the younger members of the movement to carry the march through. When Dr. King, who had met with Pres. Lyndon Johnson and received assurances of support, came out in favor of the march, the way was clear.

BLOODY SUNDAY

On a raw March day in 1965, demonstrators gathered at Brown's Chapel, one of the black churches that had supported and sustained them while they tried to overcome white resistance to registration. Then they lined up, six hundred of them, two-by-two, with Hosea Williams, there for Dr. King, and John Lewis from SNCC leading the way. Then they started walking to the Edmund Pettus Bridge.

Of the images indelibly stamped on the American mind, few are more vivid than the pictures of what took place that day. Marchers coming over the bridge, a thin line with no police escort, no support, no protection. And at the bottom of the bridge the troopers and the sheriff's posse, irregulars on horseback—ceremonial usually but deputized now and told to keep order. The marchers came on, expecting, according to what they understood had been agreed, that they would be stopped, allowed to pray, then turned back. But there were no prayers that day, except those screamed when the tear gas went off and the horses charged and the billy clubs cracked heads.

"It looked like war," Selma Mayor Joseph Smitherman later said. And everyone who had a TV set agreed. It seemed almost as if the troopers and posse had staged things for the cameras, so perfect was the footage, so clear was the assault, so horrifying was the carnage, almost as if the forces of law and order had wanted the nation to see it, and be warned. But the warning was not heeded. Dr. King was in Atlanta, and from there he issued a call for people to join him in Selma to carry the march through. The call, like the film of Bloody Sunday, went out all over the country. Then, according to Mayor Smitherman, "the people, the wrath of the nation came down on us."

Selma now became the epicenter of the movement. Dr. King arrived and began rallying the troops. In Montgomery, Governor Wallace declared that he would "enforce state law" that prohibited dangerous demonstrations, only to find himself facing a federal court ordering him not to interfere with the march. Then President Johnson invited (some say summoned) Wallace to Washington and challenged (some say ordered) him to protect the demonstrators. By then there had been another murder. James Reeb, a white clergyman in town to join the demonstration, had been assaulted and killed by local thugs. Now there was a national outcry for the federal government to do something. It did. After Wallace left, Johnson announced that he would shortly send a bill to Congress that would "strike down all restrictions used to deny the people the right to vote." He was good to his word, and on the evening after the bill arrived, the President of the United States went on national television to tell Americans that they must support the black struggle for freedom. He finished with the promise that was the anthem of the movement. "We," he vowed, "shall overcome."

The choice of words was not lost on either blacks or whites. C. T. Vivian heard the speech and called it "a victory like none other . . . an affirmation of the movement." For Mayor Smitherman and the white community "it was like you'd been struck by a dagger in your heart."

SO THEY MARCHED

Wallace still tried to stop them, tried to convince his old friend and current enemy, Judge Frank Johnson, that it was against state law for people to march from Selma to Montgomery along a busy highway, tie up traffic, and cost the state thousands of dollars. But Johnson would have none of it, and at the SCLC's request he issued an injunction forbidding Wallace from interfering.

So the governor turned to, of all people, Lyndon Johnson and on the telephone told him how "people [were] pouring in from all over the country," how they were "flying in nuns, priests, and hundreds of bearded beatniks," and how things were getting out of hand. "I know you don't want anything to happen that looks like a revolution," the governor warned, "but if these people continue to pour in here and conduct themselves in the manner they are, why, it's going to take everyone in the country to stop something."

But Johnson offered neither help nor hope, so Wallace declared that the state could not afford the cost of protecting "communist-trained anarchists" and washed his hands of the matter. In response President Johnson put some two thousand Alabama National Guardsmen under federal authority and sent in another two thousand army troops plus about two hundred FBI agents and federal marshals. With that action the stage was set.

On one point Wallace was right. There was no shortage of players. From all over the nation they came—well, not many from the South, but from most everywhere else, all to march for the right of black folks to vote. Their presence, and their lack of concern for southern racial traditions, disturbed and outraged Selma citizens. A slick-paper booklet published later, under the title *The True Selma Story: Sex and Civil Rights,* made this clear. Pictures of interracial couples embracing, of young people unsouthern in "beatnik" attire, and of

Dr. King consorting with "known communists" were interspersed with accounts of public indecency and white females "building up their sexual desires with Negro males." The girls were, of course, not from Selma, or even Alabama. Where the men were from did not matter. What mattered was that they were black.

It is hard to say how many of these occurrences were true and how many of them were the product of rumor, speculation, and an overactive imagination. Some of them probably happened. But more than four thousand people marched, and most took no part in such goings on. Still, since interracial sex was among the Black Belt's greatest taboos and public indecency regardless of race ranked pretty high on the list of social sins, it is hardly surprising that the stories became part of the folklore, the white folklore, of the march. They would be told again and again to explain and justify why it was right to oppose what the rest of the nation believed was a noble crusade, told to reveal what local whites considered the underside of the movement, a side so dark that it negated all that was positive, all that was right. Only thing was, fewer and fewer people, fewer and fewer Alabamians, were convinced.

On Sunday, March 21, they began. King was in the lead, and as they crossed the bridge they could hear over a loudspeaker set up in one of the buildings, strains of the song "Bye, Bye, Blackbird."

They reached Montgomery four days later, the hardcore marchers. There the others joined, so more than twenty thousand entered the city. But the jubilation among the leaders was tempered by word that segregationists were going to make an attempt on King's life, maybe even try to shoot him down at the head of the procession, at his moment of triumph. So what to do? They knew King would march, threat or no threat. Then they hit upon a plan.

There was Dr. King, resplendent in his "good-preacher blue suit." And among the crowd were other preachers, similarly dressed. "We just had to kind of believe that it was true when white folks said we all looked alike," Andrew Young later explained, "so everybody that was about Martin's size and had a blue suit, I put in the front of the line with him." Young did not tell them why they were put in the place of honor, nor did he tell upset dignitaries why they were shuttled further back, "but all the preachers loved the chance to get up in the front of the line with Martin Luther King." "I don't think," Young reminisced, "to this day most of them know why they were up there."

So they entered the city, passed the Dexter Avenue Baptist Church, and mounted Goat Hill. There, in front of the capitol, with the Confederate flag flying from the dome, King spoke of how the vote sets everyone free and how from that freedom will come "a society at peace with itself, a society that can live with its conscience." Inside, in his office, Governor Wallace watched, brooding, waiting for the expected delegation to arrive and deliver the expected petition. But when they came, they were told that the governor wasn't in. His executive secretary received them, took the petition, and went away.

The marchers went away as well, returned to the work at hand. So did the murderers, for in the days that followed desperate segregationists renewed their campaign of violence and intimidation. Viola Liuzzo, a woman from Detroit down to lend her support, was shot and killed by Klansmen as she took one of the marchers back to Selma. And later that summer Jon Daniels, a young seminarian from New England, who had come down to register voters, was shotgunned in a Lowndes County store by a local man "maddened by the prospect of Negroes' voting." The jury ruled it was self-defense. White citizens of Lowndes County felt the verdict was fair. Black citizens didn't.

The movement, however, had taken a turn and was about to enter a new phase. Jon Daniels was not the last martyr in the struggle, but in a sense he was the last to fall in Alabama. One can argue that his murderer sincerely believed that he was protecting his society, his world, from alien invaders who would do more damage than segregation had ever done and that the jury agreed. One cannot underestimate the fear that gripped many white people as the old order crumbled around them, nor underestimate their resolve to defend that order. Today we can see they were wrong. Back then, things were not so clear. That was the tragedy.

WHITHER WALLACE?

So George Wallace refused to receive the marcher's petition that day in Montgomery, refused to confront, face, a movement he helped create and whose success owed so much to him. Most everyone knew, maybe even Wallace, that his preening and posturing had done as much to popularize the cause as did the eloquence of King or the bravery of those who absorbed the blows. Every successful revolution needs an adversary, an enemy to personify all that is wrong with the system revolted against, someone to remind the revolutionaries what revolt is all about. Wallace gave them that. The Civil Rights movement might have succeeded without him, but he made its success much, much easier.

By the time the petition arrived, opposing segregation in Alabama was no longer at the top of the Wallace agenda, so it was fitting that he sent an aide to deal with the matter. One can even imagine Wallace, looking out at the sea of faces stretching down Dexter Avenue, and not really seeing them. One can imagine his mind drifting off to his upcoming trip to New York and appearance on the *Today* show. Or maybe thinking about all those letters piling up in the mail room, letters from around the nation praising his stand against the subversive forces that were surely behind the march and the movement. Or maybe he was recalling his reception in the North when he made a tentative run for the presidency the year before. And one can imagine, as journalist Douglas Kiker imagined, after the governor's warm greeting up there, how he lay asleep and was "awakened by a white, blinding vision" that explained why so many Yankees wanted to be his friend. "They all hate black people," the vision revealed. "All of them. They're all afraid, all of them." And that is when it came to Wallace: "Great God! That's it. They're all Southern! The whole United States is *Southern*!"

Realizing this, Wallace also realized, or believed, or at least hoped, that he could become president of that United States, a nation of southerners, so he took to running. Between 1962 and 1974 George Wallace, or his wife for him, ran for governor or for president seven times. Add to these attempts another brief campaign for the presidency in 1976 and his election as governor in 1982, and you have the record of a man who liked the race as much as, maybe more than, the office. And it was during these years, years when he was consumed with campaigning rather than governing, that white and black Alabamians had to figure out just what equality meant. It was a time when Alabama needed a governor who could calm the waters, help its citizens through the transition, but no governor was there for them. Yet since Wallace was governor, maybe that was for the best.

INTEGRATION

So Alabama integrated. The Voting Rights Act, passed by Congress in the wake of the Selma to Montgomery march, added thousands of black voters to the rolls and, in time, in some counties changed the complexion of the courthouse gang, though not necessarily its tactics. Around the state the "white only" signs came down, and the two races began to eat in the same restaurants (and even sometimes at the same tables), drink from the same water fountains, and go to the same restrooms. Despite earlier warnings of what might happen, life went on pretty much as it always had.

Oh there were those moments where people acted the fool. In one town it happened when blacks asked (whites said demanded) that in the annual Christmas parade their floats be mixed in with the rest, rather than once again relegated to the rear. I don't know if they asked (or demanded) that there be only one Santa, rather than the traditional two, or whether St. Nick should be black or white, for the negotiations probably never got that far. White organizers canceled the event. Local children of both races were disappointed. Also disappointed, someone suggested, was the one whose birth was being celebrated. Still, looking back it is remarkable how quickly most of the visible symbols and conventions of Jim Crow faded away.

And the ones that remained were often ignored. In one town there was this "Laundromat" where local women went to wash and dry their clothes. There were two rows of washing machines, with signs that indicated which side was for "our colored patrons" and which was for the whites. The owner, a staunch segregationist, refused to take them down. But by the early 1970s the women no longer paid attention. They just came in and took the first available washer. Convenience won out over racism. The Civil Rights movement had set everyone free.

But let's not make it sound too simple. There was still the matter of the schools. The *Brown* decision had hit the white South like a body blow because it threatened the most important institution on which the segregationist house of cards rested—the public schools. While the more rabid racists raised the cry that school integration would lead to miscegenation and the end of the race, there were other fears that haunted whites. White supremacy was based on the notion, the belief, that whites were superior where it counted—intellectually. Therefore, the argument went, quality education would be wasted on black students, and of course Alabama politicians deplored waste. So you have a self-fulfilling prophecy of sorts. Whites predicted that blacks could not learn as well as whites; therefore blacks were given less education than whites, which meant that blacks learned "less" than whites, which "proved" that blacks could not learn as well as whites. The fact that blacks were not given an equal chance to prove their ability was, to whites, beside the point.

Then, in what must in hindsight be seen as the most audacious argument in an era of audacity, whites claimed that integration was a bad idea because if the two races went to school together, blacks would "pull whites down to their level." The idea that equal education might enable blacks to reach their full potential, and might even help whites in the process, never seemed to enter the segregationist mind. It couldn't. Simply put, if black students, finally given the chance, turned out to be as able as, or more able than, their white counterparts, that would prove once and for all that white supremacy was a farce. Segregationists could not accept that.

Blacks, on the other hand, were at times less enthusiastic about integration than portrayed, for they knew, understood, that integration would probably come on white terms, terms that would work to blacks' disadvantage, just as terms always had. So black Alabamians watched and waited, watched whites try gimmicks like "freedom of choice" and "tokenism" and waited for the gimmicks to fail, which of course they did. All black Alabamians wanted was for the state to give their children the same advantages, the same opportunities that the state gave white children. And if the only way to get this was to put them together in the same schools, so be it.

Looking back, the students tell me, they were not so sure.

We forget that the real shock troops in the integration of Alabama were not the marchers, not the people who crossed the bridge and were beaten, not the people who faced the dogs and the fire hoses, not the people who went to jail. The real shock troops were the students who faced a situation that would not end in a few days, one that went on, week by week, year by year, a situation of confrontations and compromise, minuscule when compared to the great moments captured on film and shown throughout the land. But just as important—maybe more important. The students were the ones who made integration work.

Though the process varied from community to community, school to school, a line ran through the story that gave it a consistency, no matter where it was played out. It went like this:

The day came and whites could put it off no longer. The order was signed; the schools would be integrated. It was left to local officials, whites mostly, to decide just how to do it. So they did what blacks expected them to do. Everyone went to the white high school. The black high school became the elementary school, or a middle school, and the younger children went there. Black principals became assistant principals. Black coaches, some of them with legendary won-lost records, were told to coach the junior varsity, or assist their white counterparts. Black teachers were assigned the worst classrooms and the lowest-achieving classes, which white officials made sure were filled with blacks. In some schools two students, one white and one black, were chosen for every office, every honor. Some elected two homecoming courts. Others dropped beauty pageants altogether. As much as possible, white authorities kept the races separate, even though they were under the same roof.

And the kids had to deal with this, and more. White students watched their world invaded and, it seemed to them, taken over. Though the school still had its old name, its old mascot, its old traditions, cheers, and songs, it was no longer their school. And they resented it.

Black students watched their world destroyed, torn down, or reinvented. They were being told, or so it seemed, that their songs, cheers, traditions weren't good enough. If they wanted to mix with whites they would do it on white terms. White folks seemed to be saying what a white official reportedly said to a black educator as they watched the bulldozer reduce to rubble a school that been the center of the African American community since Reconstruction, "I hope you're happy now."

But we are not talking about happiness here. We are talking about fairness, opportunity, the future. So while white students grumbled over what they believed they had lost, black students tried to sort out what they hoped they had gained. And what is significant here is that the two groups did it, for all intents and purposes, alone. Today when students need help—the death of a classmate, the loss of a teacher, a conflict that needs resolving—counselors and consultants, preachers and parents, descend on the school. Back then, few adults knew what to do, what to say, so the students took the lead. Integration's success or failure depended on them.

Some, of course, would have none of it. In some communities white parents simply refused to comply, pulled their children out of the public schools, and set up private "academies," where white supremacy would be maintained in an all-white environment. Though some would argue that "quality education" was the issue, the timing made it clear that the real reason was race. Named after Confederate heroes or nicknamed the "Rebels," these schools drew the line in the dust as surely as Wallace had done, and in the end they were more successful at thwarting integration than the governor was. But at the same time it should be noted that in an ironic way these "seg academies" helped integration, for they took many children of hard-core segregationists, children who might have caused trouble, and isolated them. It was one of the reasons why, despite all the defiant talk, Alabama schools integrated so peacefully.

Still this resegregation hurt the communities where it occurred. Less-affluent whites saw school choice as a matter of class as well as race, which one of the schools made obvious when it chose the name "Patrician Academy." So they saved for the tuition, made the old car last a few years longer, did not buy appliances and such, cut back wherever they could, and in the process took money out of the local economy. At the same time private-school parents became less and less likely to support local initiatives to improve the public schools, less inclined to support candidates who made funding public education their first priority. In the communities where private academies rose, they undercut support for public education. It was yet another price that Alabama paid for integration.

Despite dire warnings that they would never make it, the private schools, at least most of them, survived. They did this, in part at least, because in time they were able to attract elements in the white community for whom race was not the only issue.

Let me explain. Played out against the drama of the Civil Rights movement was another revolution, one that disturbed many Ala-bamians as much as desegregation. For decades evangelical Christian parents had been uneasy over the secularization of public education. In particular, they opposed the teaching of evolution instead of the biblical account of creation. (It should be noted that according to polls, most Alabamians pick the Bible over Darwin; they just don't make a big deal about it.) Then in the early 1960s, the United States Supreme Court began handing down rulings that limited religious activities (especially prayer) in state-supported schools. That was too much. It was one thing for their ancient enemy, the federal government, to turn public schools into laboratories for social experiments like integration, but now it seemed that Washington was undertaking an all-out effort to secularize students. It was time to get out.

But where to go? Some "seg academies" offered themselves as that place. These resegregation supporters told uneasy evangelicals that it was all part of a plot to destroy the southern way of life— "They took God out and put the niggers in," was how one of them explained it. So the academies began to tout "Christian education" as part of their curriculum, and some Alabama parents took their children out of the public schools for that. But others organized their own schools, set up classes in their churches, announced that they would teach what they wanted to teach the way they wanted to teach it, and quietly let it be known that anyone who believed as they believed was welcome—even if they were black.

Meanwhile, most public schools weathered the storm and emerged from it stronger than before. Of course, pockets of segregation remained. As elsewhere in the nation, inner city schools were soon black schools, while suburban schools were mostly white. Still, by the mid 1970s things had settled down, and in most of Alabama's towns and villages, black and white students routinely went to school together. In another generation, many students and even some of their parents would wonder why there had been so much fuss in the first place. And that, in Alabama, is how you measure progress.

EMERGING FROM THE STORM

Thus it followed that in the mid 1970s Alabamians looked around them to see just what the Civil Rights movement had accomplished. Dr. King was dead, shot down in Memphis in 1968. But his legacy lived among his constituents. They could vote now, hold office, become part of the political establishment they once feared. Their children were no longer relegated by law to the state's worst schools, were no longer forced to endure the humiliations of Jim Crow, no longer expected to accept less because of the color of their skin. Though whites still controlled the state's economic and political establishment, there were fewer impediments that blacks had to overcome. It was a hopeful time.

The year 1968 was also the year Gov. Lurleen B. Wallace died. Now some might find it odd that a male-dominated political system such as Alabama's would elect a woman governor, but the state had shown that gender did not always stand for more than ability. After Hattie H. Wilkins left office in 1923, fifteen years passed before another woman, Sibyl M. Pool of Linden, was elected to the legislature. Pool proceeded to became a one-woman political dynasty. Re-elected to the house of representatives, during her second term she was appointed secretary of state, a post to which she was elected two years later, which made her the first woman voted into a state-wide office. Four years later she ran for state treasurer, carried sixty-five of the state's sixty-seven counties, and polled more votes than any candidate in state history. Then in 1954 she ran for, and was elected to, the Public Service Commission—winning every county in the process. By 1966, the year Lurleen Wallace was elected, some political insiders were suggesting that if times were not what they were, Sibyl Pool might well have been the state's first woman governor.

But times were what they were. Lurleen B. Wallace, Mrs. George Wallace, had offered herself (or maybe was offered, it is hard to say) as a candidate because her governor husband could not get the Alabama constitution changed so he could succeed himself. Elected on the promise that George would be the power behind the throne, Mrs. Wallace nevertheless proved a popular chief executive, and in some fields, mental health for example, she actually did some good. How much good she could have done, we'll never know. She was treated for cancer in 1965 and believed cured. Not long after her inauguration the disease returned, and this time there was no relief. She died in May of her second year in office.

Albert P. Brewer, lieutenant governor and a recognized "Wallace man," took over when the governor died, and to the surprise and delight of many proved a capable and effective administrator. With an attention to the details of governing that George Wallace never showed, Brewer initiated a number of reforms, especially in public education, and his mild demeanor and conciliatory style may have helped his state through the trauma of integration. It certainly did not hurt.

It was not without reason, therefore, that Brewer believed he could be governor in his own right in 1970. Besides, word was out that Wallace, with his sights set on the presidency, would not run. But the word was wrong. Finding he needed a state base to support his national aspirations, Wallace decided to challenge his former ally, and at almost the last minute threw his hat in the ring. Undaunted, Brewer put together a coalition of middle-class whites, who saw the former governor as a greater threat to peace and prosperity than were integration and newly enfranchised blacks, and to the surprise of most came in first in the Democratic primary. But there was no majority, and in the runoff that followed, Wallace, or at least his operatives, conducted one of the most vicious campaigns in this state's history.

Spreading rumors about immoral goings-on in the Brewer family and playing the race card for all it was worth, the former governor proved he was still a hero to state segregationists. But Wallace had also added to his constituency by promoting industry and expanding educational opportunities through a network of trade schools and junior colleges. Though these efforts also offered exceptional patronage opportunities for the governor, or at least for the cronies who ran the state while he was out tilting at liberal windmills, the fact remains that many Alabamians, black and white, benefited as well. All these factors combined to give George Wallace a narrow victory over Albert Brewer and ended the political career of one of Alabama's most progressive governors.

Back in office, Wallace began once again to campaign against Washington and for the presidency. However, the inclination to violence that struck down Dr. King emboldened other assassins, and in May of 1972, while the governor was campaigning in Maryland, he was shot. Paralyzed and in pain, Wallace returned to his state and began to reconsider his options. With the Alabama constitution amended to let him succeed himself, he could and would run for governor again. But in the race with Brewer, Wallace realized that black voting strength was growing, and if he wanted to be reelected, he would have to find another card to play. George Wallace was good at that game.

SO WHAT CAME OUT OF THE '60S?

Depends on whom you ask. No one can doubt today that Wallace-inspired segregationist intransigence left its mark on the state and its people. Birmingham lost nearly two decades of economic growth because businesses did not want to relocate to a city whose reputation included Bull Connor's dogs and the murder of children. This image, plus the antiunion attitudes of some of the city's largest employers, caused federal and private projects to seek other locations. As a result, Atlanta, the "city too busy to hate," flourished. "Bombingham" did not.

Other cities—Mobile, Montgomery, Selma—suffered from the state's reputation. Only Huntsville, with the Redstone Arsenal and Marshall Space Flight Center, seemed to overcome the disadvantages and thrive, an interesting (and ironic) commentary on the impact the dreaded federal government could have on the local economy.

But white Alabamians did have one thing in which to take pride—football. Alabamians, black and white, love the sport. And though their devotion may be no greater, or no more frenzied, than that found in other states, Alabamians believe it is.

During the '60s it was. Especially for white folks. During that decade about the only place one could find the national press saying something positive about the state was on the sports page. In 1961, 1964, and 1965 Coach Paul ("Bear") Bryant and his team of "skinny little boys" from the University of Alabama won national championships. The fact that he did this with all-white squads was not lost on segregationists, but that was only part of the reason why so many people who never set foot inside that university, or any university, proudly wore the crimson and white and yelled "Roll Tide."

Bear Bryant gave Alabama whites something of which to be proud, he "stood up for Alabama" more successfully than Wallace ever did, and three national championships only added to his legend. Later, when Bryant finally integrated his team, black Alabamians joined his devotees. Although the University of Alabama and its arch rival, Auburn University, have about the same number of alumni, polls show that since the 1960s, the U of A has had a far greater following among the general public. These "pickup truck alumni" were Bear Bryant folks. Most of them were also Wallace folks. And given a choice between the two, most of them would have gone with the Bear.

14

The Age of Wallace and After

It can be argued, successfully I think, that Alabama changed more in the two decades after *Brown v. Board of Education* than it did in the seventy-five years preceding it. The Civil Rights movement altered things in ways that Alabama liberals of the 1930s and 1940s could hardly have believed possible. Moreover, and some may take issue here, the movement accomplished its goals with relatively little violence.

That's right, little violence. Relatively. Though previous chapters have cataloged all sorts of outrages against black Alabamians, when one considers what the Civil Rights advocates faced—the vows whites made to resist at all costs, the way public officials ignored and sometimes encouraged assault and murder—it is remarkable that more people were not killed. Today, in Montgomery, at the Southern Poverty Law Center, a memorial lists the name of forty-one individuals who died during those bitter years. Many of them died in Alabama. Many other Alabamians were brutalized, beaten, abused, harassed. Their names are not listed. And still, those who lived through it, who heard the talk and saw the hatred, cannot help but conclude that, in the end, Dr. King's nonviolence worked. That by absorbing the blows, those struggling to free black Alabamians from Jim Crow wore down the oppressors, exhausted them, forced a pause that led to reflection that led, in the end, to peace. The forty-one martyrs were surely too many. But how many more would there have been if violence had answered violence?

Integration, however, was not the only change. By the 1970s the old man with the little cotton patch was gone. So was the mule. No one remembers which went first. One day they just weren't there, and his farm belonged to someone else, who pulled down the shed and crib, planted the patch and feed lot in pines, and used the house for storage. A few years more and the house fell over. Trees and kudzu filled the blank spaces, and soon the only way you could tell that anyone had lived there was by a piece of broken crockery next to the one surviving stone pillar on which one corner of the house had rested. By then only a few neighbors, old people, could recall the man's name. None of them remembered the mule's. It was Betty.

Deserted farms sprinkled the countryside. Sharecropping was a thing of the past. So was tenant farming. One person, one family, could no longer make a living from the land. At mid-century there were more than two hundred thousand farms in the state. In the 1980s the number dipped below fifty thousand. Yet as the number of farms decreased, the size of surviving farms grew larger. Federal farm policies had done what they were designed to do—turn farming into agribusiness.

Reacting to this trend, and benefiting from it, the old farm bureau transformed itself into the Alabama Farmers Federation (ALFA), shifted its focus to selling insurance, and became a household name in the state. But ALFA executives still were Bourbons at heart, so with the money they made they hired lobbyists, and with the help of the Alabama Forestry Commission, they did what their Bourbon ancestors had done—kept property taxes low and social services starved.

Meanwhile, out away from towns, a family could drive for miles on Jim Folsom roads and seldom see a soul. You would hardly believe folks had ever lived out there, at least until spring, when daffodils push up in rows and clumps where a farm wife, hoping for a bit of beauty, had planted them long ago.

Alabamians were moving. During the 1970s and 1980s more than half the counties lost population. Rural areas suffered the most, as their people were siphoned off to Birmingham, Mobile, Montgomery, and Huntsville, where the jobs were, or at least where the wanderers hoped they would be. But there was another migration, more insidious and debilitating, that took some of Alabama's best and brightest out of the state. For reasons only they could explain, scores, hundreds, maybe thousands of young, well-educated Alabamians decided here was not where they wanted to live and raise their families. During this period the goal of many promising professionals trained in Alabama was to get a job out of state. Pundits called it a brain drain. Politicians complained that Alabama taxpayers were footing the bill and other states were getting the benefits. But no one seemed to know what to do about it.

And yet, amid all this uncertainty, some things in some places seemed to be turning around. Birmingham, after watching itself pilloried in the press, after seeing the steel industry collapse amid recession and retrenchment, and after witnessing its leaders miss chance after chance to improve the city and its reputation, began to find itself. Or maybe reinvent itself. Maybe that is what it did. Either way, a biracial city government with a new economic outlook began to focus Birmingham's energies on its service economy and on the medical complex growing out of the University of Alabama campus downtown. People, black and white, were finding out that the Magic City was a good place to live.

Huntsville, with its federally financed military-industrial complex, prospered as well, and Mobile, despite white flight to the eastern shore of the bay and Baldwin County, began an aggressive effort to revive downtown and make the city a desirable place to visit and to call home. Other towns, especially in North Alabama, also enjoyed real, if uneven, prosperity, so that by the end of the century it could be said, guardedly, that in parts of the state the much-anticipated "New South" finally had arrived.

BUT WHAT ABOUT POLITICS?

Of all the changes wrought in and on Alabama in the wake of the Civil Rights movement, the most dramatic, the most revolutionary, and in many ways the most historically consistent was the emergence of a two-party political system. Okay, some would say the emergence of a "no-party" political system, and they have a point. However, the fact remains that while Alabama's "parties" seldom showed the unity of position and philosophy, much less the organization and loyalty that one usually associates with a political party, folks here began identifying themselves by competing party labels. In other words, some Alabamians began calling themselves Republicans.

And that was something new.

ENTER THE GOP

Different people at different times have tried to ferret out the origins of Alabama's Republican Party. Some point back to the 1928 revolt against Catholic-wet-urban-Yankee-Al Smith, when evangelical Protestants, suburban conservatives, and die-hard southerners bolted the party rather than vote for someone so unlike themselves. Others note conservative concern over New Deal racial policies and Gov. Frank Dixon's 1942 warning to Alabama Democrats that the national party was "dynamiting their social structure." Dixon, like many other white Alabamians, became a Dixiecrat six years later and raised the banner of states' rights to halt Truman's "federal gestapo" and those "who would destroy our civilization and mongrelize our people."

But we would be wrong to believe that race alone drove Alabamians out of the Democratic Party. Prominent among the disillusioned were businessmen, the big mules and their ilk, who believed that a federal government empowered in civil rights might soon be a federal government capable of rewriting labor laws, contractual obligations, and the rights of property to favor the masses. Thus it was no surprise to find Alabama corporations including in their goals a statement of opposition to "all socialistic and communistic economic systems" and warnings about the dangers of "One World Government." Race mattered, but not exclusively.

So the steady erosion of Democratic strength that began earlier gained momentum in the 1950s when some prominent businessmen actually admitted they were Republicans and endorsed GOP candidate Dwight D. Eisenhower—twice. "Ike" lost the state both times, but returns showed Republican strength growing in the Black Belt, where race mattered most, and in the urban counties, where future business leaders were settling into upscale suburbs. Still, old ties were strong, and some citizens organized into committees of States' Rights Democrats in an effort to remain in the party of their fathers. But for them the effort was futile, and the committees became little more than whistle stops on their route to the GOP.

Getting Black Belt planters and big mules to switch parties was one thing. Getting the general population to make the move was another matter. While some folks might cite their grandfathers' hatred of Reconstruction Republicans as cause sufficient to vote Democratic—"Granddaddy would turn over in his grave if I . . . "—more often they remembered it was Hoover who "hollered 'all aboard'" when "business went to hell" in '29. FDR, the Democrats, and the New Deal had saved them, or so they believed, and that was enough.

Besides, back then Republicans were an odd lot. Small-town children growing up in the '40s and '50s, even in the '60s, can recall being told, in hushed tones, "he's one," and turning to see someone shuffling down the sidewalk, alone, an outcast, and asking "one what?" and being told "a Republican." Later grown up, children learned that Republicans weren't that bad, really. But in a culture where being in the mainstream was so important, to cut oneself off from the cultural center by choice, to deny oneself the acceptance that was given every Democrat, seemed to suggest mental imbalance at best—at worst, moral degeneracy.

And still the Republicans marched on. Reorganized and refocused, in 1962 they put a candidate in the field against Lister Hill, the distinguished senator whom Alabamians could thank for TVA, rural hospitals, libraries, and a host of education initiatives. Hill's opponent, Gadsden businessman James D. Martin, did not run against this record, but rather against the senator as a Democrat, a "liberal," and a lackey for the Washington establishment. Borrowing from George Wallace, and in some cases anticipating him, Martin made states' rights, southern chauvinism, and fiscal conservatism his issues, leaving Hill with little but tired populist rhetoric to inspire the troops. Had Wallace himself not joined the fray on behalf of the Democrat, Hill might well have lost, but his narrow, sixty-eight-hundred-vote margin of victory unnerved the senator, and he retired at the end of his term.

Wallace's entry into the contest helps explain why Republican pioneers, the ones who created the party in the 1960s, hated George Wallace. Though any comparison of Wallace's rhetoric with that of the state's rising Republicans reveals that they were singing from the same song sheet, Wallace ignored the connection and fought the GOP almost as hard as he fought Washington and the federal government. Except for a brief flirt with independency in 1968, George Wallace spent his political years as a Democrat. Which meant that Alabama voters, Alabama white voters, stayed with the party as well. But would this loyalty survive Wallace? That was the question.

HUGGING THE ELEPHANT

Despite Wallace, Republicans made headway in the state. In 1964 the GOP nominated Sen. Barry Goldwater of Arizona as its presidential candidate. Goldwater's fiscal conservatism endeared him to big mules, while his vote against the Civil Rights Act of 1964 made him something of a hero among Black Belt planters, even though they knew the vote was cast over constitutional quibbles and not racial reservations. But Goldwater's appeal was broader than that, so broad, in fact, that he could overcome missteps that would have cost other candidates dearly.

Visiting North Alabama during the campaign, Goldwater suggested that the time had come to get the federal government out of private business and that it might be a good idea to sell TVA. Word of the remark spread, and soon bumper stickers appeared all along

the Tennessee Valley—"Sell TVA, Hell, I'd Rather Sell Arizona"—
but what was once heresy was heresy no longer. Goldwater carried
Alabama with nearly 70 percent of the vote. Arizona, Alabama, and
three other Deep South states went Republican. Those five were all
he got.

As far as Alabama Republicans were concerned, it was a great
day. Goldwater's coattails carried in five GOP congressmen and
nearly a hundred local office seekers. Democrats were not so happy,
as one revealed in a note of congratulations she sent to a Republican
friend:

> The election is over,
> Let hard feelings pass.
> I'll hug your elephant
> And you kiss my ass.

Meanwhile, newspapers throughout the state heralded the arrival
of two-party politics. The newspapers, however, were wrong. Wallace, running his wife's campaign for governor, reinvigorated the
Democrats and, in 1966, that party recaptured many of the local
offices it had lost and a couple of congressional seats in the bargain.
Though Republicans vowed a comeback, they would have to wait
until Alabama was no longer Wallace country.

Then the ex-governor was off again, running against "pointy-
headed bureaucrats" in Washington who wanted to tell hardworking
taxpayers who could live in their neighborhoods, where they could
send their children to school, and whom they could serve in their
stores. Around the country he went, ranting and raving about law
and order, welfare cheats, communists, hippies, and our "socialistic" government's "blueprint for federal control of education." And
middle-class and lower-middle-class Americans—because they were
"all southerners" now, because (as one journalist noted) they all "feel
they are left out in the cold while the country's leadership pampers
the undeserving shiftless"—listened and believed.

Republicans listened too, and nationally did what the party could not do in Alabama. They borrowed (some would say stole) a page from the Wallace campaign book and from it fashioned the "southern strategy" that put Richard Nixon in the White House. From the ruins of George Wallace's 1968 and 1972 runs for the presidency, a new GOP emerged, and the "Solid South" that was once Democratic became, in a short time, Republican.

EXCEPT FOR ALABAMA

Wallace returned home, wounded politically and physically, to an Alabama that was still his if he wanted it—which, of course, he did. Republicans watched in dismay as the folks on whom GOP hopes depended rallied to their hero and in 1974 reelected him governor. So complete was the Democratic victory on the state level that four years later, when candidates came out of the woodwork to succeed Wallace, the best the GOP could find was Guy Hunt, a Cullman County probate judge who was also a Primitive Baptist minister, small farmer, and one-time Amway salesman—hardly representative of the big mules and planters who ran the party.

But the Republican establishment had no cause for concern. In 1978 Hunt was crushed by Forrest "Fob" James, a former Auburn football great and millionaire businessman whose political career underscored the GOP's problem. Starting out a Republican, James realized that with Wallace running the state, only a Democrat could be elected governor, so he switched parties—a move that required no philosophical readjustment, since white Democrats and Republicans believed much the same things. This, however, can be said about the James campaign: For the first time in years, race was not a significant issue. Touring the state in a yellow school bus to emphasize his support for education, James vowed to run Alabama like a business and put an end to "insider" politics—priorities most voters shared.

When he won, reform-minded Alabamiams took hope. But as had happened so often before, just when Alabama seemed about to break away from its past, forge a place for itself in what progressives were calling the "New, New South," something went wrong. And once again, the fault lay both in our stars and in ourselves.

During the James administration the nation sank into a deep recession, and nowhere was it deeper than in Alabama. With unemployment rates among the highest in the country and tax revenue falling, there was little James could do to carry out educational reforms. But even if the money had been there, the governor would have had a difficult time getting his bills passed. Unwilling (or unable) to cultivate legislative support, more inclined to command than to seek consensus, and often inattentive to the day-to-day business of governing, Governor James's popularity sank so low that after four years in office he washed his hands of the whole thing and returned to private life.

WALLACE REDUX

Coincidental with James's decision not to run in 1982 was news that, once again, George Wallace was getting into the race. But the perennial candidate was a sickly shadow of his former self, and though he still could command a core of supporters, many of them holdovers from the old segregationist days, Wallace knew that the politics of race could no longer win the Democratic nomination in a state where black voters were increasingly important in the political equation. So to no one's surprise, with Alabama still reeling from the recession, the former governor returned to populist themes, castigated corporations, their lobbyists, and the Republicans as enemies of working men and women, and vowed to bring in new industries and create jobs. This time Wallace did not leave African Americans at the back door with their hats in their hands. Acutely aware that he could not win the nomination without their support, George Wallace tearfully apologized for his racist past and vowed that in the future he would "represent the average man and woman, black and white."

And average men and women, black and white, believed him. In the primary and the runoff Wallace received more than half of the black votes cast, and that was enough.

Then he faced the Republicans in what was surely the first real, toe-to-toe two-party contest for the governorship since Reconstruction. The GOP rallied behind Emory Folmar, Montgomery's "law and order" mayor who many believed could "out-Wallace Wallace." But though they had the organization and had the money, the Republicans were no match for the former governor. Injecting class into the campaign to a degree unseen since the days of Jim Folsom, Wallace attacked the Republicans as a "rich elite" who would govern at the expense of the little man and promised that his administration would be fair to everyone, regardless of race or status.

And he won, taking some 58 percent of the votes cast. But what really drew attention was the way black Alabamians rallied around their former enemy. When the votes were counted it was found that Wallace had carried all ten of the state's majority black counties— most of them by a two-to-one margin. George Wallace owed his election to the very voters that he had earlier tried to disfranchise. Of all the ironies in Alabama political history, this is one of the greatest.

REPUBLICAN REDIVIVUS

Although the Wallace comeback was surely discouraging to Republicans, some saw in the situation the seeds of future victories. Where once the Democrats were the "white man's party," that 1982 election revealed that the most dependable Democratic voters were now black. Moreover, in much of old Democratic North Alabama, the party of Roosevelt and Truman no longer held the loyalties of blue-collar folks. Just as national Republicans had discovered ways to appeal to working-class Americans, ways to turn them into "Reagan Democrats," Alabama Republicans discovered that Wallace's years of castigating national Democrats for neglecting common people's concerns had born fruit. All Alabama Republicans had to do was figure out a way to get Alabamians to focus their antiestablishment outrage on the Democrats. Or to put it another way, Alabama Republicans had to figure out how to become heirs of Wallace without admitting it.

This trick proved easier to do nationally than on the state level. Ronald Reagan's 1980 presidential campaign captured the imagination of white Alabamians of all classes, and "liberal" became the ultimate political pejorative. Reagan carried Alabama then and again in 1984, and Republicans remained prominent in the state's congressional delegation. Equally important, Democratic senators and congressmen who remained held their seats by acting more and more like Republicans. But back home Democrats continued to control the courthouses, the legislature, and the governor's office. Nothing short of a political miracle could dislodge them.

In 1986 that was what the Republicans got. Of course, it didn't look that way at first. Even though Wallace had announced he would not seek reelection, the Democratic field was so crowded with popular contenders that few Republicans thought a run for the state's highest office was worth the trouble. So they turned once again to Guy Hunt to carry the party standard. Then GOP leaders watched with glee as the Democrats self-destructed.

It was an unusually bitter primary, even for Democrats, but after the election and runoff it seemed that Attorney General Charles Graddick, a former Republican, had narrowly defeated longtime Democratic loyalist Lt. Gov. Bill Baxley for the nomination. But Baxley did not concede, and shortly his supporters filed a protest with the Democratic Party, claiming that Graddick had won with illegal crossover votes cast by Republicans trying to influence the outcome. Party officials, most of whom supported Baxley, set up a committee to investigate, and thus began a series of hearings and rulings that soon tried the patience of even the most interested observer. Finally, as is so often the case in Alabama, it was left to the U.S. Department of Justice to resolve the matter, and in August 1986, a three-judge federal panel announced that Graddick had indeed been elected illegally and that the Democratic Party could either hold another election or give the nomination to Baxley.

The public wanted a new election. Party regulars wanted Baxley. So Bill Baxley got the nod, and Guy Hunt was on his way to the governor's mansion.

Outraged Graddick supporters first considered a write-in campaign, and for a while the candidate encouraged their efforts. But he could see it was a losing cause. So when a group of wealthy businessmen and lobbyists offered to help pay his campaign debts if he would drop out, Graddick decided to give it up. Returning to the Republican fold, the defeated Democrat campaigned for Hunt, who systematically attacked Baxley as a "liberal" and warned that in office he would be overly influenced by "special interests"—the powerful Alabama Education Association and the Alabama Democratic Conference, which spoke for black interests in the state. This injection of race into the campaign upset some voters, but old Wallace loyalists found comfort in it, saw Hunt as one of their own, and lined up behind him. The Wallace folks proved the difference, and Guy Hunt from Holly Pond became Alabama's first Republican governor since Reconstruction.

REPUBLICAN ALABAMA

As I said, Guy Hunt was not what founders of Alabama's modern Republican Party had in mind when they envisioned one of their own in the governor's office. Even the Democrats during the campaign had pointed out that he was a little short of expectations, short on style, short on education, and short on administrative experience. They also observed, gleefully in some cases, that unlike the GOP big mules, what little business acumen the candidate possessed came from a brief, not-too-successful career as a salesman. But Hunt instinctively knew and said what Wallace had known and said, that salesmen and such were "much more highly regarded than both lawyers and politicians."

Guy Hunt was no Black Belt planter or big mule patrician. He was a man of the people and proud of it.

But if Hunt knew his election was a fluke, an accident, he didn't act like it. He went right to work, dismissed most of the old Wallace crowd, filled appointments with as many Republicans as he could find, and set out to strengthen the party all the way down to the county level. Again, his instincts were right, for he knew that until Republicans could establish themselves locally, Democrats would continue to control the courthouses and put their folks in the legislature.

That stirred up a hornet's nest. It was one thing for the governor to want to shake up the executive branch, but anything beyond that was meddling. So for four years Governor Hunt fought with the Democratic house and senate and in most cases lost. At the same time, he had to contend with factions within his own party. Urban business groups, suburban ("white flight") interests, and rural agricultural allies had united as Republicans to get rid of the Democrats, but beyond a general commitment to fiscal and social conservatism, they could not completely agree on what to do and how to do it. So for the most part they did nothing.

And that pretty well sums up the first Hunt administration.

BOURBONISM REDUX

But let's not blame Hunt entirely. He had to play the hand history dealt him. Bourbon Democracy, that political philosophy on which the Constitution of 1901 was based and which made low taxes, scant social services, and white supremacy the law of the land, was still alive and well. It had survived two world wars, a depression, decades of social upheaval, and economic readjustment to reemerge as the foundation on which Alabama's Republican Party was built. Sure the planks of the platform had been rearranged a bit. Higher taxes were acceptable so long as they had little impact on those with property—agriculture and timber interests mainly. Social services could be expanded so long as they did not cost too much or reward sloth (or Democrats). As for white supremacy, federal laws and economic realities had made open, mean racism both illegal and unprofitable, but it did not take long to see that in Alabama the GOP was the white man's party. Nor did it take a political genius to realize that blacks could expect little from Republicans.

Having gone full circle, Alabama returned to where it started, which gets us back to Guy Hunt. Like the hill country Republicans who were his political ancestors, Guy Hunt was more a populist than a Bourbon, so when he ran for reelection in 1990, he (and his advisors) crafted a campaign that played on his folksy image and on the general belief among many Alabama voters that, despite a lackluster record, the governor was guiding the state in the "right direction." Or to put it as Hunt himself did in one of his early commercials, conditions in Alabama were just "fine."

Hunt's opponent was Paul Hubbert, head of the Alabama Education Association (AEA), who had survived a rough primary election to capture the nomination. Like Hunt, he was not a particularly exciting candidate, and when asked the difference between the two, one local philosopher without portfolio replied:

"What you got here is a Primitive Baptist (Hunt) running against a member of the Church of Christ (Hubbert). It's all a question of whether you want to have your feet washed or sing without music."

But it was more than that, really. Or at least it could have been. It could have been a contest between a progressive moderate who wanted to use state resources to improve the lives of its people, which was essentially what Hubbert intended to do, and a well-meaning reformer, Hunt, who felt he could satisfy the Bourbons in his party without compromising his own populist instincts.

That is what it could have been. What it became was a campaign characterized by one candidate (Hunt) calling himself a conservative, denouncing his opponent as a liberal, and forcing the accused (Hubbert) to spend time defending himself against charges of being soft on crime, tolerant of homosexuality, and a tool of special interests, which was what Republicans called the AEA. And when the accused challenged the accuser to a debate so that all of this could be aired before the public, the accuser refused. Instead Hunt's campaign treated Alabama voters to a series of TV commercials showing a cigar-smoking Hubbert sitting in the back seat of a car with Joe Reed, one of the most powerful black politicians in the state.

That's right, *black*. Combining the ultimate populist ploy with basic Bourbon strategy, Republicans played the race card, and won. In November Guy Hunt took 52 percent of the votes cast, a margin of victory made possible by support from small-town Alabamians on whose loyalty Democrats had always counted. Hunt had done in Alabama what Ronald Reagan had done nationally—get the lower-middle-class vote. "Wal-Mart Republicans," one writer called them. And that's what they were.

REPUBLICANS IN CRISIS

The problem with Guy Hunt's election was just that. It was his and only his. Despite his popularity, Hunt's coattails were short, and few Republicans benefited from his victory. So he took office facing a legislature filled with Democrats spoiling for a fight. Actually, it was not so much the Republicans and Democrats who were ready for a tussle, but the lobbyists who financed the campaigns and, more often as not, called the shots. Behind the Republicans were ALFA, committed to low taxes, and the Business Council of Alabama, clamoring for tort reform, while on the Democratic side were AEA, searching for more revenue for education, and the Alabama Trial Lawyers Association, which never saw a tort it didn't like. Sprinkle among these a whole host of other "special interests," and you have something of a shadow government, a bunch of behind-the-scenes string pullers who could, or at least claimed they could, get bills passed, appointments made, and people elected. Alabama, some pundits suggested, actually had four branches of government—executive, legislative, judicial, and lobbyist.

But circumstances, and the state ethics commission, saved Guy Hunt the trouble of having to deal with any of them. Not long after he was sworn in, Hunt was accused of illegally transferring money from an inaugural fund to his own personal account. Though the governor swore that his advisors assured him the switch was legal, the court found otherwise, and in April 1993 Guy Hunt became the first sitting governor to be convicted of a felony and removed from office. Summing up the situation, a supporter and member of a Primitive Baptist church where Hunt had once preached observed "Brother Guy wouldn't have done what he did if he had knowed what he was doing," a statement that, some folks figure, is a pretty good assessment of Alabama politics and politicians.

Replacing Hunt was Lt. Gov. James E. Folsom Jr., "Little Jim," son of "Big Jim" and heir to what passed for liberal (make that moderate) hopes in the state. However, "Little Jim" could not motivate people the way his father had, so when he sought the governor's office on his own, he was unable to turn the Democratic nomination into victory. Instead, in 1994, Alabamians elected Fob James once again—this time as a Republican.

That's right. James had returned to the GOP, and under the banner of "no new taxes" had captured the nomination. Carrying his brand of Bourbon-populism to the people, he united the big mules, Black Belt planters (who were raising more trees than cotton now, not that it mattered), and the Wal-Mart Republicans to end "Little Jim's" hopes of following in his father's footsteps.

James's coattails were a little longer than Hunt's, but Republican gains, and there were many, were less the result of the governor's popularity and more a matter of circumstances. After a public fallout with President Clinton over the chief executive's proposed budget, Alabama's Sen. Richard Shelby left the Democrats for the GOP, a move some said made little difference, since Shelby voted with the Republicans on most matters anyway. When he sought reelection Alabamians told Shelby he had done the right thing and sent him back to Washington for another term. Then to make sure our Republican senator was not lonely up there, state voters sent another Republican, Attorney General Jeff Sessions, to join Shelby in the Senate. Across the hall, in the House of Representatives, most of Alabama's congressional delegation was in the GOP camp. It was a fine example of the Republicanization of Dixie.

Republicans were also making gains in the legislature, but Democrats continued to control both houses, so GOP legislators could not help Governor James very much. Not that he seemed to need it. Or for that matter, want it. More often than not, the governor appeared to be operating in a world where normal rules of conduct and accepted political priorities no longer counted for much. Rejecting conventional wisdom time and again, James based decisions on personal standards and beliefs that many Alabamians found bewildering—and when it comes to political matters, Alabamians aren't bewildered very often.

Convinced that a state with one of the highest incarceration rates in the nation was "coddling criminals," James ordered offenders put in chain gangs and set to work on the public roads, a decision that sent the state's business boosters, industrial recruiters, and image makers into fits of apoplexy. But not James. And not the "law and order" conservatives, inside and outside the state, who applauded the move. However, many Alabamians felt it was a bad idea. They didn't want others to think that they were the sort of people who would chain convicts together and put them in the hot southern sun. They believed chain gangs were something they had moved beyond.

What it comes down to is this: Somehow or other James and his supporters seemed to have missed the moment, a few years back, when other southern states had elected progressive, "New South" governors. Those chief executives wanted to shake off the past and move their states into a future where education was a priority, social services were sufficient, and jobs were plentiful and well-paying. It was not that the James people did not want these things for Alabama; it was just that they weren't able, or willing, to do what it took to get them. Or maybe they really believed, as they said they did, that these things could be had by following the old ways rather than adopting the new—as crime could be reduced by putting chain gangs on the road.

Problem was, it had not worked before, and it didn't work again. James's Bourbonesque pledge of "no new taxes" left the state unable to meet its obligations, so the governor was forced to make heavy cuts in state services, especially higher education. This step naturally outraged educators, who now had to do more with less, and upset a normally pro-James business community desperately in need of trained (and trainable) employees. But it also upset middle-class voters who reasoned that the higher tuition they were paying to send their children to college was a heavier burden than any proposed tax increase might have been.

Looking back, it is apparent that by the second year of his term, James was in trouble. Old South solutions to New South problems simply were not acceptable to progressive elements in the state. Though the governor still had a solid core of followers among Wal-Mart Republicans and agricultural interests, his business supporters were beginning to waver.

Still, James might have held his coalition together if he had spent more time governing and less time on locally popular but unproductive causes like school prayer and the public display of the Ten Commandments. Though many Alabamians agreed with the governor that students should be allowed to pray in school and that the commandments should hang on courthouse walls, they were a little uneasy when James took to telling federal judges that the Bill of Rights somehow did not apply to the state. It seemed, once again, that Governor James had missed something—in this case about a hundred years of constitutional law.

But it was not so much what the governor said, or what he did, but how he said and did it. In other words, image mattered. It was one thing for the *New York Times* to call James a "genius of bumpkin publicity." That was to be expected from the *New York Times*. But when one of the state's own journalists, writing about the governor's trip to Israel to recruit business and visit religious shrines, could suggest that a meeting between our governor and their prime minister would be a confab between "our yahoo and their Netanyahu," well, you could see where things were going.

Even James's own party was worn out. After four years of legislative deadlock and executive ineffectiveness, moderate Republicans deserted the governor. Some supported respected businessman

Winton Blount III for the GOP nomination. Others rallied to Ann Smith Bedsole. The first Republican woman elected to the Alabama House of Representatives and the first woman of either party elected to the state senate, Bedsole was seen by many as the most progressive candidate in the race. James faced his challengers, pressed the attack, played both the race and gender card, and emerged from the bitter primary victorious but burned out. Still, Bedsole and Blount's challenge, and its near success, revealed a shift in Alabama politics which, if carried to what seems a logical conclusion, suggests that significant changes were in the offing.

Both Blount and Bedsole drew their support from the state's substantial, solid middle-class, bourgeois Bourbons who, for most of the century, had defended the status quo—social, economic, and especially racial—as if it were sacred. Given their history they should have voted for James, but they didn't. Why? Because of all the things that had changed in Alabama over the last few decades, the outlook of folks like these might be the most significant. Their eyes on the future, they rejected what seemed to them policies from the past and deserted the governor in droves. And when, after that bitter and divisive primary, James captured the nomination, many of these opponents vowed to stay home on election day or, horror of horrors, vote for the Democrat.

Governor James seemed to sense the sand shifting under his feet. Though he campaigned right up to the November general election, those close to him noticed how the old spark, the old combativeness no longer was there. As a result the lieutenant governor, Don Siegelman, a seasoned Democratic politician who had held most of the important executive offices the state had to offer, carried the day, and Fob James, perhaps a relieved Fob James, went hunting and fishing in Canada.

ALABAMA 2000: DÉJÀ VU ALL OVER AGAIN?

At the center of Don Siegelman's campaign was one issue—a lottery. That's right, a lottery. Following the example of Georgia's successful entry into state-sponsored gambling, candidate Siegelman promised that a similar lottery would bring in money to upgrade educational resources and provide college scholarships for deserving students. These were things Alabamians needed and here was a way for Alabamians to have them.

In the lottery scheme one could see the political mind of Don Siegelman at work. Coming to office as one of the most politically savvy governors in Alabama's history, Siegelman understood that no matter how progressive a plan might be, conservative forces would block the initiative if it meant new taxes. A lottery was a way around that obstacle. So what if gambling promised to place the burden on the backs of Alabama's poorer citizens? That was the way things had always been done in Alabama.

And because the lottery was his principal issue, and because he won handily, it was widely assumed that the constitutional amendment needed to make everything happen would be approved without a hitch. That assumption was wrong.

First of all, a lot of people had voted for Siegelman not because of the lottery but because he wasn't Fob James. Others, disaffected Republicans mostly, sat out the election. And then there were those who, once the new governor was in office, had second sober thoughts about the whole thing. In other words, there was a large block of undecided and ambivalent voters out there, ready to vote for whichever side was able to convince them to support its cause.

All this was to be played out in a highly partisan context, unlike anything run-of-the-mill Alabamians had ever seen before. Despite losing the governor's office Alabama's GOP was in some ways stronger than before, and many in their ranks were ready to take Siegelman on. The newly elected Republican lieutenant governor, Steve Windom, angered by an attempt by the governor to strip him of his power as the presiding officer of the senate, ran the opening session with an iron hand and held his opponents at bay till a compromise was worked out. Anyone who watched what went on was treated to a bizarre bit of absurdist theater that featured a resolute

Windom refusing to surrender the gavel even to go to the restroom and instead (secretly) "relieving himself" in a jug behind the podium. In a state where historical precedents are easy to come by, this was surely a first, and when the tactic was revealed one wit noted that here was a case where "someone did in the Senate what the public would like to do on the Senate."

But behind the show serious politicking was going on. Already on record opposing the lottery, Windom now doubled his efforts, and soon many progressive Republicans joined him. It was not that they were against gambling. Most weren't. And though some said they were troubled because a lottery placed a financial burden on the poor, social implications did not appear a critical concern. Instead, as plans for the lottery became clearer, Republicans who might have voted for it grew uneasy over the prospect of so much money coming in to be handed out by a Democrat. Playing on this fear, and on Alabamians' basic distrust of the people who governed them, lottery opponents produced commercials showing cigar smoking good-ol'-boy politicians sitting around the table dividing up the spoils. These advertisements struck a chord, and soon the word on the streets was that the opportunity for corruption was too great and the lottery should be defeated.

But Republicans were not Siegelman's most potent opponents. Preachers, not politicians, proved the governor's undoing. Not since the days of prohibition had Alabama's churches united to address a political issue, to express the matter in moral terms, and to challenge their congregations to do the right thing. The bulletin board outside a small, central Alabama church may have put it best:

The Governor says yes.
God says no.
What do you say?

Little room for debate, that's what I'd say.

So the churches, especially the evangelical Protestant churches, came together, denounced gambling as a sin, spread the word that a lottery would exploit the poor and the weak, and called on their members to crush it. And they did. Polls showed that those who saw the lottery as a political issue were narrowly divided. But those who felt gambling was a moral matter were overwhelmingly against it. They turned the tide. The lottery lost.

AND WHAT GOOD CAME OF IT AT LAST?

In the chaos and confusion that followed, modern Bourbons, still strong under the one-hundred-year-old, much-amended constitution, moved back to center stage. Meanwhile the governor, stung by his plan's rejection, began to sound like a Bourbon himself. Declaring his opposition to new taxes, Siegelman announced that education could be improved with income from economic growth and set out to recruit new industries and make the business climate more hospitable. Conservatives were skeptical, but with the state benefiting from one of the longest periods of prosperity in American history, it looked for a while like the governor might pull it off. A Mercedes-Benz plant near Tuscaloosa, a Honda plant in Lincoln, and expanded industries in Autauga County, Huntsville, Sylacauga, and McCalla seemed to herald a new age for the state. Optimistic citizens even approved a constitutional amendment to use a portion of offshore gas royalties for economic development, infrastructure improvements, and the expansion of the state docks in Mobile—another way to get things done without raising taxes.

The governor was on a roll. And because he was, he was able to dismiss calls for a constitutional revision and tax reform, say he had other things he needed to do first, and tell those concerned that it would take a "grass roots movement" to get those issues on his agenda.

But the issues would not go away. Take tax reform. Over the years conservative forces had taken the advantages given them by the 1901 Constitution and slowly but surely had constructed a financial arrangement that built Alabama budgets on sales taxes and on income levies that fell heavily on families living below the poverty line. It was, by most measures, one of the most regressive tax systems in the nation. And it was created and maintained with little protest from most Alabamians. But the lottery controversy made the issue difficult to avoid. In the heat of the debate lottery supporters began asking opponents how it was that they could claim to oppose gambling because it hurt the poor and the powerless, yet continue to support a tax structure that did the same thing. Churches in particular were open to the charge, and for some it became a moral dilemma not unlike segregation had been. So they acted. The year after the lottery's defeat Alabama's United Methodist Church conferences and the Alabama Baptist Convention, the state's largest denominations, passed resolutions favoring tax reform. Then in 2001 the Episcopal Diocese of Alabama joined them and urged "the governor and the state legislature to provide relief and hope especially for our most vulnerable citizens and our poorest counties." Tax reform advocates began to believe a new day was dawning.

So did those who wanted a new constitution. Truth was, tax reformers and constitutional revisionists were often the same folks. Aware that a tax code favoring property over people grew naturally from the Bourbon-written 1901 Constitution, members of both groups argued that in order to have a fairer Alabama, the constitution needed to be rewritten. But it was not all about taxes. Reformers also emphasized that a new constitution would give local authorities more control over local matters, streamline the legislative process, and improve the efficiency of one of the nation's least efficient governments. To bring this about, the movement's leaders advocated a popularly elected convention—a democratic solution to the problems created by one of the nation's most undemocratic constitutions.

But calls for reform fell on deaf ears. So long as times were good, so long as the revenue was rolling in, and so long as funds for major projects could be found without asking the public to sacrifice for them, tax reformers were easily ignored. Churches discovered that folks in the pews just could not get as worked up over tax reform as they could over the lottery, so despite encouragement from their leaders congregational enthusiasm waned. As for constitutional reform, though a poll showed that a majority of the legislature claimed to support a rewrite, the few legislative plans that surfaced seemed to favor in-house-generated editorial changes in the document and scant changes in the status quo.

Then, as the year 2000 drew to a close, the economy turned sour. Sales tax receipts, on which the education of Alabama's children depended, came up short. Constitutionally required to balance the budget, the governor and the legislature knew their choices: find some way to bring in additional revenue or scale back programs. The dilemma was hardly a new one. Neither was the solution. In February 2001 Governor Siegelman, standing by his "no new taxes" pledge, announced that state schools would have to get by with 6.2 percent less than they had been told they would have.

Soon word spread that over a thousand teachers might lose their jobs, that more students would have to be crammed into classrooms, and that computer upgrades and Internet expansion would have to be delayed for who knows how long. Then, horror of horrors, some school systems announced that they might have to cancel football season in the fall. This was getting serious. As concern grew there were more calls for tax reform, more calls for constitutional revision, and more explanations and excuses why changes could not, should not be made.

And Alabama entered the twenty-first century.

FINDING THE NEW ENEMY

What happened next should come as no surprise to anyone who has read this far. Governor Siegelman, his back to the wall, began looking for the source of the problem—or if you believe his critics, began looking for someone or something to blame it on. He found both in the Constitution of 1901. In what some called a political epiphany, and others called a conversion of convenience, the governor joined the reformers. Claiming this most recent crisis had convinced him that Alabama's underfunded schools, starved social services, and frequent budget shortfalls were constitutionally created, he announced that now he favored a rewrite.

What's more, the governor let it be known that he believed a convention was the way to go. Almost immediately the issue shifted from what to do to how to do it. Lobbyists for interests that had thrived under the old constitution found the convention debate a convenient way to delay and maybe even derail the reform movement. Skillfully avoiding the merits of constitutional revision, these supporters of the status quo and their legislative allies attacked the details, raised fears of what could happen if the "wrong" people got control of the convention, and convinced other legislators to oppose a resolution that would have put the convention question to a popular vote. Ironically, black legislators, who seldom agreed with conservatives, concluded that their interests would not be served by a convention either and joined the opposition. This odd alliance blocked the measure and with it constitutional reform.

For the moment.

Bloodied but unbowed, reform interests vowed to continue the fight. Nervous opponents began plotting ways to stop them. And uncommitted politicians started trying to figure out which enemy to oppose, which cause to champion, if they wanted to stay in office.

THE ELECTION OF 2002

Don Siegelman was one of the politicians who wanted to stay in office, but he knew it would not be easy. With the help of equally desperate legislators, he cobbled together a few new taxes, shifted some money about, and took some sting out of the budget cuts. But with the economy getting no better, he knew he had to find a way to raise more revenue without upsetting any members of the coalition that had become Alabama's Democratic Party. So he quit blaming the constitution for a moment and announced that the state was in such sorry shape because misguided interests had rejected the lottery and selfish corporations were using loopholes to avoid paying taxes. Then, those enemies identified, he promised that, if reelected, he would bring the lottery back and close the loopholes once and for all.

No talk of constitutional reform, apart from references to being for it. And nothing on tax reform, other than to say the system was unfair. Just a safe attack on the Democrats' ancient adversaries—big mules and narrow minds—to hold party loyalists together and get them to the polls.

In a hard-fought primary the Republicans picked three-term congressman Bob Riley from Ashland to carry their standard. Free from ties to the political culture of Montgomery (and unencumbered by state political experience), Riley offered himself as an alternative to the policies of the past, policies that had gotten the state into the mess it was in, policies that were, he suggested, the real enemy.

It was a bitter contest, marred by personal attacks on both sides and marked by a near-universal avoidance of the issues voters said they wanted discussed. So on election day the committed and the confused went to the polls and, for a moment there, it looked like Siegelman had won. Then an error was found in the Baldwin County returns, and the election swung to Riley—by just over three thousand votes. The Siegelman camp cried foul, demanded a state recount, and showed every indication of being willing to fight the outcome as long as it took. Then they gave it up, quit. Siegelman announced that for the good of the state he would step aside, and he did.

Some said it was a noble thing to do. But others, quietly, speculated that the real reason was that the governor finally saw the future for what it was and decided he didn't want to be governor any more.

And who could blame him? Things were that bad.

SO, WHAT NEXT?

Governor Riley inherited a host of problems, but at the core of it all, this is his dilemma. Although new auto plants and such brought in new jobs, old industries (especially textiles and paper) had been hemorrhaging workers for years. As a result, according to U.S. Census Bureau reports, Alabama families were getting poorer. Yet thanks to the way taxes were collected, these poorer families were expected to generate the revenue necessary for the state to see after the health, education, and welfare of its citizens. They couldn't, of course, so the new governor would be faced with budget shortfalls in almost every agency.

To the casual observer the choice seemed simple—raise taxes or cut services. But nothing is ever simple in Alabama. If social services, starved by years of underfunding, were cut again, public safety, public health, and public education would be seriously undermined, and Bob Riley's political career would come to an inglorious end. That leaves higher taxes. But lower- and middle-income folks in Alabama were already overtaxed, while constitutional and legislative restrictions made it difficult for needed money to be raised from the people who could afford to pay.

So, like it or not, Bob Riley and the Alabama legislature (for they were in it too) were going to have to confront the real enemies—the constitution and the tax system it created. Or so it seems as I bring this to a close. Will it happen? By the time this book is published, we might know. But if it hasn't happened, some folks should be asking why.

Epilogue

To Sum It Up

SWEET HOME ALABAMA

And there you have it.

As the new century begins, Alabama might be, could be, on the verge of changing the system that most observers credit with keeping the state at or near the bottom of just about every ranking that progressive folks don't want to be at the bottom of. OR, Alabama might be, could be, on the verge of rejecting reform, of clinging to the status quo, and continuing to operate under a constitution that, if nothing else, has accomplished what its authors wanted to accomplish. Those mighty men of 1901 wanted a state where the poor and powerless stayed poor and powerless, where the propertied and privileged stayed propertied and privileged, and where the majority in the middle helped keep it that way. That is what they wanted, and that is what they got.

And that is what Alabama has.

But one wonders if people and politicians realize just what constitutional revision will really require? As reformers go through the document and its amendments, they will be forced again and again to deal with the reasons, the rationale, that put the offending articles there in the first place. And the interests that have benefited from provisions that reformers find offensive will have to defend what is there as they rally to protect what is theirs. Alabama's constitution and its amendments are like the rings of a tree, layer upon layer added to protect the central core, a core made up of groups that believe themselves entitled to special treatment. Peeling off the layers will demand a reevaluation of the rules, regulations, incentives, and exemptions these interests have fought for, have accumulated, and are determined to keep. To change all this, or just some of it, will require Alabamians to discuss what was done, understand why it was done, judge whether it should have been done, and, if it needs righting, set it right. In other words, Alabamians will have to confront the past and, if the past is found wanting, chart a new direction for the future. Can Alabamians do it?

I don't know.

But recently something happened that gives me hope.

A LITTLE TOWN SHALL LEAD THEM

Recall that in the early 1920s a number of Alabama towns raised monuments to local soldiers who gave their lives in what was called then "The Great War." One of these was a little county-seat community down in the southwest corner of the state.

It was the county's first war memorial. Although the region sent its share of its sons to fight in the southern war of rebellion, citizens never put up anything to commemorate the Lost Cause. After Appomattox the local newspaper editor advised readers to "yield to the stern logic of events and make the best of the situation." Apparently that did not include spending what little money they had on something to memorialize defeat.

But after World War I folks in the county decided that those who fell in that conflict needed to be remembered. So they raised $1,650 by public subscription, and in 1924 they put a memorial in place. It was a simple slab of granite, set down on a mound in front of the courthouse. On it they carved the names: twenty-six whites on one side, thirteen "colored" on the other.

Looking back, one is inclined to consider such segregation as yet another example of the racism of the era, and perhaps it was. But a little digging reveals something else. There were some towns in the state whose monuments listed only white soldiers. This town could have gone that way, but it didn't. Maybe it was because blacks as well as whites contributed to the memorial fund. Why else would Dr. G. G. Daniel, the "Colored Extension Service Farm Demonstration Agent" for the county, have been invited to "represent the colored people" at the dedication and make some "brief remarks"? Now Dr. Daniel's role was probably regulated according to his race; however his being there made the ceremony truly a community event and the monument a memorial to the living as well as the dead.

In time, however, Dr. Daniel was forgotten, and the monument, by then the center of a traffic circle that confused even local drivers, was remarkable only for its inconvenience. Except for the occasional pep rally held there by students from the white high school, no one paid the monument much mind. In the early 1960s, when African Americans staged the county seat's only Civil Rights demonstration, the speaker addressed the crowd from the courthouse steps, not from the monument, and as best people there that day can recall, no mention was made of the segregated slab.

So whites figured blacks didn't care.

And once again, whites were wrong.

The Civil Rights movement changed attitudes, perceptions in the black community, and in time the monument became a sore spot, a visible symbol of segregation and a constant reminder of the pain of the past.

Then, finally, in the spring of 2001, someone decided to do something about it. Members of the local NAACP chapter got one of the county commissioners to approve replacing the old marker with one that listed all the fallen on the same side—alphabetically. Now it is significant to note that the county commissioner who did this was black, which not only explains why the official was sympathetic to the NAACP's position but also reveals how the Civil Rights movement had give black Alabamians a voice in local government.

Ignoring the fact that a single commissioner lacked the authority to issue such an order, someone (no one would say who) had the new marker made, put on a truck, and taken to the county seat. Then, in broad daylight, with local citizens (black and white) looking on and a policeman directing traffic, they took down the old and put up the new. Those watching (including the policeman) assumed it was all on the up-and-up, figured the old one was chipped or something—until they looked more closely.

And then the talk began.

The first criticism came over aesthetics. The new marker did not match the rest of the monument. Then someone noticed mistakes in the carving—a flag turned the wrong way, a name misspelled. Then someone got around to asking who authorized and carried out the change. That's when things began to get hot.

Discovering that the switch was made without public discussion and commission approval, some whites demanded that the old memorial be put back. Blacks countered that though the switch could have been, should have been handled better, the first marker was a daily insult to African Americans, and returning it was not an option.

At that point it could have gotten nasty, but it didn't. Other whites listened to what black citizens were saying and understood why they felt the way they did. Other blacks considered white objections and found merit in some of them. So the two sides began searching for a solution.

They formed a biracial committee—four "good folks that are sort of level" was how one observer described them—and it set to work. Now this state has seen its share of biracial committees, and has seen them collapse along racial lines. But not this one. Maybe it survived because it decided at the outset not to try to ferret out who was responsible for the removal and replacement. Aware, as the old adage goes, that "some swamps just don't need draining," members decided there was nothing to be gained from such an investigation and moved on. They also decided that all of the fallen should be treated equally. At the first meeting one of the white members, a veteran of Korea and Vietnam, pointed out that "everyone bleeds red when shot." From then on it was not a matter of what to do, just how to do it.

This forced the members to ask some really hard questions. Instinctively they understood that no matter how distasteful the old marker was, it was a historic document, one that proved that segregation once permeated southern life and death. Would it be right, some wondered, to remove it, hide it away, and replace it with one that listed the fallen as we wish they had been listed back then? Would it be right, honest, to imply in stone that things have always been as they are? The committee also realized that the segregated marker called citizens to consider how words mean different things to different people at different times. Today "colored" is offensive to many Alabamians, blacks mostly, but some whites as well. But in 1924 "colored" was widely accepted by both races as a polite and proper designation, as in the National Association for the Advancement of *Colored* People. Was this something Alabamians needed to remember, or something they needed to forget? And what, members asked each other, would be lost by lumping everyone together? With African Americans still struggling for their share of history, who would know, looking at an integrated marker, the sacrifice black soldiers made? These were not questions that Alabamians, white or black, were used to asking themselves, much less each other. But the committee, and through it the community, asked them.

About a week later the committee handed the commission its solution. A new marker would be ordered, just like the one removed, except all of the names would be listed alphabetically on one side. On the other side would be a note explaining that this was not the original marker and suggesting that those who wanted to see it could go around the block to the county museum. There they would find the segregated stone along with a simple text telling how, though the dead were divided by race, to have even listed black soldiers back then was an accomplishment for both communities. To this would be added the observation that though the marker reveals some racial toleration, "it is a relic of segregation past and a reminder that all citizens are considered equal now."

AND WHAT DOES THIS PROVE?

It proves Alabamians can do it, can face the past, understand why things were done then, and have the courage to declare that things will be done differently from now on. It proves that even in a state where interests attached to the status quo are so powerful, where attitudes are often so archaic, and where traditions are clung to for security, change is possible. And it gives Alabamians who want change a reason to be optimistic.

It was a little incident, but in it we find evidence of how far Alabama and Alabamians have come. And in considering our journey, where we began, where we are now, and where we are going, we can find comfort in a prayer one preacher, maybe an Alabama preacher, once prayed:

Dear God:
We ain't what we ought to be.
We ain't what we gonna be.
We ain't what we wanta be.
But, thank God,
We ain't what we was.

No, thank God, we ain't.

Bibliographical Essay

The decision to present readers with the following bibliography rather than identify sources in traditional academic footnotes was based on a number of considerations. First, this is not a traditional, academic study. It is not based on exhaustive primary research in archives, courthouses, and family trunks. Instead, I have relied on secondary studies by historians who have ransacked these sources, and I believed that acknowledging my debt to them in this way was appropriate. Moreover, a great deal of what I have written is based on doing what teachers always do—reading a lot and working what is read into lectures and making it their own. The result is often interpretation layered upon interpretation, twisted together in such a way that the original source would be difficult, if not impossible, to discover. In other words, if I honestly tried to tell you where I got some of it, the footnote would go something like this: "I read this somewhere, or somebody told me. I can't remember where or who, but I think it was ———." This intellectual imprecision would have been maddening to scholars preoccupied with sources but would have mattered little to the general reader, for whom footnotes are at best inconvenient and at worst discouraging. Not wanting to do either, I decided against detailed documentation.

Like most historians, however, I found that academic training carried with it a healthy dose of academic responsibility (and academic guilt), so it is impossible for me simply to list possible sources and leave it at that. What follows, therefore, is a compromise. I have pointed out the studies that were most helpful to me and where their impact was significant in what I have written. I have also given credit to people who told me the stories, taught me the songs and poems, and passed along the observations that I absorbed over the years. However, if a story is not identified, an insight not credited, I probably got it from my daddy.

That said, let me begin.

Over the years scores of studies have influenced the way I interpret Alabama's history. Many of these can be found in the bibliography of *Rivers of History: Life on the Coosa, Tallapoosa, Cahaba, and Alabama,* which I wrote in 1995. Although in some cases I have forgotten from which of them I learned what, points they made have found a way into my understanding, and today I often treat their ideas as my own. Albert James Pickett's *History of Alabama and Incidentally of Georgia and Mississippi, from the Earliest Period* (1851) and Albert Burton Moore's *History of Alabama* (1934) are surely two of these. More recently William Warren Rogers, Robert David Ward, Leah Rawls Atkins, and Wayne Flynt, in *Alabama: The History of a Deep South State* (1994), provided readers an exceptional account of the subject, and whenever I needed information and/or insight, it was to this book that I turned. Also helpful in my work was Samuel L. Webb and Margaret E. Armbrester, eds., *Alabama Governors: A Political History of the State* (2001), which is an indispensable handbook for anyone interested in Alabama politics. And for me, like so many others of my generation, the influence of W. J. Cash's *The Mind of the South* (1941) is apparent and appreciated.

Rather than try to recall the many authors and books to which I owe some debt, I will confine this essay to the ones that I consulted (time and again) while preparing this manuscript. For example, my account of early Alabama relies heavily on the work of Charles Hudson—*The Southeastern Indians* (1976) and *Knights of Spain, Warriors of the Sun: Hernando de Soto and the South's Ancient Chiefdoms* (1997). At the same time I think it is important to acknowledge those individuals who provided information and guidance that shaped the way I look at Alabama and Alabama history. In that regard I am indebted to Douglas E. Jones of the Alabama Museum of Natural History for his pig DNA suggestion as a way to clear up the mystery of where de Soto actually went. Harry Holstein of Jacksonville State University invented the DeSoto hubcap story.

For information on the Indian trade and its impact on Native Americans, I turned to Kathryn E. Holland Braund, *Deerskins and Duffels: Creek Indian Trade with Anglo America, 1685–1815* (1993). Claudio Saunt's *A New Order of Things: Property, Power, and the Transformation of the Creek Indians, 1733–1816* (1999) provided an insightful analysis of the impact the plans of Benjamin Hawkins had on the Creek Indians and greatly shaped my thinking about this important period. Primary material found in William Bartram, *Travels*, ed. Francis Harper (1791; reprint, 1958) and C. L. Grant, ed. *Letters, Journals, and Writings of Benjamin Hawkins* (2 vols., 1980) added to my understanding and to the story I am telling. Saunt's work, along with Frank Lawrence Owsley Jr., *Struggle for the Gulf Borderlands: The Creek War and the Battle of New Orleans, 1812–1814* (1981) helped me understand events from both the Indian and the American perspective. An older, but still very interesting, interpretation of this conflict can be found in H. S. Halbert and T. H. Ball's, *The Creek War of 1813 and 1814* (1895). I also frequently consulted Henry deLeon Southerland Jr. and Jerry Elijah Brown, *The Federal Road through Georgia, the Creek Nation, and Alabama, 1806–1836* (1989). The saga of Sarah Merrill is a staple story in southwest Alabama. My version combines accounts told to me by my father and my cousin-in-law Kathryn Tucker Windham. Ed Williams pulled many of the threads together, including interviews with descendants, for an article, "Sarah Merrill: Lone survivor of an Indian raid, her story still lives today," which was published in *The South Alabamian* (May 1976).

Of the many studies of Alabama from statehood to secession, none explained things better for me than J. Mills Thornton III, *Politics and Power in a Slave Society: Alabama, 1800 to 1860* (1978). As for the almost comic maneuvering of political factions in the state, see

Daniel Dupre, "Barbecues and Pledges: Electioneering and the Rise of Democratic Politics in Antebellum Alabama," *Journal of Southern History* (August 1994), which contains the "Barbacuensis" assessment of the relationship between pork and politics. Also important to my understanding of the period was Harriet E. Amos Doss, *Cotton City: Urban Development in Antebellum Mobile* (1985); Elizabeth Fox-Genovese, *Within the Plantation Household: Black and White Women of the Old South* (1988), which gave me insights into the life and world of Sarah Haynsworth Gayle; James Benson Sellers, *Slavery in Alabama* (1950), and the chapter on William Lowndes Yancey in Eric H. Walther, *The Fire-Eaters* (1992). My appreciation of antebellum Alabama was greatly enhanced by period pieces such as Joseph G. Baldwin, *The Flush Times of Alabama and Mississippi* (1853); Philip Henry Gosse, *Letters from Alabama, (U.S.) Chiefly Relating to Natural History* (1859); Fletcher M. Green, ed., *The Lides Go South . . . And West* (Columbia, S.C., 1952); and Johnson Jones Hooper, *Adventures of Captain Simon Suggs, Late of the Tallapoosa Volunteers* (1858). Anyone hoping to grasp the impact that slavery had on the people who were enslaved should consult George P. Rawick, ed., *Alabama and Indian Narratives*, vol. 6 of *The American Slave: A Composite Autobiography* (1941), and E. A. Botkin, ed., *Lay My Burden Down* (1945).

My indispensable guide through Civil War Alabama has been Malcolm C. McMillan, ed., *The Alabama Confederate Reader* (1963). Also important were William Warren Rogers, Jr., *Confederate Home Front: Montgomery During the Civil War* (1999); Arthur W. Bergeron Jr., *Confederate Mobile* (1991); James Pickett Jones, *Yankee Blitzkrieg: Wilson's Raid Through Alabama and Georgia* (1976); and Sarah Woolfolk Wiggins (ed.), *The Journals of Josiah Gorgas, 1857–1878* (1995). On-the-scene insights into the impact of war are found in Rawick's *The American Slave*, vol. 6; Anna M. Gayle Fry, *Memories of Old Cahaba* (1908); Thomas C. DeLeon, *Four Years in Rebel Capitals* (1890); and William Howard Russell, *My Diary, North and South* (1863).

When writing on politics and society in postwar Alabama, I drew on Jonathan M. Wiener, *Social Origins of the New South: Alabama, 1860–1885;* Richard Bailey, *Neither Carpetbaggers Nor Scalawags:*

Black Officeholders during the Reconstruction of Alabama, 1867–1878 (1991); Sarah Woolfolk Wiggins, *The Scalawag in Alabama Politics, 1865–1881* (1977); Allen Johnston Going, *Bourbon Democracy in Alabama, 1874–1890* (1951); William Warren Rogers, *The One-Gallused Rebellion: Agrarianism in Alabama, 1865–1896* (1970); and Sheldon Hackney, *Populism to Progressivism in Alabama* (1969). A recent study by Samuel L. Webb, *Two-Party Politics in the One-Party South: Alabama's Hill Country, 1874–1920* (1997), helped me understand the diversity and persistence of populism in the state. How these issues played out against the background of industrial development in the state was explained in Henry M. McKiven Jr., *Iron and Steel: Class, Race, and Community in Birmingham, Alabama, 1875–1920* (1995). Also helpful was Grace Hooten Gates, *The Model City of the New South: Anniston, Alabama, 1872–1900* (1978). By this time readers will have noticed a southwest Alabama slant in some of the narrative, revealed in a reliance on material from T. H. Ball, *A Glance Into The Great South-East, or, Clarke County, Alabama and Its Surroundings from 1540 to 1877* (1882), and Isaac Grant's *The Clarke County Democrat,* which, except for a few issues during The War, has been in continuous publication since 1856.

Although its scope is broader than the postwar period, Malcolm Cook McMillan's *Constitutional Development in Alabama, 1798–1901: A Study in Politics, the Negro, and Sectionalism* (1955), was particularly helpful on constitutional development during and after Reconstruction. Recent efforts to rewrite Alabama's 1901 Constitution have produced a number of assessments of the origins of that document. The latest scholarly treatment will be found in H. Bailey Thomson, ed., *A Century of Controversy: Constitutional Reform in Alabama* (2002). John Simpson Graham, *History of Clarke County* (1923) is a fine example of the Bourbon interpretation of history applied at the local level, while a pamphlet by James Oscar Prude, *Importance and Growth of Genealogical Work in the South* (1895), is remarkable in its candidly Bourbon analysis of slavery, Civil War, Reconstruction, and redemption. I learned much about the role of women during this and later periods from Mary Martha Thomas, *The New Woman in*

Alabama: Social Reform and Suffrage, 1890–1920 (1992), and from the biographical sketches of those inducted into the Alabama Women's Hall of Fame. *Stepping Out of the Shadows: Alabama Women, 1919–1990* (1995), which Professor Thomas edited, was also helpful, as were the candid comments on women's suffrage by delegates to the 1901 Constitutional Convention, which may be found in the *Official Proceedings of the Constitutional Convention of the State of Alabama, May 21, 1901, to September 3, 1901* (1901). These proceedings also contain some of the most candid white supremacist language found in a public document of the era as well as enlightening comments on class and culture at the turn of the century. Information on the Mitcham War came from my collaborative effort with Joyce White Burrage and James A. Cox, both from Clarke County. The story first appeared as *The Mitcham War of Clarke County, Alabama* (1988) and was told in Harvey H. Jackson, "The Middle-Class Democracy Victorious: The Mitcham War of Clarke County, Alabama, 1893," *Journal of Southern History* (August 1991).

The story of David Crutcher was found in the material collected by the Alabama Historical Commission to support efforts to put his property on the National Register of Historic Places. The saga of Emmett Kilpatrick was pieced together from contemporary newspaper accounts and family papers by Tommy Walker and published in the *Clarke County Democrat* ("Alabama militia almost fought Bolshevik Army to free Wilcox countian," 3 May 1990). Of the many accounts of small-town and rural life at the turn of the century, none is better than Viola Goode Lidell, *With a Southern Accent* (1948), although it should be admitted that my view of this world has been greatly influenced by stories handed down through my family, many of whom were members of that bourgeois Bourbon class that dominated small-town life in the period. The "Heflin blew the whistle" poem was taught me by my father, who learned it from his grandfather. Daddy also told me about the children, his classmates, who packed their lunch pails with hickory nuts and a rock. Illustrations like that stay long with a boy.

Any study of politics in the twentieth-century South must begin with V. O. Key's *Southern Politics in State and Nation* (1949), ably updated and expanded by Earl and Merle Black's *Politics and Society in the South* (1987). However, to understand better how things were "on the ground" in Alabama, I drew on Theodore Rosengarten, *All God's Dangers: The Life of Nate Shaw* (1975); Carl Carmer, *Stars Fell on Alabama* (1934); Clarence Carson, *90 degrees in the Shade* (1935); and James Agee and Walker Evans, *Let Us Now Praise Famous Men* (1941). I rounded out this reading with Wayne J. Flynt's *Poor But Proud: Alabama's Poor Whites* (1989); then I returned to the politics of the period with Robin D. Kelley, *Hammer and Hoe: Alabama Communists During the Great Depression* (1990) and Dan T. Carter's *Scottsboro: A Tragedy of the American South* (1969). For a critical yet sympathetic account of the accomplishments and shortcomings of liberals and liberalism during this period, I turned to John Egerton, *Speak Now Against the Day: The Generation Before the Civil Rights Movement in the South* (1995). Also helpful were Virginia Van der Veer Hamilton's *Hugo Black: The Alabama Years* (1972) and *Lister Hill: Statesman from the South* (1987). I found a glimpse into the Alabama that local liberals wanted outsiders to see in *Alabama: A Guide to the Deep South,* which was compiled by the Writers' Program of the Work Projects Administration and published as part of the American Guide Series in 1941. For insight into the most powerful religious group in the state, I consulted Wayne Flynt, *Alabama Baptists: Southern Baptists in the Heart of Dixie* (1998). And for a look at the darker side of Alabama, I went to Glenn Feldman, *Politics, Society, and the Klan in Alabama, 1915–1949* (1999).

For World War II and the changes it brought to Alabama, I consulted Alan Cronenberg, *Forth to the Mighty Conflict: Alabama and World War II* (1995); Mary Martha Thomas, *Riveting and Rationing in Dixie: Alabama Women and the Second World War* (1987); and Robert J. Jakeman, *The Divided Skies: Establishing Segregated Flight Training at Tuskegee, Alabama, 1934–1942* (1992). In covering this topic the essays in Webb and Armbrester, *Alabama Governors,* were especially helpful. The story of the Hurts comes from Herman C. Nixon, *Lower Piedmont Country: The Uplands of the Deep South* (1946). Insight into the changes that took place in Mobile society and culture can be gained from reading Eugene Walter (as told to Katherine Clark), *Milking the Moon: A Southerner's Story of Life on This Planet* (2001). The "we must be husbands-in-law" story has been repeated so often and in so many ways that I am not sure of the origin. However, I do recall hearing it once from the late R. A. Duke of Sandflat, Alabama. Observations on the decline of the cotton culture come from cited studies and from my own experiences helping my "field-man" father measure cotton when I was a boy.

My understanding of postwar Alabama was greatly enhanced by William D. Barnard, *Dixiecrats and Democrats: Alabama Politics, 1942 to 1950* (1974), while the career of Alabama's most prominent postwar politician was explained to me in George Sims, *The Little Man's Big Friend: James E. Folsom in Alabama Politics, 1946–1958* (1985), and Carl Grafton and Anne Permaloff, *Big Mules and Branchheads: James E. Folsom and Power Politics in Alabama* (1985). I learned the details of one of the great scandals of the era from Margaret Anne Barns, *The Tragedy and the Triumph of Phenix City, Alabama* (1998). Fuller Kimbrell's *From the Farm House to the State House: The Life and Times of Fuller Kimbrell* (2001) provided insights into the inner workings of the Folsom administration. Today, "Big Jim" is part of Alabama folklore. "She was poor but she was honest" was taught to me by Ann Feathers, who at the time was, like me, an expatriate Alabamian living in Georgia. The story of Big Jim on the aircraft carrier appears in many forms. This one was told to me by Jerry Brown, who got it from an Associated Press reporter, who was there.

Though I lived through it, many aspects of the Civil Rights movement escaped my notice until I read Taylor Branch's *Parting the Waters: America in the King Years, 1954–1963* (1988). Other studies that have expanded my understanding of those critical years are Howell Raines, *My Soul Is Rested: Movement Days in the Deep South Remembered* (1977); J. L. Chestnut and Julia Cass, *Black in Selma: The Uncommon Life of J. L. Chestnut Jr.* (1990); Glenn T. Eskew, *But for Birmingham: The Local and National Movements in the Civil Rights Struggle* (1997); Andrew M. Manis, *A Fire You Can't Put Out: The Civil Rights*

Life of Birmingham's Reverend Fred Shuttlesworth (1999); Deborah E. McDowell, *Leaving Pipe Shop: Memories of Kin* (1996); Jimmie Lewis Franklin, *Back to Birmingham: Richard Arrington Jr. and His Times* (1989); Paul Hemphill, *Leaving Birmingham: Notes of a Native Son* (1993); Virginia Foster Durr, *Outside the Magic Circle,* ed. Hollinger F. Barnard (1985); William A. Nunnelley, *Bull Connor* (1991); David J. Garrow, ed., *The Montgomery Bus Boycott and the Women Who Started It: The Memoir of Jo Ann Gibson Robinson* (1987); Sheyann Webb and Rachel West Nelson, *Selma, Lord, Selma: Girlhood Memories of the Civil-Rights Days* (1980); Charles W. Eagles, *Jon Daniels and the Civil Rights Movement in Alabama* (1993): Nancy Callahan, *The Freedom Quilting Bee* (1987); Ellen Sullivan and Marie Stokes Jemison, eds., *An Alabama Scrapbook, 32 Alabamians Remember Growing Up* (1988); J. Mack Lofton Jr., ed., *Voices From Alabama: A Twentieth Century Mosaic* (1993); Jay Lamar and Jeanie Thompson, *The Remembered Gate: Memories of Alabama Writers* (2002); Frank Sikora, *Until Justice Rolls Down: The Birmingham Church Bombing Case* (1991); S. Jonathan Bass, *Blessed Are the Peacemakers: Martin Luther King Jr., Eight White Religious Leaders, and the "Letter from Birmingham Jail,"* (2002), and Diane McWhorter, *Carry Me Home: Birmingham, Alabama, The Climactic Battle of the Civil Rights Revolution* (2001).

The story of the cancellation of the Christmas parade was told to me by Ed Williams. The peacefully integrated laundromat was in my home town, Grove Hill, and my mother and her friends were among the integrationists. Wayne Flynt deserves credit for making the connection between Bear Bryant's success during this era and "pick-up truck alumni" loyalty to the University of Alabama. The story of "Bye, Bye, Blackbird" being played to departing freedom marchers came out in a conversation with some Black Belt friends, but for the life of me I can't remember who told it.

On George Wallace and the impact he had inside Alabama, there is no shortage of commentary. The best is Dan T. Carter's *The Politics of Rage: George Wallace, The Origins of the New Conservatism, and the Transformation of American Politics* (1995), although the author's focus on the impact Wallace had on the national scene often leaves questions about what was going on in the state at the time. Stephen Lesher's *George Wallace: American Populist* (1994) fills in some of the gaps, but not enough. There is still much to be done on the Alabama created by Alabama's most famous politician.

Once past the Civil Rights era and the last Wallace administration, material on Alabama generally came from newspapers and other contemporary sources. As the year 2000 approached, the state's press published a variety of articles and special issues on the past century, and these proved invaluable in my work. In addition, the movement to write a new constitution inspired a host of assessments of the impact that the old constitution has had on the state, and I drew heavily on these. However two books—Peter Applebome's *Dixie Rising: How the South Is Shaping American Values, Politics, and Culture* (1996); and Clinton McCarty, *The Reins of Power: Racial Change and Challenge in a Southern County* (1999)—have greatly helped my analysis of the impact the Civil Rights movement had on the communities it tried to change. Applebome's assessment of what has taken place in Selma and Montgomery since the days of Dr. King was both enlightening and troubling. However, Clinton McCarty's account of what happened in Wilcox County, in the heart of the Black Belt, after political power shifted from white to black gets closer to the heart of the matter than anything I read on the subject.

Others who have entertained and enlightened me with stories and observations on modern Alabama politics include the late Wilson Norris ("I'll hug your elephant"), Joe Franklin ("have your feet washed or sing without music"), Philip Rawles ("Wal-Mart Republicans"), the late Ron Casey ("our yahoo"), and the late B. J. Richey ("some swamps just don't need draining"). I also learned a lot one evening, sitting at dinner with a group of old Montgomery hands that included former governor John Patterson and former legislators Fuller Kimbrell and Pete Mathews ("if it was right I wouldn't need your vote"). And of course, there is my daddy. You can pick up plenty just listening.

A number of local histories were especially valuable in preparing me to write this. Among the most helpful were Alston Fitts III, *Selma: Queen City of the Black Belt* (1989); Michael V. R. Thomason, ed., *Mobile: The New History of Alabama's First City* (2001); Ronda Coleman Ellison, *Bibb County, Alabama: The First Hundred Years, 1818–1918* (1984); and Val L. McGee, *Claybank Memories: A History of Dale County, Alabama* (1989). Other books that have been both entertaining and enlightening but do not fit into any particular category are Frye Gaillard, *Lessons From the Big House: One Family's Passage Through the History of the South, a Memoir* (1994); Thomas R. Allison, *Moonshine Memories* (2001), which contains the story of the sheriff who hit the man because he "forgot he was a nigger"; Dennis Covington, *Salvation on Sand Mountain: Snake Handling and Redemption in Southern Appalachia* (1995); Rick Bragg, *All Over but the Shoutin'* (1997); Judith Hillman Paterson, *Sweet Mystery: A Book of Remembering* (1996); Roy Hoffman, *Back Home: Journeys Through Mobile* (2001); and Paul Hemphill, *The Ballad of Little River: A Tale of Race and Restless Youth in the Rural South* (2000).

Anyone wanting to know anything about historic buildings in the state should consult Robert Gamble, *The Alabama Catalog: A Guide to the Early Architecture of the State* (1987). If you are interested in newspapers, see King E. (Ed) Williams Jr., *The Press of Alabama: A History of the Alabama Press Association* (1997). For a look at material culture in general, see E. Bryding Adams, ed., *Made in Alabama: A State Legacy* (1995). And if you would like to know what Alabamians think about their state, see Patrick R. Cotter, James Glen Stovall, and Samuel H. Fisher III, *Disconnected: Public Opinion and Politics in Alabama* (1994).

Over the years a number of books devoted to historic photographs have been published, and these visual images of the state were especially valuable when I tried to reconstruct life at a particular time and in a particular place. Among the best of these are the pictures assembled and explained by Michael V. R. Thomason in *Trying Times: Alabama Photographs, 1917–1945* (1985) and *To Remember a Vanishing World: D. L. Hightower's Photographs of Barbour County, Alabama, c. 1930–1965* (1997). Although published to provide a window into Wilcox County just after the Civil Rights movement had run its course, the photographs taken by Bob Alderman, which appeared in *Down Home* (1975), have become part of the historic record of the region, and a remarkable record at that.

Recently a number of very fine documentaries have appeared and are available on video cassette. Some that were particularly helpful to me were *From Fields of Promise,* produced by Auburn Television; *Big Jim Folsom: The Two Faces of Populism,* which was produced for Alabama Public Television; and two programs that are part of National Public Television's *The American Experience* series— *Scottsboro: An American Tragedy* and *George Wallace: Settin' the Woods on Fire.*

Anyone wanting to really get inside Alabama should read anything written by my cousin-in-law Kathryn Tucker Windham. My particular favorites are *A Sampling of Selma Stories* (1991) and *Twice Blessed* (1996). But there are many more.

As for the moving of the monument, that episode occurred in Grove Hill, Alabama, my hometown. Jim Cox, editor-publisher of the *Clarke County Democrat* and one of my most faithful "poutin' house" buddies, supplied me with information on this and a whole host of other things.

The prayer comes from *Roy Blount's Book of Southern Humor* (1994), p. 653. Which is about as close to a traditional footnote as you are gonna get.

Index

African Americans, 130, 148, 160. *See also* Black Alabamians; Slaves; *names of individuals*

Alabama, state of: statehood, 51–52; secession, 86–89; Civil War elections, 97–98; invaded, 98, 99, 102

Alabama Education Association (AEA), 180, 287, 289, 290

Alabama Farmers Federation (ALFA), 277, 290. *See also* Farm Bureau Federation

Alabama Federation of Women's Clubs, 150

Alabama Platform, 84

Alabama Power Company, 162, 185, 186, 214

Alabama River, 9, 15, 22, 26, 30, 32, 41, 49, 50, 54, 55, 60

Alabama Territory, 44–49

Banks: Planters and Merchants, 55, 56; state bank, 57, 61, 72; national, 75

Bibb, William Wyatt, 50, 53, 54, 60

Big mules, 168, 170, 178, 187, 189, 190, 191, 211, 212, 214, 220, 223, 279, 280, 287, 291

Birmingham, 125, 149, 175, 176, 177, 190, 193, 194, 205, 210, 229, 274; during the Civil Rights movement, 252–56; Sixteenth Street Baptist Church bombing, 256–57; after the movement, 277–78

Black Alabamians: response to freedom, 104, 108–10; in Republican Party, 112–15;

voting, 115, 116, 137, 148, 258–59; Bourbon view of, 141–42; under Jim Crow, 151–52, 154, 155, 160, 170, 174, 177, 224–27, 228–30, 231–46; during New Deal, 186; during World War II, 197, 202–03, 220, 221; after the Civil Rights movement. *See also* African Americans; Black Belt; Civil Rights movement; *names of individuals*

Black Belt, 1, 41, 46, 50, 52, 54, 59, 61, 65, 75, 79, 80, 159, 172, 190, 193, 197, 202, 210; during the Civil War, 90, 96; post–Civil War, 111, 121, 128, 131, 133; voting in, 134, 135, 136, 139, 258–59; opposition to reform, 166, 167, 172, 212, 214, 225, 237, 257–58; during the Civil Rights movement, 258–59, 263, 276; post–Civil Rights movement, 280, 287, 291. *See also* Selma

Black Warrior River, 3, 13, 50

Bloody Sunday, 260–61. *See also* Civil Rights movement; Selma; *names of individuals*

Bottle Creek, 3, 4

Bourbons, 122–23, 124, 125, 127, 128, 129, 131, 133–37, 139, 140, 147, 149, 182, 208; view of history, 140–44; small town, 149–55; as Republicans, 288–91, 297. *See also* Democratic Party; Republican Party

Breckinridge, John C., 86, 87

Brewer, Albert P., 272–74

Brown v Board of Education of Topeka, Kansas, 223, 236, 250, 276

Burnt Corn, 32, 35

Cahaba River, 43, 50

Cahawba, 9, 44, 50, 51, 53, 54, 55, 59, 60, 81, 90

Canoe fight, 35, 40

Cherokee Indians, 11, 36

Chestnut, J. L., 245, 259

Chickasaw Indians, 11, 26

Child labor, 157, 159, 170, 188–89

Choctaw Indians, 11, 16, 26, 36, 37, 49

Chotard, Sarah F. Williams Willis, 43, 44

Churches, 27, 47, 108–09. *See also* Religion

Civil Rights Act of 1964, 257, 289, 281

Civil Rights movement, 229–30, 245–26, 252–65, 266–71, 278

Civil War: casualties, 94–95, 96, 97; desertions, 97; *See also* Alabama, state of

Claiborne, 43, 60

Claiborne, Gen. Ferdinand L., 33–37

Class conflict, 51–53, 56, 62, 227; barbecues, 57–58; during the Civil War, 93; post–Civil War, 110–11, 144–48, 152; during the Depression, 187; during the Civil Rights movement, 256; post–Civil Rights movement, 285

Comer, Braxton Bragg, 157, 158, 159

Connor, Eugene "Bull," 252, 253, 255, 274

Constitutions of Alabama: 1819, 51–53, 56; 1868, 111–13, 115; 1875, 121–22, 134; 1901, 135–140, 145, 148, 182, 212, 214, 220–21, 288; efforts to reform, 297–301

Convict leasing, 129, 130, 157, 164, 167, 169, 170

Coosa River, 1, 8, 11, 13, 15, 16, 20, 36, 37, 38, 59

Cotton culture, 24, 25, 26

Creek Indians, 11, 16, 17, 21, 22, 23, 26, 42; Lower Creeks, 16; Upper Creeks, 16, 20, 30; prophets, 29, 39. *See also* Red Sticks

Crutcher, David, 155–56

Dale, Sam, 34, 35, 39, 40, 59

Democrats: Jacksonian, 46, 61, 62, 75, 121; divisions in 1860, 83, 84, 86; Reconstruction, 112, 114; Redeemers, 114, 122, 115, 121; Bourbon Democrats, 125, 127, 131, 132, 133, 135, 136, 140, 145, 147, 156, 208; and Constitution of 1901, 159, 161, 164; election of 1928, 171–73, 177, 190, 192; post–World War II, 210, 211, 212, 221, 282; post–Civil Rights movement, 280, 284, 285

Depressions: Panic of 1819, 55, 56; Panic of 1837, 77; Panic of 1873, 113, 116; Great Depression, 173, 174, 175–194, 200

de Soto, Hernando, 6–10

Dixon, Frank M., 187, 190–193, 197, 210, 279

Dunn, Loula Friend, 188–89

Education, 134, 143, 159, 164–66, 168–70, 179–81, 228; integration, 241–42, 267–71; post–Civil Rights movement, 273, 274, 283, 284, 293, 299. *See also* Alabama Education Association

English (British), 14, 15, 21

Farm Bureau Federation, 180, 214, 227. *See also* Alabama Farmers Federation

Farmers' Alliance, 125–29, 132, 136, 138. *See also* Populists

Federal Road, 26, 28, 59

Folsom, James E. "Big Jim," 211–23, 225–51; civil rights, 236–38, 241–43; programs and reforms, 238–40

Forrest, Nathan Bedford, 95, 96, 100

Fort Jackson, 38, 39, 41

Fort Mims, 32–36, 38

Fort Sinquefield, 31, 33, 34

Fort Toulouse, 15, 38

French, 13–15

Gayle, John, 64, 66; challenges Jackson, 67–68, 70, 73–74

Gayle, Sarah Haynesworth, 64–71

Georgians, 21, 27; Broad River Group, 27, 50

Graham, John Simpson, 124–25, 147–48, 163–64

Graves, Bibb, 161, 166, 167, 170, 171, 178, 187–90, 193, 211

Graves, Dixie Bibb, 167, 168

Hawkins, Benjamin, 11, 23, 24, 28, 29

Heflin, Tom, 162, 171–73, 178, 192

Henderson, Charles, and the Russell Sage Foundation, 164, 166, 167

Hill, Lister, 188, 280, 281

Holy Ground, 36–37

Horseshoe Bend, 38

Hunt, Guy, 283–84, 286–91

Huntsville, 27, 28, 44, 51, 57, 116; post–Civil Rights movement, 78; Civil War, 91; impact of World War II, 205–06, 274

Indians: Woodland, 2; Mississippian, 2–5, 11, 12; contact with Spanish, 5, 8–10, 13–15, 30; epidemics, 10–12; contact with French, 13–15; contact with Americans, 12, 23, 24, 67–70, 73, 74; contact with English, 13–15, 19, 30; contact with Scots, 13, 19, 21

Jackson, Andrew, 43, 67, 68, 73, 74; Creek War, 36, 38, 39

James, Forrest "Fob," 283, 284, 291–94

Johnson, Frank, 251, 262

Jones, Thomas G., 129–31

Kilby, Thomas E., 166

Kilpartick, Emmett, 160–61

King, Martin Luther, Jr., 232, 234, 235, 245, 253–55, 260, 261, 263, 264, 271, 276. See also Birmingham; Civil Rights movement; Montgomery; Selma

King, William Rufus, 74, 75, 80–82, 84, 85

Kolb, Reuben F., 127–31, 133, 145. See also Farmers' Alliance; Populists

Ku Klux Klan, 110, 169, 170–72, 178, 187–88, 191, 235–36, 255. See also Lynching; Violence

Labor, 125, 157–59, 164, 181, 192, 210, 214, 223, 274

Lafayette, Marquis de, 58–60

Le Moyne, Bienville, 13, 14, 15

Le Moyne, Iberville, 13, 14

Lewis, Dixon Hall, 72–75, 80–84, 87, 125. See also States Rights

Lewis, John, 259–60

Liberalism, 183, 188, 193, 215, 222–23, 251–52; congressmen, 188, 208–211; on race, 240–43; post–Civil Rights movement, 286–87, 289

Lynching, 130, 181, 191. See also Ku Klux Klan; Violence

McGillivray, Alexander, 20–22, 25

Mabila, 9, 54

Merchants, 116–18, 119, 136, 178

Mestizos, 21, 25, 29, 30

Miller, Benjamin Meek, 178–82, 187

Mims, Samuel, 26, 31

Mississippi Territory, 20, 25, 27, 44, 48, 49

Mitcham War, 131–33, 145–46

Mobile, 60, 149, 182, 193, 274; founded, 14, 15, 18; fall to Americans, 31, 32, 41, 49; Civil War, 91–93, 99; Reconstruction, 116; impact of World War II, 195–97, 203–05, 228; at end of century, 277–78

Mobile Bay, 5, 6, 14; during Civil War, 92–93

Mobile River, 3, 4

Montgomery, 11, 48, 59, 149, 228, 274, 276–77; Confederate capital, 89, 91; Civil War, 99, 101–02; Reconstruction, 116; bus boycott, 230–37. See also Civil Rights movement; King, Martin Luther, Jr.; Nixon, E. D.; Parks, Rosa; Robinson, Jo Ann

Moundville, 3, 4

Narvaez, Panfilo, 5, 6

Native Americans, 8, 16. *See also* Indians

New Deal, 182–86, 188, 191–93, 219. *See also* Roosevelt, Franklin Delano

Nixon, E. D., 233, 235, 245

North Alabama, 79, 87, 107, 111, 136, 215, 278, 285

Oates, William C., 134, 136, 164

Parks, Rosa, 232–33

Patterson, John, 244–46, 249–50

Pelham, John, 90–91, 95

Pensacola, 13, 18, 32

Persons, Gordon, 222–23

Pickens, Israel, 55, 56, 59, 61, 72, 87, 125, 171, 176, 207, 212

Plantation economy, 21, 29, 44, 45, 51; post–Civil War, 165–66; post–1901, 174; post–World War II, 206–07. *See also* Depressions

Planter class, 61, 62, 65; post–Civil War, 107, 113, 117; post–1901, 164, 166; post–1928, 174, 175, 177, 189, 190, 191; post–World War II, 211, 220

Pool, Sibyl M., 272

Poor whites, 152, 153, 154, 165, 166, 208. *See also* Class conflict; Yeomen

Pope, Leroy, 27, 52, 55, 56

Populists, 125, 127, 132, 140, 144, 145, 148, 156, 157. *See also* Farmers' Alliance; Kolb, Reuben F.

Powell, Adam Clayton, 237–38

Progressives, 150, 156, 166, 167

Prohibition, 158, 159, 164, 167–69, 171

Prude, James Oscar, 140–45, 147, 148

Rabbits' Wedding, The, 246–48

Reconstruction: Bourbon interpretation, 106–07; revisionist interpretation, 107–08. *See also* Republican Party

Red Sticks, 29–32, 34, 36, 38

Religion, 58, 65, 68, 71, 153–54, 169–72, 178, 225–26, 228, 296–99

Republican Party, 85, 88; Reconstruction, 109–10, 112–14; election of 1928, 172–73, 177; post–World War II, 208; post–Civil Rights movement, 279–302. *See also* Hunt, Guy; James, Forrest "Fob"; Riley, Bob

Riley, Bob, 301–02

Robinson, Jo Ann, 231, 234, 245

Roosevelt, Franklin Delano, 182–84, 186–88, 191–92, 208

Royal Party, 56–58, 72, 207

Sansom, Emma, 96

Scotts, 13, 19. *See also* Mestizos

Scottsboro Boys, 181–82, 188

Selma, 59, 228, 274; during Civil War, 89–91, 100–01; during Civil Rights movement, 258–60, 262–63; Bloody Sunday, 260–62; Selma to Montgomery march, 260–64

Sharecropping and tenant farming, 118–121, 154–55, 164, 174–75, 193, 201, 277

Shuttlesworth, Fred, 245, 253

Siegelman, Don, 294–95, 297–301

Slavery, white Alabamians obsession with, 55–56, 83–84

Slaves (Slavery), 13, 21, 25–27, 44–46, 52, 63–66, 70, 71, 75, 76; as a political issue, 78–80, 83–85, 87–88; during the Civil War, 98

Southern Christian Leadership Conference (SCLC), 235

Spanish, in Alabama, 5–8, 10, 12, 15, 18–21, 26, 31

St. Stephens, 26, 34, 48–51, 55

Stars Fell, 69

States Rights, 67, 68, 70, 73–76, 82, 110, 279–80. *See also* Bourbons; Democratic party

Steamboats, 49, 50

Tallapoosa River, 1, 8, 11, 13, 15, 16, 20, 37, 38, 59

Taxes: on slaves, 62; Reconstruction, 111–13;

Bourbons, 129, 134; on income, 179–81; on gasoline, 179; corporate, 181; sales, 189; property, 191; opposition, 290, 292, 295, 299; reform, 299, 300. *See also* Constitutions of Alabama: of 1875, 1901

Tecumseh, 30, 31

Tennessee Valley, 1, 25, 27, 28, 36, 52, 54, 56, 57, 185

Tennessee Valley Authority (TVA), 185–86, 192–94, 281–82

Texas, 76–81

Tombigbee River, 13, 25, 27, 34, 48–49

Tunstall, Loraine Bedsole, 166

Tuscaloosa, 50, 61, 65, 166

Tuscaluza (Chief), 8, 9, 12

Tutwiler, Julia, 150

Unionists, 94

University of Alabama, 1955 attempt to integrate, 241–42; Wallace stand in the school house door, 255; football, 274–75

Violence, 47, 82–83, 112–13, 230, 235–36, 260–61, 264–65, 276. *See also* Lynching

Voting rights movement, 258–260

Wallace, George: early career, 244–45, 249–50; elected governor, 250–52; assessment of, 251–52; in office, 252–56, 281–82; opposition to voting rights, 260–66; programs, 273–74; post–Civil Rights movement, 282–85

Wallace, Lurleen B., 266, 272

Washington, Booker T., 137

Weatherford, William ("Red Eagle"), 33, 37, 39

Whigs, 61, 62

White Alabamians, response to emancipation, 105–108

White Citizen's Council, 236, 246–47

White Supremacy, 124, 138, 148, 152, 190, 225, 233

Wilkins, Hattie Hooker, 168, 272

Wiregrass, 52, 87, 136, 211

Women, 43, 44, 63; slave, 63–64; upper class, 64; Lady's bill, 66; Civil War, 90, 92, 95–97, 142; middle class, 150; reformers, 150, 158, 166, 168–70; 1920s, 162–64; suffrage, 162–64; New Deal, 188–89; World War II, 194, 198, 200–06; World War II, 203–04, 225; Civil Rights movement, 231–32, 234; in politics, 272, 294

Yancey, William Lowndes, 80–87, 110, 125, 176, 207, 212

Yeomen, 45, 46, 52, 55, 61, 79, 90, 113